Olson offers his readers a timely and powerful defense of a distinctively Christian metaphysics and teases out its implications for theology, apologetics, and cultural dialogue. It is a rich and rewarding read and will do much to reassure its readers of the intellectual credentials of the Christian faith.

ALISTER E. MCGRATH, Andreas Idreos Professor
of Science and Religion, University of Oxford

Just as war is too serious to be left to generals, so philosophy is too important to be left to philosophers. At least philosophy in the hands of a theologian like Roger Olson is too important to be left to philosophers. Though my understanding of philosophy is not the same as Olson's, I learned much from his stimulating account.

STANLEY HAUERWAS, Gilbert T. Rowe Emeritus
Professor of Divinity and Law, Duke University

THE
ESSENTIALS
OF CHRISTIAN
THOUGHT

Also by Roger E. Olson

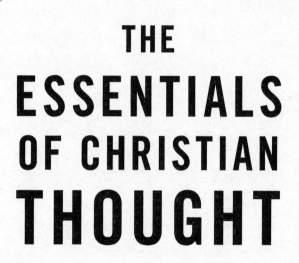

THE
ESSENTIALS
OF CHRISTIAN
THOUGHT

SEEING REALITY THROUGH
THE BIBLICAL STORY

ROGER E.
OLSON

ZONDERVAN®

ZONDERVAN

The Essentials of Christian Thought
Copyright © 2017 by Roger E. Olson

This title is also available as a Zondervan ebook.

Requests for information should be addressed to:
Zondervan, *3900 Sparks Dr. SE, Grand Rapids, Michigan 49546*

Isbn 978-0-310-52155-6

Art direction: Tammy Johnson
Cover photo: 123RF Pogonici
Interior design: Denise Froehlich

Printed in the United States of America

17 18 19 20 21 22 23 24 25 26 /DHV/ 10 9 8 7 6 5 4 3 2 1

Contents

Preface

This book grew out of a concern for Christians who either shun philosophy altogether as hostile and antithetical to vital, robust Christian faith or absorb unbiblical, and therefore unchristian, views of reality into their own perspectives on life and reality. The world, including America, is filled with alternative, competing visions of reality—what is ultimately and "really" real behind what everyone sees every day. These visions of reality are philosophies of life, worldviews, or metaphysical perspectives. This book proposes to help especially Christians devoted to the Bible as God's Word understand its implicit philosophy of reality—what is really real behind and beyond appearances. And it proposes to help them distinguish between the Bible's implicit vision of reality and competing ones—some of which are sometimes even labeled "Christian" or "compatible with Christianity."

A secondary purpose of this book is to provide administrators and faculty members of Christian institutions of higher education with a relatively simple elucidation of the "faith" part of "faith-learning integration"—a central reason for such institutions' existence. Numerous Christian colleges and universities, sometimes even Christian high schools, expect their faculty members to practice faith-learning integration. However, that project is often poorly explained. Many administrators and faculty members want to know what the faith part of that project includes. For most Christian thinkers involved in explicating faith-learning integration, the faith part is not a whole system of doctrines or inward spirituality but the biblical-Christian view of reality—that is, basic biblical-Christian philosophy.

This book contains an archeology of the implicit philosophy of the Bible—the Bible's assumed view of reality. It is called *The Essentials of Christian Thought* because this philosophy is foundational to everything the Bible teaches, and orthodox, thinking Christians of all denominations throughout the centuries have believed it. The meaning of the title will be more fully explained in the Introduction.

I thank Zondervan, and especially editors Madison Trammel and Stanley Gundry, for inviting me to write this book. Thanks also goes to the writer's assistant Jared Patterson and to many blog commenters who have stimulated me to compose this book. Finally, much thanks goes to my late mentor John Newport (d. 2000), who planted the seeds of the book in the writer's mind during seminars at Rice University in the late 1970s. This book is dedicated to his memory.

Introduction: Why This Book

This book is primarily intended for Christian believers, although others are more than welcome to read it. The intended audience is people who believe the Bible is a truthful and trustworthy guide not only to spirituality and ethics but also to the nature of ultimate reality. That is, it is especially for people who believe the Bible is more than just a book of human wisdom or even an expression of God's moral will. This book is for people who believe the human authors of the Bible were instruments of God, albeit active and not passive ones, in revealing what would otherwise be his secrets. What secrets? The true nature of ultimate reality—the realities behind appearances. Philosophers call the study of such secrets *metaphysics*, but more about that later. Don't let a word scare you away.

This book presupposes that the Bible is God's narrative, God's story, about himself and his relationships with people. It also presupposes that, like every story, the biblical narrative about God and people in history past, present, and future has certain hidden features that need to be explored and drawn out. They are not hidden by design as in esoteric religion. They are hidden because they are taken for granted—by God and by his human instruments, the Bible's authors. *Hidden* may be a misleading word; no intentionality to hide is intended. The hiddenness of certain truths within the Bible is not intentional; it is due to the fact that God and his human authors simply told a story; they did not deliver a book of philosophy or theology. However, certain philosophical and theological truths are *implied* by the story.

This book is an *explanation* of the hidden background within the biblical narrative. It is written for believers who really would like to know what *vision of ultimate reality* lurks, as it were, within the Bible. Who would want to know that? Inquiring Christian minds want to know. Especially those inquiring Christian minds who desire to distinguish biblical truth about ultimate reality—the mysteries of God and the universe—from the plethora of competing visions about ultimate reality floating around in pluralistic culture.

Here's a question to pique your curiosity: What does the Bible imply about *time*? Is time only a matter of perception? Is time only an illusion of finite existence? Is time negative, something to escape in salvation? A hymn speaks of a time when "time shall be no more." Will there be time in heaven? Does God experience time? These are issues that have perplexed philosophers and theologians for centuries, and they have taken radically diverse positions. Does the biblical narrative provide any guidance to a biblical, and therefore Christian, view of time? There is no chapter or verse that directly addresses the subject, and there is no definite "Christian doctrine of time." And yet, it is a subject of great perplexity and consternation for inquiring Christian minds.

This book intends to be a guide for the perplexed Christian—for the Christian who believes the Bible is in some sense God's holy Word but is confused about its message about *the nature of reality*. Unfortunately, the Bible is not always as clear as we would like it to be—especially about philosophical subjects. And yet Christians living in a pluralistic society filled with competing worldviews and visions of the nature of reality need guidance about how to sort them out biblically.

The Bible's Implicit Philosophy

A basic presupposition of this book is that *the Bible does contain an implicit metaphysical vision of ultimate reality—the reality that is most important, final, highest, and behind everyday appearances.*

That vision of reality has been called various things such as "biblical theism" and "biblical personalism." Perhaps "biblical personal theism" or "biblical theistic personalism" would be good terms for it. The point is to emphasize that ultimate reality is a personal God who acts, shows, and speaks. "Biblical relational theism" is another inadequate but useful term for the Bible's implicit vision of ultimate reality. Ultimate reality is *relational*.

Contemporary Western society is awash in competing visions of ultimate reality. Christians who do not know any better often absorb beliefs about reality from worldviews completely alien to the Bible and in radical conflict with it. This is known as *syncretism*. There is both conscious and unconscious syncretism. Conscious syncretism is when a person willingly and knowingly attempts to combine radically disparate belief systems in eclectic fashion—often looking for a new worldview made out of preexisting ones. Unconscious syncretism is when a person unknowingly absorbs radically disparate belief systems into his or her basic belief system (for Christians, that of the Bible and Christian tradition). This should create cognitive dissonance, but often it does not because our pluralistic culture tends to promote eclecticism. Biblically committed Christians, however, *should* want to purify their worldview of beliefs radically alien to and in conflict with the worldview implied in the biblical story.

This book, then, is a guide for Christians who want to know and understand the *basic philosophy of the Bible*. Here *philosophy* simply means "vision of ultimate reality"—a view of what is really, ultimately real and what is not. Swiss theologian Emil Brunner (1889–1966) helpfully pointed to this meaning of philosophy, especially that branch of it called *metaphysics*, in his *Philosophy of Religion*, where he emphasized the importance of seeing *connections* that do not appear but are necessary for a holistic understanding of things that do appear.[1]

---

1   Emil Brunner, *The Philosophy of Religion*, trans. A. J. D. Farrer and Bertram Lee Woolf (London: James Clarke, 1958), 57.

What does "essentials of Christian thought" mean? Certainly *not* "what a person must believe to be Christian." Many good Christians are simply unaware of the Bible's basic, foundational ideas about reality. Rather, essentials of Christian thought refers to *bedrock Christianity* in terms of worldview, life and world perspective, the Bible's implicit understanding of the nature and meaning of life and reality, and *basic Christian philosophy*—that which lies underneath and undergirds as a foundation the truths explicitly revealed in the Bible and tenaciously held by Christians for two thousand years. It is what every Christian *should* think about the reality behind everyday appearances, but many don't. Why don't they? Again, because they have been confused by the plethora of competing visions of reality in culture.

I have taught Christian theology to hundreds, perhaps thousands, of students in universities and churches over more than three decades. One thing I have discovered is that many God-fearing, Bible-believing, Jesus-loving Christians are confused about the nature of ultimate reality—what here will often be called "biblical metaphysics." They may know their church's catechism forward and backward and yet have absorbed and embraced a vision of ultimate reality totally alien to the Bible and to Christian tradition. There are three reasons for this common condition.

Why Many Christians Miss the Bible's Philosophy

First, as said earlier, the Bible is a story and not a book of philosophy. Even the most astute Christian philosophers and theologians have struggled to discern its implied vision of ultimate reality in all its details. There has been some significant disagreement about the details even as the vast majority of Christian thinkers throughout the centuries have agreed about the basics.

Second, many churches never touch on even the basics of the biblical-Christian vision of reality. Gradually over the last century most American churches (and perhaps others) have largely dropped any teaching about Christian philosophy or theology and emphasized only matters of worship and lifestyle. Christian people are left adrift, as it were, to fill in the gaps from other sources, and there are plenty of other, competing sources offering their visions of reality for that purpose. An example is the so-called "New Age movement" that flourished in America especially in the 1980s and 1990s. Many sincere Christians with inquiring minds turned to it for philosophical and even spiritual guidance, not knowing that much of what they were absorbing from it was totally alien to biblical truth about reality.

Third, cultural pluralism and a cultural emphasis on tolerance that often implies relativism seduces many Christians to create their own syncretistic blends of life and world philosophies—answers to life's ultimate questions.

Out of this set of problems arises a situation where Christians increasingly need guidance back to a basic biblical-Christian view of reality-behind-appearances. Everyone wants to know something about reality-behind-appearances. Life's ultimate questions are all about that. Is there life after death? If so, what is it like? Is the mind more than the brain? Is everything some form of matter, or is there a spiritual reality behind material reality? What is the soul? What does it mean to be human? What is evil? These are ultimate questions, questions about *metaphysical reality*—what is unseen but nevertheless important.

This writer once heard a Christian pastor and theology professor speak to a college audience about "Christian Buddhism" and "Buddhist Christianity." He quoted the influential English philosopher Alfred North Whitehead (1861–1947), who famously said that whereas Christianity is a religion seeking a metaphysic, Buddhism is a metaphysic generating a religion.[2] Of course Whitehead meant that slightly tongue-in-cheek, but he created a metaphysic, a

---

2   Alfred North Whitehead, *Religion in the Making*, Lecture 2: "Religion and Dogma" (Cambridge, UK: Cambridge University Press, 1926), 39–40.

philosophy about ultimate reality called "process thought," that he believed filled the gap for Christianity in the modern world. The Christian pastor and theologian this writer heard touted a version of Buddhism from Japan as his metaphysic for his Christian religion. It may be shocking to hear such from a Christian minister and theologian, but many ordinary Christians have unthinkingly done something similar—absorbing non-Christian and even unbiblical beliefs about reality into their Christianity.

Why should Christians, or anyone, read a book about biblical-Christian philosophy? Think of it as an exercise in developing an examined faith. Think of it as a challenge to bring all thoughts into conformity with God's revelation. If you are a committed Christian, devoted to the truth of Scripture, think of this book as a guide to deeper thinking about God and the universe, including your own existence, and to avoiding syncretism. This book is *not* especially *for* scholars of religion or theology; it is *for* ordinary Christians untutored in philosophy or theology. It does not presuppose previous training in philosophy or theology.

The Project of Integrating Faith with Learning

There is another audience for this book—one perhaps included in the above but that may not recognize themselves in that description. This book is also, and perhaps *especially*, for teachers and students in Christian liberal arts colleges and universities who are curious about *faith-learning integration*. (If you are *not* such a person, don't run away! You may need guidance in integrating your Christian faith with your discipline or profession too!)

I have taught in three Christian universities and edited a journal dedicated to "the integration of faith and learning" or "the integration of faith and the disciplines"—meaning the subjects of research and teaching found in most universities—the arts and sciences. In and through all of that I have discovered a *great deal of confusion* about the meaning of that project. That confusion has led to unnecessary consternation and conflict on many Christian faculties. The faith part of faith-learning integration refers to the subject of this book—*basic Christian philosophy* or *Christian metaphysics*—"essentials of Christian thought" in the sense of "bedrock Christian life and world perspective." Some have called it "the Christian worldview" so often that it has become a cliché worn out by overuse.

Too many teachers and students jump to wrong conclusions about faith-learning integration. They assume it means putting research into a kind of dogmatic straitjacket, limiting what questions can be asked and conclusions drawn from solid research. Many fear it means teaching only "Christian mathematics"—whatever that would be!—or "Christian sociology" or "Christian art." Perhaps in some Christian institutions that has been a misuse of the concept of faith-learning integration. One motive (and motif!) of this book is to develop and explain the faith aspect of faith-learning integration. What is it that Christian university administrators should expect faculty members to believe and use in integrating Christianity with their subjects of research and teaching? Well, certainly *not* every Christian doctrine! What then? Most integrationist scholars have intended, even if they have not explained very clearly, that the faith part of faith-learning integration be the subject of this book—*the basic, bedrock, biblical view of God and the universe (creation) and especially humanity in it.*

The point is that *if Christianity is compatible with anything and everything it is nothing.* Christian institutions of higher learning are dedicated to the truth of the biblical narrative *and the worldview it implies.* Need an example? How about this: *Ultimate reality is personal, not impersonal, and humans reflect that ultimate reality in their created constitution—what they are.* Here we will call that "Christian humanism." It is not "secular humanism." In fact, from a biblical-Christian perspective, it is *true humanism!* How many Christians know this or think about human existence like that? Like what? Like this: *Because human persons reflect the nature of ultimate reality and are loved by it (him) they are of infinite dignity and value, which is why they should never be treated as means to an end but always as ends in themselves.* The great philosopher Immanuel Kant (1724–1804) is the one who said that it is always right to treat persons as ends in themselves and never as means to an end. He called it the "categorical imperative" and thought it was purely rational. Many have disagreed and thought it perfectly rational to use power to dominate, enslave, and oppress other persons. From a biblical-Christian perspective *the reason why* it is right to treat persons as ends in themselves and never as means to an end (in other words, not to manipulate and oppress them to enhance one's own happiness) is *because* they are created in the image and likeness of ultimate reality—the personal Creator God of the universe.

Administrators of Christian schools want faculty members in all disciplines to know and respect that basic, bedrock truth of the biblical narrative, of Christian metaphysics. They want them to integrate it into their teaching about humanity in the arts and sciences. They do not want (hopefully) any contrary philosophy used to teach about humanity—such as secular humanism, which says human beings are highly evolved, conscious matter but only products of impersonal natural forces and processes. Theories about humanity that are rooted in secular humanism are to be eschewed, not taught as truth. But that does *not mean* there can be no truth in theories such as sociobiology, which emphasizes the influence of natural forces and processes on human life. Humans are also *not* "godlets"—divine beings above nature trapped in matter as some non-Christian worldviews would have it.

In other words, faith-learning integration is not about using a highly systematic theology, a dogmatic system, as a straitjacket to hinder academic freedom. It is about *developing discernment* about what theories about reality are compatible with the Bible and what theories are not—or what aspects of a theory are compatible and what aspects of it are not. It is also about enriching the relevance of the basic biblical perspective on reality with fresh insights about reality from objective research in the arts and sciences. Fresh research can also help refine our understanding of the essentials of Christian thought—by, for example, purifying interpretations of them that are literally impossible.

Needed: A Guide for Perplexed Thinking Christians

This book, then, is especially for *every inquiring Christian mind*. It is intended as a guide for all perplexed Christians—Christians perplexed by the reticence of the Bible about some subjects, perplexed by cultural pluralism of competing visions of reality, or perplexed by lack of teaching in their churches about the nature of ultimate reality as implied by revelation in the Bible.

Some knowledgeable, tutored readers will be put off by the claim that the Bible itself conveys, however obliquely, a philosophy—a metaphysical vision of ultimate reality. Especially among modern Protestant Christian scholars there exists a profound bias *against* metaphysics. There are several reasons for this. First, metaphysics is often wrongly viewed as the distraction of speculation from pure faith; it is assumed to be rationalistic and devoid of revelation. This book works with no such bias. Here *metaphysics* is simply another word for investigation into the nature of ultimate reality. It carries no baggage smuggling particular philosophical schools of thought such as Platonism or Aristotelianism or process thought. Second, metaphysics is often wrongly associated inseparably with Catholic tradition. There is no good reason why a Protestant cannot think metaphysically. Third, metaphysics is supposed to have been devastated once and for all by the skepticism of Kant, but that assumes that Kant's epistemology (theory of knowledge) is sound. It has been extremely influential, but that does not equate with it being correct! Fourth, and finally, metaphysics is often assumed, especially by Protestants, to be a distraction from the main point of Christianity, which is assumed (under the influence of Kant) to be ethics, spirituality, and/or faith.

The simple point is that the modern Protestant bias against metaphysics is just that—a bias based on distorted ideas of what it means and on its abuses, also perhaps on commitment to Kant's reduction of religion to ethics or Friedrich Schleiermacher's (1768–1834) reduction of religion to spirituality. (Schleiermacher was the father of modern Protestant theology who tended to equate religion, including Christianity, with feeling.) Metaphysics as here understood and explicated means *only* a vision of ultimate reality—reality behind everyday appearances and common sense notions. Here it is assumed that the Bible contains and implies a metaphysical perspective on that reality, and that belief in the truth of the Bible points one toward having a certain perspective on the really real. Christian theologian H. Richard Niebuhr (1894–1962) expressed this writer's belief concisely: "The Christianity of the gospels" (this writer would add "of the Bible") is not a "metaphysical creed" but it "presupposes the metaphysics of a Christlike God."[3]

Some Guides to Discerning the Bible's Philosophy

In many ways this book was inspired by and is a continuation of the projects of two eminent Christian theologians of the 1950s and 1960s: French Catholic thinker Claude Tresmontant (1925–97) and American Protestant thinker Edmond La Beaume Cherbonnier (b. 1918). Both dared to suggest that the Bible itself contains a philosophy, and they meant a metaphysical vision of reality—a suggestion rare among modern Protestants. According to Tresmontant biblical thought implies a concealed metaphysical structure.[4] He did not

---

3   H. Richard Niebuhr, *The Social Sources of Denominationalism* (New York: Meridian Books, 1958), 278.

4   Claude Tresmontant, *Christian Metaphysics*, trans. Gerard Slevin (New York: Sheed & Ward, 1965), 29. Also, elsewhere, Tresmontant wrote, "There are certain metaphysical exigencies implied in revelation, and organically pre-adapted to the theological message delivered by the inspired books [of the Bible]." *A Study in Hebrew Thought*, trans. Michael Francis Gibson (New York: Desclee, 1960), 146.

mean its concealment is intentional but only that it is not formulated there in a technical or explicit manner as in a philosophical treatise.

Tresmontant was Catholic, so his belief in a Christian metaphysic is not very surprising in and of itself, but what is notable is his apparent belief that the basic ingredients of the Christian metaphysic are *all* found in Scripture and are *not* dependent on Greek, that is Aristotle's, philosophy. (Catholic theology, especially since Thomas Aquinas in the Middle Ages, is traditionally heavily dependent on Aristotle's philosophy.)

Cherbonnier, who taught many years at Trinity College in Hartford, Connecticut, was a strong opponent of antimetaphysical Christianity as well as of Christianity that wed itself to Greek philosophy. He was critical of both Karl Barth (1886–1968) and Paul Tillich (1886–1965), two twentieth-century Protestant theologians who he thought were guilty of promoting an antiphilosophical Christianity (Barth) and a Christianity dependent on nonbiblical and even antibiblical philosophy (Tillich). He defined metaphysics as it is here defined simply as "the quest for ultimate reality."[5] He admitted that "biblical metaphysic" is often treated as a "contradiction in terms" but denied that, arguing instead that the Biblical metaphysic is simply the development of underlying hints and assumptions within the Bible.[6] He sought to develop what he called a "genuine *philosophia Christiana*"—a genuine Christian philosophy as an alternative to so many metaphysical visions that have been *imposed* or *superimposed* on the Bible and Christianity over the centuries by theologians (for example, Plato's philosophy) who have wrongly assumed that all metaphysics must be Platonic.[7] According to him, this bias has caused many, if not most, Christian theologians to deny the distinctly biblical metaphysic a fair hearing.

---

5   Edmond La Beaume Cherbonnier, "Is There a Biblical Metaphysic?" *Theology Today* 15, no. 4 (January 1959): 460.

6   Ibid., 454.

7   Ibid., 468.

Certainly Tresmontant and Cherbonnier are not the only two modern Christian thinkers who have argued for and sought to develop a genuinely biblical philosophy, a metaphysical vision of reality. A more recent example is Scottish theologian Neil B. MacDonald in *Metaphysics and the God of Israel: Systematic Theology of the Old and New Testaments* (2007).[8] Others could be mentioned, including Jewish philosopher-theologian Abraham Joshua Heschel (1907–72). (Cherbonnier was inspired by Heschel and referred to his books often.) However, Tresmontant and Cherbonnier stand out as thinkers who rejected any idea that biblical truth is devoid of philosophical-metaphysical implications or that Christianity must depend on other philosophies and metaphysical visions outside the Bible for its basic perspective on reality.

In fact, both Tresmontant and Cherbonnier argued very cogently that the biblical philosophy is holistic, not requiring supplementation by extrabiblical philosophies (which is not to say they are all untrue in every aspect), and that the biblical philosophy is fundamentally contrary to Greek philosophies. Tresmontant boldly proclaimed that the metaphysic assumed by the biblical narratives fundamentally conflict with Greek thought's typical ideas about reality including time.[9] Nearly all of Cherbonnier's writings criticize Christian theology's traditional dependence on Greek philosophical methods and categories. Of the latter he wrote that they do not adequately protect or articulate basic Christian truths.[10] Compared with Greek philosophical theology, he wrote, "the wisdom of the Bible is almost uncanny."[11]

This is not a book of Christian apologetics; its purpose and goal

---

8   Neil B. MacDonald, *Metaphysics and the God of Israel: Systematic Theology of the Old and New Testaments* (Grand Rapids, Mich.: Baker Academic, 2007).

9   Tresmontant, *A Study in Hebrew Thought*, 142.

10   Edmond La Beaume Cherbonnier, "Biblical Metaphysic and Christian Philosophy," *Theology Today* 9, no. 3 (October 1952): 361.

11   Ibid., 369. Neither Tresmontant nor Cherbonnier were influenced by liberal Protestant theologian Adolf Harnack, who famously attempted to de-Hellenize Christianity by reducing it to a few simple platitudes about ethics.

is only to explicate biblical-Christian philosophy which, in agreement with Tresmontant and Cherbonnier, will often turn out to be contrary to Greek metaphysics. However, some account of Christian knowledge will be helpful. Why are Christians justified in finding truth in the biblical narrative and how should that be done? These are, of course, questions the answers to which would take volumes. The first chapter of this book, however, will be devoted to a brief discussion of biblical-Christian epistemology (theory of knowledge) and hermeneutics (interpretation). The thesis there will be that *in this postmodern age* every philosophy is rooted in some story and tradition based on it, and that for the Christian "the Bible absorbs the world"—the biblical story, narrative, is the lens through which the Christian *sees* reality *as* God's good creation (for example). On, then, to that (wholly inadequate) discussion so necessary before plunging into the meat of the book—the explication of the essentials of Christian thought.

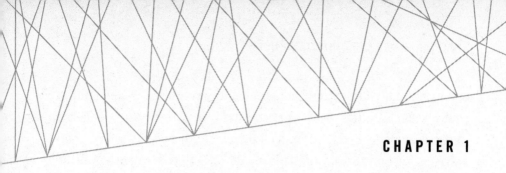

CHAPTER 1

Knowing Christianly: Seeing Reality through the Biblical Story

M any Christians consider philosophy and the Bible as contraries, antithetical to each other. Yet, literally, *philosophy* simply means "love of wisdom." If there is wisdom in the Bible, and if we love that wisdom, then we are automatically philosophers in the literal sense of the word—especially if we seek to understand that wisdom using our God-given reasoning minds. Some will agree with that much but object to talk of metaphysics in the Bible and wish to disassociate the Bible and Christianity from metaphysics. Again, much depends on how metaphysics is understood. Literally it simply means "what goes before the physical." It could be understood simply as love of that wisdom about ultimate reality revealed in the Bible. Surely the Bible does not presuppose that the physical is ultimate reality; something came before and underlies the physical, the natural. As soon as one talks about anything "supernatural" one is in the realm of metaphysics. *Supernatural* is another problematic word that will be used in this book, but it will be carefully defined later to clear up misconceptions that cause much confusion about it.

Epistemology: Thinking about Knowing

One branch of philosophy is *epistemology*, thinking about knowing: What can we know and how can we know it? All kinds of questions arise in epistemology such as: Can we have absolute certainty about anything? There is no room here for a complete discussion of epistemology; that would consume many volumes. Modern philosophy especially has been obsessed with questions and concerns about knowledge. Traditionally epistemology comes before metaphysics in handbooks of philosophy, and that sequence will be followed here somewhat reluctantly. "Reluctantly" because it is our conviction that every epistemology assumes some account of reality and thus metaphysics. Put otherwise, the *hows* and *whys* and *whats* of *knowing* depend on some understanding of reality itself—on a worldview. Epistemology always assumes some framework of reality itself. There is an inescapable *circularity* in philosophy between epistemology and metaphysics.

Here, however, before delving very deeply into essential Christian thought (basic, foundational, biblical-Christian metaphysics), a bare-bones kind of account of Christian knowing will be offered. A certain perspective on knowing about ultimate reality, metaphysics, will be presupposed throughout the rest of the book, and therefore the reader is owed an account of it up front. The underlying question here is: How are Christians justified in believing the Bible to be a true account of reality?

Our account of knowing, our Christian-based epistemology, will diverge considerably from the main modern one which is commonly called foundationalism. Until the dawn of the modern age with the Enlightenment (approximately 1650), most philosophers, like ordinary people, believed that knowing truth depended on a combination of faith, tradition, and reason. Reason was commonly understood as common sense observation and logic. When it came to metaphysics, truth about ultimate realities, certain traditional philosophies and theologies held sway for most people. Authority was heavily invested in, for example, a combination of Greek philosophy and traditional church teaching about the Bible's meaning. Knowledge and belief were not separated.

Then came the Protestant Reformation, which shook the foundations of Christian civilization, including philosophy and theology, and triggered the devastating Wars of Religion between Catholics and Protestants. One philosopher was especially disillusioned by the Wars of Religion and determined to find a new way of establishing knowledge even in religion. René Descartes (1596–1640) is usually considered the father of modern philosophy because of his revolutionary ideas about knowledge. He is famous for advocating doubt rather than faith as the beginning point for knowing. The one thing he could not doubt was his own existence: "I think; therefore I am." He deduced an entire system of knowledge, including metaphysics and the existence of God, from his own existence.

Foundationalism is the epistemology begun by Descartes and carried forward by later Enlightenment thinkers. Basically, foundationalism depicts knowledge as a pyramid with indubitable truths of evidence and/or reason at the bottom and everything else flowing upward from them by induction or deduction (observation and/or logic).[1] Many modern philosophers adopted some form of foundationalism because it seemed to offer an objective, universal, rational path to knowledge that eliminated faith, revelation, and reliance on authority. At its most extreme, foundationalism claims that *knowledge* is a term reserved for what can be proven rationally; all else is "belief," "opinion," or "superstition." Of course, one result has been that those three categories *tend* to collapse together into one for foundationalists: "subjectivism." Only the foundational method, rationalism, is thought to yield objective knowledge. The result, of course, was a crisis for religion. Many religious philosophers and theologians scrambled to adapt religion to foundationalism using natural theology—knowledge about God and religious matters based on reason alone. But many affirmed foundationalism for the physical and human sciences while taking religion into the realm of subjective belief divorced from reason and knowledge (fideism).

---

1   For further reading about foundationalism and postfoundationalism—the postmodern approach to knowledge—see John H. Thiel, *Nonfoundationalism* (Minneapolis: Augsburg Fortress, 1994). There are, of course, numerous other good books on modern and postmodern epistemology. This is a relatively brief and simple-to-read one this writer recommends.

Enlightenment foundationalism created a crisis for religion; religious responses were wildly diverse. None seemed to satisfy the rationalists, who disagreed among themselves about many things, such as whether it was possible to have knowledge about metaphysics. Kant argued that metaphysics was off limits to reason because pure reason could know nothing except appearances and the categories the mind uses to organize the data of the five senses. The upshot of it all was extreme skepticism about metaphysics and religion—unless they were relegated to the realms of subjectivity or authority, in which cases their truth claims should not be labeled "knowledge."

The ultimate reach of Enlightenment-based skepticism toward metaphysics and religion relegated them totally to the realm of subjectivity and mere opinion (at best) and came in the early twentieth century with a type of rationalism called positivism. Positivism, led by philosophers A. J. Ayer (1910–89) and Antony Flew (1923–2010), dictated that all statements of fact were meaningless unless they could be empirically (using the five senses) verified (Ayer) or falsified (Flew). This meant that religious truth claims not only did not constitute knowledge but were meaningless—unless they could be verified or falsified. Ayer, Flew, and other positivists claimed they could not be verified or falsified objectively and empirically. This was true for all metaphysics as well. Metaphysics, which had long been held to be a necessary part of theology, was declared dead. At best, even its supporters admitted, it had become the "sick man of philosophy"—virtually ignored, considered a relic of a distant, premodern past.[2]

The Decline of Modern Rationalism

The irony is that not long after ascending to the pinnacle of modern philosophy, positivism itself became sick. It was attacked from all sides for many reasons. One main reason was that its own principle

---

2   The phrase "sick man of philosophy" was probably derived from the common claim after World War I that the Ottoman Empire (Turkey and its dependent territories) had become the "sick man of Europe." It means "unworthy of serious attention" and/or "on life support and destined to die out."

was itself unverifiable and unfalsifiable![3] In other words, critics pointed out, if positivism is true it is meaningless—an example of what is called in philosophy a "self-referentially absurd claim." Of course, positivists came back with defending arguments and critics provided many alternative accounts of how truth claims can be meaningful even if not provable or falsifiable. The 1950s was either the high point or the low point, depending on one's perspective, of modern philosophical analysis of metaphysical and religious language.

During this drawn-out debate over language and meaning, one philosopher gradually became the leading voice against positivism, but he was much more than that. Austrian-born Cambridge University philosopher Ludwig Wittgenstein (1889–1951) proposed that language, including truth claims, was being misunderstood and misrepresented by the positivists (even though he had once associated himself with them). According to Wittgenstein and his followers, there is no one "language game" that is normative and that has the authority to determine the meaning and validity of all others. For him, there are multiple language games with different grammars and rules. What is meaningful in one is not meaningful in another. Each has its own rules for meaningfulness. Most shocking, to positivists and other foundationalists, was Wittgenstein's claim that religion is its own language game not to be judged by other language games such as the empirical sciences. In other words, Wittgenstein was denying a universal rationality that covers and judges all thought and speech. Whether he intended to or not he extended a philosophical olive branch, as it were, to metaphysics and religion, both of which had been under incredible attack in philosophy since the dawn of the Enlightenment but especially

---

3   The account here given of the demise of positivism and gradual rise of nonfoundationalist epistemologies in modern/postmodern philosophy relies heavily on a blockbuster edited volume entitled *New Essays in Philosophical Theology* edited by Antony Flew and philosopher Alasdair MacIntyre (London: SCM Press, 1955). This volume of essays has become a classic in modern/postmodern epistemology especially as it relates to metaphysics and religion. The essays provide wildly diverse defenses and criticisms of positivism.

by positivists who seemed to rule especially British and American philosophy in the first half of the twentieth century. If Wittgenstein was right, so it seemed, metaphysics and religion had new leases on life.

Several of the authors of essays in *New Essays in Philosophical Theology* (1955) offered what could be considered *postmodern* approaches to epistemology. Certainly they were *postfoundationalist*. One of the book's editors was Catholic philosopher Alasdair MacIntyre (b. 1929) who began then and went on to advocate an approach to knowledge that borrowed heavily from Wittgenstein but added in the dimensions of *story, community,* and *tradition*. MacIntyre has argued persuasively in his many volumes of philosophy that *all knowledge, including scientific knowledge, is shaped by a tradition-community and its governing story.* By *story* he does not mean "fiction" but narrative account of reality. His argument gained great support when philosopher of science Thomas Kuhn (1922–96) demonstrated in *The Structure of Scientific Revolutions* (1962) that even the "hard" experimental sciences do not operate solely by evidence and reason but are driven or held back by paradigms—another word for what MacIntyre meant by story. (Kuhn's groundbreaking work in the philosophy of science drove a nail in the coffin of modern foundationalism and opened the door further to postfoundationalist epistemology.)

Another author of an essay in *New Essays* was R. M. Hare (1919–2002), an Oxford University professor of philosophy who coined the term *blik* for world perspective—a way of "seeing the world as" something—existing independently of verification or falsification. In other words, according to Hare, everyone tends to "see" reality "as" something or other, and such basic visions of ultimate reality are never amenable to mere evidential or logical verification or falsification. In fact, as many of Hare's followers pointed out, positivism itself depends on and articulates a blik!

The Rise of Perspectives in Thinking about Knowing

This word and concept *blik* merits further attention here. While not all postfoundationalist philosophers like the word, it seems to cover a lot of potential territory in postfoundationalist epistemology. A simple illustration is often used to explain it. Imagine, for example, a drawing of an animal that might be seen as *either* a duck or a rabbit. (There is a famous illustration of such found in Wittgenstein's 1953 book *Theological Investigations*.) The mind tends to see it either as one or the other, although it could be either. A blik is when one sees it as a duck, not a rabbit, or vice versa. Of course, this is a simple illustration of something much more complicated. According to Hare and other Wittgensteinian philosophers, all knowing is blik-dependent. That is not to say, they would all caution, that it is impossible to break out of one's blik and see reality "as" something else. Only extreme Wittgensteinians think bliks, language games, are private and incorrigible—that is, imprisoning such that one cannot look at reality differently. The point is only that *all knowing tends to be influenced by perspectives*. This can be called "post-foundationalist perspectivalism." The relevant point for religion is that it introduces something akin to *faith* in all knowing. If it is true, then knowing is always shaped by "seeing as," by unprovable and unfalsifiable perspective.

This postmodern, postfoundationalist, perspectivalist approach to epistemology, however, might not be of any help to either metaphysics or theology because both, by definition, seek to discover and state what is true about reality *for everyone, always, and everywhere*. In other words, metaphysics, especially, can never be private or personal in the sense of merely relative or true only for one person or group. By definition metaphysics attempts to explain *ultimate reality—what is really real* and not just for one person or a group of people. So while Wittgensteinian postfoundationalism might crack open the door to religious discourse once again being meaningful and might take away foundationalism's claim to own the category *knowledge*, how does it help metaphysics?

Uniting Perspectivalism with Metaphysics

A too-little noticed but very insightful answer was published by philosopher James Richmond in 1971: *Theology and Metaphysics*. Richmond brought together *perspectivalism* and *metaphysics* by redefining both. In other words he softened perspectivalism to avoid sheer subjectivism and relativism in truth and knowledge and softened metaphysics to allow for an element of subjectivity.

Richmond went against the stream of post-Kantian antimetaphysical theology so prominent in modern Protestant theology, which has tended to reduce Christianity to ethics or spiritual feelings. He boldly stated his thesis that Christian theology and ethics cannot dispense with some metaphysical vision that draws together into a rational whole human experience of and knowledge about reality.[4]

Richmond defined *metaphysics* as "existential map-making."[5] In other words, a "metaphysical vision" means a mental image of the terrain of life, of reality. *Existential* means it matters to the individual for finding his or her way around in the world and interpreting experience. One of religion's functions, according to Richmond, is to provide just such an existential map of reality—a "heuristic picture of the world as a whole."[6]

Richmond turned to Wittgenstein to argue that metaphysics, so defined, has not been ruled out by reason—as so much modern philosophy argued—or by faith—as much modern Protestantism seemed to believe. Wittgenstein's idea of language games and of theology as grammar, he averred, cancelled the positivist argument against metaphysics as meaningless. And he strongly implied that

---

4   James Richmond, *Theology and Metaphysics* (New York: Schocken Books, 1971), xi.
5   Ibid., 137.
6   Ibid., 68.

modern Protestant theology's turn away from metaphysics into fideism was an unnecessary escape from the ravages of rationalist philosophies.[7]

Following Wittgenstein and Hare, Richmond sought to rescue metaphysical theology's rational credentials as knowledge by appeal to *perspectives.* All "facts," in other words, "are not simply seen, but 'seen as.'"[8] Seeing the world *as* something is inescapable; all observations and experiences are interpreted through some blik, some "explanatory hypothesis," some "apprehension of reality," some pattern of thought to be observed in reality as experienced. The point is, according to Richmond—following Wittgenstein and post-positivist philosophers influenced by him— that the search for truth is never purely objective based solely on empirical observation and logical interpretation. Something like *faith* always lies in the background of research and its conclusions. And there is no single language game that rules all research and knowledge.

Even more to the point, for our purpose here, is Richmond's insightful argument that *belief in the supernatural* (something above and free from nature and nature's laws) is no more a matter of faith, "seeing as," than *belief in naturalism* (that nature and its laws are all that are real).[9] The thrust of modern rationalism, culminating in positivism, was to enforce belief in naturalism and rule out belief in the supernatural as meaningless gibberish. Naturalism, a product of Enlightenment rationalism, is placed on the same plane as supernaturalism or theism—belief in a personal God. Both are *bliks*! Neither one can be proven by facts or ruled out of court as superstition. *Both* are world perspectives, what sociologists of religion call "plausibility structures," that determine what counts as evidence and what doesn't.

---

7   Ibid., 33.
8   Ibid., 68.
9   Ibid., 88.

Richmond was not, however, an advocate of radical Wittgensteinian fideism—the belief espoused by some postfoundationalists that language games and bliks are incorrigible, incapable of being supported or undermined by observation or reason. Following English philosopher of religion Ian Ramsey (1915–72), Richmond argued that there are special areas of experience relevant to metaphysical maps of the universe, even though all of them have the character of prerational bliks. They are not immune from being critically examined and supported or undermined by lived experience or what might be called "empirical fit." (Here *empirical* does not mean only experience of the five senses; it refers to experience as a whole, including nonsensory experiences.) According to Richmond, bliks can be tested by their ability to illumine or explain moral experience, human existence, history, and nature—all spheres of experience any worldview ought to explain. According to Richmond, religious experience is also a sphere of human experience that any metaphysical map of reality ought to explain. A worldview or metaphysical perspective on the whole of reality that cannot explain these special spheres of experience is thereby undermined. That worldview or blik that most adequately accounts for them is thereby supported.[10]

Even Ramsey, however, admitted that *coming to see reality as*, coming to hold a certain blik or world perspective, is never just a matter of evidence or reason; it usually happens in a kind of "Aha!" moment that Ramsey referred to as "the penny dropping." Suddenly a person *sees* the drawing *as* a duck and not *as* a rabbit. Both ways of seeing it are plausible. People who look at it are looking at the same thing even if, as often happens, they interpret it, see it *as*, entirely different. It is not permitted, in post-Wittgensteinian philosophy, to say that only one way of seeing it *as* is meaningful or valid. Both are. And yet, one must not say two people who see it *as* something different are both right. That is the error of relativism which

---

10   Both "empirical fit" and "adequacy to experience" are concepts used by Ramsey and borrowed by Richmond. See Richmond, *Theology and Metaphysics,* 137.

Wittgenstein never intended even if some of his radical interpreters (and many lazy postmoderns!) took him to that extreme.

Knowing Reality Itself as "Metaphysical Map-making"

Richmond strongly believed, as do many theistic believers influenced by Wittgenstein, that even though the basic biblical-Christian metaphysic, the God-centered worldview, cannot be proven evidentially or rationally, seeing reality *as* such need not be a sheer leap of faith without rational support. But, one might ask, if all metaphysical visions are bliks and if all language games including religious ones are independent, then how would it ever be possible to convert a person from one to another? A partial answer was touched on above, and Richmond explained the answer further by asking how a metaphysical map-maker can communicate his way of seeing reality "as" to a skeptic. According to Richmond, he might ask the skeptic to use his imagination to try to see reality "as" that and ask if this does not perhaps appear more reasonable overall than alternatives.[11]

In other words, Richmond suggested, sheer natural theology and rationalistic apologetics may be ruled out by Wittgensteinian epistemology, but that does not mean metaphysical visions such as personal theism are irrational or incapable of support. (Natural theology includes the so-called "proofs of the existence of God" from reason and evidence, and rationalistic apologetics is the project of proving theism, if not Christianity, true by appeal to historical evidences such as the resurrection of Jesus.) Protestant theologian Brunner called Richmond's dialogue approach "eristics."[12] Ramsey

---

11 Ibid., 118–19.

12 See Emil Brunner, "Nature and Grace" in *Natural Theology*, trans. Peter Fraenkel (London: Geoffrey Bles: The Centenary Press, 1946), 35. Some readers may know that this essay by Brunner sparked a heated debate with Barth, who responded to it with his own essay entitled simply "No!" (which is included in the same volume). Although Brunner used the phrase "natural theology," what he was really talking about was a "point of contact" within the natural person, before and apart from salvation, for the gospel. Brunner talked about "eristics," his alternative to rationalistic apologetics, very similar to Richmond's approach, in many of his books. For him, eristics was the Christian recommendation of the biblical worldview to non-Christians on the ground that it better explained all of reality and human experience. But he did not think it was a matter of proof or that reason or argument alone could lead a person to a saving knowledge of God.

would say that in and through such dialogue, attempting to get a nonbeliever to "see" the world "as" (the Bible and Christianity sees it), "the penny might drop," or the nonbeliever might suddenly have an "Aha! moment." But theologically, from a Christian perspective, this "disclosure situation" would be a work of grace too, and not merely a human achievement. The main point, however, is that in such events of coming to *see* the world *as*, to adopt a different metaphysical vision than one's own, it is never a matter of adopting a neutral, purely objective point of view, a "view from nowhere." *There is no view from nowhere* in Wittgensteinian, postfoundationalist epistemology. *All views are from somewhere*—from within a particular blik. But people are not prisoners of their bliks; they can change them, but the change is always a kind of conversion—from one perspective to another.

From within the biblical-Christian blik, Richmond argued that *there actually is reason to believe it*; it is not merely an irrational leap of faith. A believer may not be able to convince a nonbeliever of its truth by appeal to some evidence or logic independent of any blik. Such does not exist. However, believers need not worry that their metaphysical map of reality is arbitrary or irrational. Following Ramsey and other post-Wittgensteinian Christian philosophers, Richmond suggested that the theistic metaphysical map of reality contained in the Bible and explicated by hundreds of years of Christian tradition is *supported by universal human experience* in the sense that it better answers life's universal ultimate questions than its competitors. "Neither human life nor the world carries *within itself* anything that can answer the questions or satisfy the appetites that *its existence provokes*."[13] According to Richmond, only the Christian-theistic worldview of the Bible and Christian tradition answers those questions and satisfies those appetites wholly.

This is far from proof. But if Wittgenstein and postfoundationalist philosophers are correct, there is no knock-down, drag-out

---

13   Richmond, *Theology and Metaphysics,* 118.

proof of anything outside of perhaps mathematics. Even physics, so they say, works with paradigms and models and is not simply a matter of objective observation and rational interpretation. Albert Einstein, the most famous genius of modern physics, was reluctant to give in to the mounting evidence for quantum mechanics, saying, "God does not play dice with the universe" (meaning there is no contingency in reality). Modern physics is divided—in spite of what students learn in high school and even college—between determinists and nondeterminists.

After Foundationalism: Knowing without Proving

The point of all that (above) is simply that postfoundationalist epistemology, led by Wittgenstein, has reopened the door to metaphysics as meaningful discourse and to religion as more than mere opinion or superstition. The news has not yet reached everyone, of course, and many high school and college teachers still teach as if Enlightenment rationalism, even positivism, is normative. The norm today is what Richmond called "soft perspectivism," which can be summed up most simply by saying "there is no view from nowhere." Which means that *all knowing takes place from within some metaphysical vision, some blik about reality.*

Surely that means, then, that inquiring minds should want to know about and understand their own blik, their own map of reality, their own metaphysical vision. Socrates said that the unexamined life is not worth living. By extension that means the unexamined belief system is not worth believing. The mature believer, the serious, conscientious truth seeker, should at least want to know the ins and outs of his or her map of reality. As mentioned in the introduction, however, a serious problem arises in a pluralistic culture because many individuals *do not seem to have a coherent map of reality.* That is, they piece together absolutely *incommensurate* pieces of radically divergent maps of reality, creating, whether consciously or unconsciously, incoherent worldviews that then result in absurd cognitive dissonance.

This should be a matter of concern especially for Christians who claim that their biblically based map of reality is true and not a figment of imagination or mere myth. But truth is a whole; truth requires consistency. And the Bible, one hopes, communicates a coherent map of reality. Something is wrong, or ought to be, when a Bible-believing Christian integrates into his or her world perspective absolutely contrary elements drawn from competing world perspectives. That's syncretism and it creates confusion. That confusion is all too common among especially postmodern people, including many Christians whose real, functioning worldview is eclectic and not wholly biblical.

Many people seem to have misinterpreted Wittgenstein (whose ideas trickle down to them through postmodern culture often in distorted forms) as saying that every individual has his or her own private language game and that Hare's bliks are individualized. That is, that everyone has a different blik. In philosophical discussions this misunderstanding is referred to as belief in "private language games." Much vulgarized postmodern culture seems to thrive on this idea, that every individual has his or her own truth and that there is no need for or value in discovering and adhering to traditional, community-based metaphysical visions and language games that transcend individuals and their personal preferences or tastes. This is postfoundationalism gone to seed into cognitive nihilism, a kind of chaotic, anarchic, individualistic view of truth and knowledge that absolutely undermines any hope of morality or ethics outside the individual. Philosophers call this anomie—a cultural condition without norms, each person believing whatever seems right based on what benefits or suits himself or herself.

Philosopher MacIntyre, mentioned earlier as one of the editors of *New Essays in Philosophical Theology* and a major postfoundationalist thinker, has spent a lifetime attempting to counter this distortion of postfoundationalist, Wittgensteinian-inspired epistemology. In books such as *Whose Justice? Which Rationality?*

(1989), MacIntyre argued that all knowing takes place within some metaphysical vision, some world perspective, as Wittgensteinian epistemology says, that all "seeing" is "seeing as" and there is no "view from nowhere." But he also argued *against* any idea of private "seeing as," purely individualized, eclectic plausibility structures, metaphysical visions of reality. Rather, according to him, all knowing is shaped by some tradition-community and its story about ultimate reality. Individuals *may* attempt to invent their own worldviews, but in the end, there are really only a few, not many. Over much time and space, human communities develop such perspectives on reality based on overarching stories about the nature of the world and the meaning of life, and then hand them on from generation to generation. All authentic metaphysical visions, then, that are worthy of serious consideration and that are more than private belief-systems invented for personal gain and benefit to suit individuals' tastes and preferences, are bound to tradition-communities and shaped by their common stories. Biblical-Christian theism is one such metaphysical vision bound up with the Christian tradition and community and inspired by, rooted in, the biblical narrative.

No Apology for Believing

Before delving into an exploration and explanation of the biblical-Christian metaphysical vision, one more philosophical-theological preface will be helpful so that readers know where I am coming from in terms of methodology. I agree with the basic epistemology laid out briefly above—the postfoundationalist soft perspectivalism inspired by Wittgenstein, Hare, Ramsey, MacIntyre, and others. The biblical-Christian vision of reality is a "view from somewhere," a blik, a revealed-to-faith perspective that, in this writer's opinion, cannot be proved true but nevertheless is no private worldview based solely on a subjective leap of faith. It is rooted in the narrative of the Bible, the main purpose of which is to identify God for all people but especially for God's own people. This blik has been discerned and developed by the people of God over two thousand years—with many variations and sometimes strong disagreements about interpretation. It is universally true, true for everyone, everywhere and at all times, but not provable by some universal rationality. And yet, in spite of its not being provable by some independent, neutral rationality (which does not exist), it better answers life's ultimate questions than any competing worldview or metaphysical vision of reality.

People who call themselves Christians ought to know and understand the biblical-Christian vision of reality embedded in, often implicitly assumed by, the biblical narrative. It is their story; it is their faith community's perspective on reality. It is the metaphysical vision attached to, underlying, and supporting their theology. It is not a denominational creed or systematic theology; it is more general and abstract that that. Most Christian creeds and systems of theology (dogmatics) assume it without always expressing it. It needs explication because our culture is pluralistic—filled with competing metaphysical stories, visions, perspectives, bliks—and unless we know ours we will inevitably be influenced by others, often to the detriment of our faith journey and competent handling of issues that arise in Christian living. Discovering and understanding it cannot help but strengthen Christian faith, which is more than feeling. Christianity includes a worldview, a metaphysical vision, and is not reducible to feeling-based spirituality.

Postliberal, Narrative Christian Knowing

A relatively recent type of Christian theology, very Protestant in orientation, that fits postfoundationalism and is indirectly inspired by Wittgenstein and soft perspectivism is sometimes poorly labeled *postliberalism*. That is my basic theological orientation as to method.[14] Postliberal theology relies heavily on narrative theology such

---

14   For some very basic explanations of postliberal theology see: Roger E. Olson, "Back to the Bible (Almost): Why Yale's Postliberal Theologians Deserve an Evangelical Hearing," *Christianity Today* (May 20, 1996): 31–34; Gary Dorrien, "A Third Way in Theology? The Origins of Postliberalism," *Christian Century* (July 4–11, 2001): 16–21; and "Truth Claims: The Future of Postliberal Theology," *Christian Century* (July 18–25, 2001):

that the two are virtually inseparable.[15] The two postliberal-narrative theologians relied on here are the movement's real guru—Hans Frei (1922–88)—and the movement's clearest popularizer (a term not meant by any means to disparage), William Placher (1948–2008). Frei's classic book that helped launch the postliberal movement was *The Eclipse of Biblical Narrative: A Study in Eighteenth and Nineteenth Century Hermeneutics* (1974). Placher's semipopular exposition of postliberalism was *Unapologetic Theology: A Christian Voice in a Pluralistic Conversation* (1989).

Placher provides a helpful, brief description of postliberal theology thus:

> Christian theology lays out how the world looks from a Christian perspective, with whatever persuasive force that account musters and whatever connections it may happen to make with other perspectives, but it does not systematically ground or defend or explicate that picture in terms of universal criteria of meaningfulness or truth.[16]

The similarity of this approach to theology to the Wittgensteinian, postfoundationalist epistemology outlined above should be obvious. For Placher, as for all postliberals, Christian theology's main task is *not* correlation with other, non-Christian worldviews or plausibility structures, but self-description of the Christian view of reality from within the Christian tradition-community inspired by the biblical story. Much modern Christian thought has been obsessed with answering to secular philosophies and worldviews and attempting to correlate Christianity with them—in order to make Christian belief plausible and relevant to non-Christians.

22–29; and George Hunsinger, "Postliberal Theology," *The Cambridge Companion to Postmodern Theology*, ed. Kevin J. Vanhoozer (Cambridge, UK: Cambridge University Press, 2003), 42–57.

15   For an excellent introduction to and overview of narrative theology see Alister E. McGrath, "The Biography of God: Narrative Theologians Point to the Divine Stories that Shape Our Lives," *Christianity Today* (July 22, 1991): 22–24.

16   William C. Placher, *Unapologetic Theology: A Christian Voice in a Pluralistic Conversation* (Louisville: Westminster, 1989), 19.

This takes us back to philosopher Whitehead's aphorism that Christianity is a religion in search of a metaphysic. Not only in modern times but in medieval and ancient cultures many Christian thinkers have sought for and adopted nonbiblical, non-Christian philosophies not only as conversation partners for theology but as frameworks for explaining and making plausible biblical-Christian belief. According to Placher and postliberals, that project has always tended to subvert Christianity, accommodating it to secular or pagan philosophies. It assumed that Christianity could not stand on its own two feet, so to speak, but depended for its credibility on some borrowed non-Christian, extrabiblical metaphysic or worldview. Placher and postliberals assume that Christianity does not need such and can stand on its own two feet in the marketplace of ideas; it does not need correlation with extrabiblical, non-Christian plausibility structures or metaphysical perspectives, whether Greek or modern Western.

Placher went on in *Unapologetic Theology* to explain that "confronted by our culture's [or any culture's] standards of what makes sense and what doesn't, postliberal theology invites Christians to say, 'We don't look at things that way,' and to nurture communities that offer an alternative vision."[17] That alternative vision is the biblical-Christian metaphysical vision of reality and basic, orthodox Christian doctrines shared by all branches of historic, classical Christianity. According to Placher and other postliberals, both conservative and liberal Protestants have *tended* to accommodate Christianity to secular culture's plausibility structures, whether they be common sense realism (conservatives) or existentialism (some liberals) or process thought (other liberals). Those options do not exhaust the many extrabiblical frameworks borrowed by both conservative and liberal Protestants to attempt to make Christianity seem plausible to non-Christians.

Behind Placher stands his theology professor and mentor Frei.

---

17   Ibid., 19.

Perhaps Frei's most basic presupposition is that *for the Christian*, "the Bible absorbs the world."[18] All postliberal theology begins there. Placher explains Frei's point succinctly:

> Frei proposes a radical solution. Suppose we do not start with the modern world. Suppose we start [in theology] with the biblical world, and let those narratives define what is real, so that *our* lives have meaning to the extent that we fit them into *that* framework. . . . If we do that, then the truth of the biblical narratives does not depend on connecting them to some other *real* world. *They* describe the real world.[19]

In other words, being Christian means, *in part*, seeing the world *as* the reality described, or presupposed, by the Bible. According to Frei, Placher, and postliberals in general, there is a certain *unfaithfulness* and *inauthenticity* in Christians starting with some extrabiblical, secular, or pagan metaphysical vision, and then using that to determine *what the Bible must really mean* if it is to be credible.

Back to the Bible without Fundamentalism

Frei was not a biblical literalist; he was no fundamentalist. He did not think a Christian is committed to taking every story found in the Bible literally. Rather, he argued that faithful Christians ought to take the Bible seriously *as* "realistic narrative." In other words, the Bible ought not to be viewed either as *history* in the modern, literal sense (viz., a textbook of facts about history) or as *myth* (symbolic representation of universal human experience). Rather, a Christian should find the *meaning* of Scripture not outside it—whether in outer history or universal human experience—but inside of it. He

---

18   Frei did not actually articulate this pithy axiom often misattributed to him. Rather it was written by his Yale colleague and cofounder of postliberalism George Lindbeck in *The Nature of Doctrine: Religion and Theology in a Postliberal Age* (Louisville: Westminster, 1984), 118. However, it nicely expresses Frei's presupposition.

19   Placher, *Unapologetic Theology*, 161.

wrote, "If one uses the metaphorical expression 'location of meaning,' one would want to say that the location of meaning in narrative of the realistic sort is the text, the narrative structure or sequence itself."[20] Put most concisely, Frei's point is that *the Bible means what it says*. That should not be interpreted, however, as an expression of literalism; the Bible contains many literary genres and some of them are not to be taken literally. Frei's point is simply that the *meaning of the Bible is not outside of it.*

What Frei and Placher and other postliberals want to say is that there is no neutral, universal plausibility structure, metaphysical vision, or worldview, independent of any story or perspective, that determines the meaning of Scripture for Christians. Rather, the Bible itself is that plausibility structure, metaphysical vision, or worldview that determines for Christians the meaning of life and reality. The Bible is our *metanarrative*, to use a word common among postmodern thinkers. It is not a *totalizing* metanarrative like an ideology that coercively imposes itself on everyone and conditions all their thoughts and actions. It is a nontotalizing metanarrative—a story of God, revealed by God through human authors, that identifies God for all people but especially for God's own people. It is the lens through which Christians view the world; it absorbs the world for us.

Placher reveals clearly his and other postliberals' agreement with, if not dependence on, Wittgensteinian postfoundational soft perspectivalism. In complete agreement with MacIntyre, for example, Placher stressed that for postliberals the truth of Christianity's basic claims about reality is not dependent on a tradition-context even though the means of justifying them are. Christian truth is not merely true for Christians; it is universally true. But there is no universal plausibility structure or rationality inside of which one can prove it.[21]

---

20   Hans Frei, *The Eclipse of Biblical Narrative: A Study in Eighteenth and Nineteenth Century Hermeneutics* (New Haven and London: Yale University Press, 1974), 280.

21   Placher, *Unapologetic Theology*, 123.

In other words, just because one cannot *prove* Christianity true to all people does not mean that it is not true *for all people*. Postliberals adamantly deny relativism of any kind even as they affirm that *knowing* is always context dependent and perspectival. In other words, Christianity is a certain *blik*, but that does not undermine its truth status.

According to Placher and postliberals generally, the Christian plausibility structure, including what counts as evidence for truth, is "all tied up with a series of stories."[22] Those stories are found in the Bible, which itself constitutes an overarching story. But there's nothing unique or different about Christianity in that; all plausibility structures are story-shaped and tradition-community handed down. According to Placher and postliberals, the biblical story contains an inner logic that theology discerns and develops. For them, "*If* I buy into the stories [of the Bible], then I have to buy into that logic."[23] That logic, I suggest, is what is meant here by "biblical-Christian metaphysics"—a definite but sometimes hidden set of truths about ultimate reality. An analogy is Jesus's parables. They both revealed and hid the truth. They had definite points; they communicated truths. But their points, their truths, were not obvious to all. The inner logic of Jesus's parables was the kingdom of God. But knowing what Jesus was saying about the kingdom of God took and still takes some discernment. So it is with the biblical-Christian metaphysic. This book is an attempt to discern and explain the definite but sometimes hidden metaphysic of the Bible.

It's important to stop and repeat here, once and for all, that this is not a book of apologetics. It is a book that seeks to explicate the biblical-Christian metaphysic, worldview, perspective on reality, or plausibility structure for Christians. I do believe the Christian perspective on reality better answers life's ultimate questions than all alternatives and that is *one reason I find it convincing*. But more

---

22   Ibid., 130.
23   Ibid., 134.

than that, it is and always has been my *blik*; I have always inhabited that story and let it absorb the world for me. I had the privilege of growing up in a church and home saturated with the Bible, a church and home that trained me to *see* the world *as* the Bible depicts it. I want others to begin also to see the world that way—as the Bible depicts it. I want Christians to free themselves of syncretisms and take every thought captive to the biblical story.

Interlude 1

Throughout this book will appear brief interludes—
explanatory essays between chapters that usually
clarify issues raised in the previous chapter and set the
stage, as it were, for what follows. This is the first one
and its subject is postmodernity—especially as it relates
to *knowledge*.

Postmodernity/Postmodernism

Many people have wrongly equated postmodernism with
relativism—the denial of any absolutes—and with *cognitive
nihilism*—the denial of any access of human minds to reality
(if not denial of reality itself!). Admittedly there are postmodern
thinkers who go to those extremes with postmodernity. However,
those extremes are not necessary to postmodernity.

Postmodernity is a cultural condition, a set of *general perspectives*, after modernity. Modernity, in this sense, refers not to
a *time* but to a set of ideas or mental habits conditioned by the
Enlightenment. One such mental habit attached to modernity,
growing out of the Enlightenment, is *foundationalism* as explained
in chapter 1. Boiled down to its essence, it is the belief that the word
knowledge should be restricted to what can be proven either with
observed evidence (empiricism) or logic (rationalism) or both. It is
often referred to simply as rationalism, and its most extreme form
is *positivism*—the claim that all propositions that are not empirically or logically verifiable or falsifiable are *meaningless*. Most
scholars believe that foundationalism, and especially positivism,
led to secularism if not agnosticism. According to foundationalism,

life's ultimate questions, including the question of ultimate reality, cannot be answered with answers amenable to proof.

In its broadest sense, postmodernity is simply disillusionment with foundationalism and with its whole obsession with *certainty* through reason alone. Postmodernity is pervasively dissatisfied with the Enlightenment's belief in the *omnicompetence of reason*. Postmodernity does not necessarily deny *reason*; but to be truly postmodern is to be *suspicious of rationalism*. An excellent single volume, easy-to-understand postmodern critique of Enlightenment rationalism and of the whole modern project in philosophy is Stephen Toulmin's *Cosmopolis: The Hidden Agenda of Modernity* (1990). According to Toulmin (1922–2009) and other postmodern critics of modernity, modernity overreached itself and ended up using rationalism to justify an oppressive social and political system in which philosophical elites ruled over everyone else. Toulmin's book is a classic example of postmodern thought; it turns reason against rationalism—casting the spotlight of suspicion on rationalism's excesses.

Another critic of modern rationalism or foundationalism is philosopher John Caputo (b. 1940), who attacks modernity's rationalism as inimical to virtue and ethics, which depend on what he calls "impossibles"—transcendent ideals beyond rational proof, such as justice and hospitality. According to him, modern philosophy has suppressed *the human*, which is more than reason, and has resulted in a stultifying naturalism that relegates everything spiritual and religious to opinion if not superstition. His book *On Religion* is a practical companion to Toulmin's *Cosmopolis* in terms of critiquing modernism. In it he rejects modernity's tendencies toward secularism and uses a postmodern method of thought to reopen philosophy's door to the sacred. For him, as for many other postmodern thinkers, postmodernity creates new opportunities for the *spiritual*.

Another way of saying all that is that *postmodernity* necessarily includes *acknowledgment of perspectives* in epistemology—the ways and means of *knowing*. There is no "view from nowhere." There are no absolute, universal foundations, and proof is elusive in matters outside of mathematics. In other words, something akin to faith appears in all knowing in the *synthetic realm*—outside of mathematics and dictionary definitions (the analytical realm).

To be sure, some postmodern thinkers have gone much farther than that and denied *objective truth itself*, but that's not necessary to postmodernity. What is necessary to postmodernity is the denial of any human, rational, direct access to *truth itself*. Another way of putting that is that postmodernity insists on *at least* critical realism—belief that all knowing falls short of proof in the Enlightenment, foundationalist sense. *Perspectives always intrude.* All knowing takes place within tradition-communities shaped by narratives. Reality and truth may exist, many postmodern thinkers believe so, but the kind of cool, detached, direct, rational access to them is not possible. All knowing is infected by some set of narrative and tradition-based values.

Postliberalism and Postmodernism

Is postliberal theology a form of postmodernism? The similarities should be obvious, even if most postliberal theologians are not themselves excited about being categorized as postmodern. Christian philosopher-theologian Nancey Murphy (b. 1951) demonstrated the postmodern impulses within postliberal theology in *Beyond Liberalism and Fundamentalism: How Modern and Postmodern Philosophy Set the Theological Agenda* (1996). Postliberal theology is postmodern *insofar as* it rejects modernity's emphasis on foundationalism and opts instead for intratextual truth—that truth, or knowledge of truth, is always found *within some narrative framework,* and for the Christian that framework is narrated in canonical Scriptures.[1]

---

1   Nancey Murphy, *Beyond Liberalism and Fundamentalism: How Modern and Postmodern Philosophy Set the Theological Agenda* (Valley Forge, Pa.: Trinity Press, 1996), 128.

At the very least, postliberal theology is *postfoundationalist* in epistemological style. A question that often arises about it is whether it is fideist—resting its truth claims on faith alone. Postliberal theologians such as Placher reject that appellation. I believe postliberal theology is inherently *softly fideist* without being a form of *hard fideism*. The latter, hard fideism, would be belief that the Christian worldview is knowable *only to faith* and therefore, in some sense, *esoteric*. Soft fideism admits that the truth of the Christian worldview, in its fullness, is *revealed* but not *irrational*. That is, it is not accessible to *reason alone—working up from below—but once grasped it is not against reason*. In fact, once revealed and grasped by faith, it is the *most reasonable of all beliefs about ultimate reality* because *it has greater explanatory power than alternatives insofar as it provides satisfying answers to life's ultimate questions*. But that is not a matter of proof. Nevertheless, neither is it esotericism. The truth of the Christian vision of ultimate reality, the Christian life and worldview, is open to all to see, if they will. But *seeing* reality *as* it is described, or assumed, by the biblical narrative requires a shift in perspective for most, perhaps all, people. The biblical narrative itself explains this phenomenon by means of the category of "hardness of heart." Christians believe that, ultimately, only the Spirit of God imparting faith to the person can fully convince him or her of the truth about ultimate reality, because *sin* causes people to be closed minded toward it.

CHAPTER 2

Ultimate Reality Is Supernatural and Personal (But Not Human)

Some years ago I had a very interesting conversation about ultimate reality, the "really real" beyond appearances, with a professor of computer science at a Christian university. (As editor of a scholarly journal dedicated to faith-learning integration, I had numerous such conversations with professors and other scholars in many disciplines.) This computer science professor explained that ultimate reality is a great cosmic computer; he called it "God." When I, as a Christian theologian, attempted to explain that, according to the Bible, God is personal, the computer science professor immediately jumped to the conclusion that I was saying God, ultimate reality, is a human being. Naturally, he objected most strenuously.

This illustrates the all-too-common problem mentioned in the Introduction—Christians, even Christian scholars, creating their own syncretistic, eclectic metaphysical visions in complete ignorance of the Bible's worldview and, worse yet, untutored in even basic Christian theology about the nature of God.

Clearing Away Distracting Underbrush

Let's begin by clearing away some inevitable and distracting underbrush. All words can create confusion, especially when they are used for reality beyond the visible, for reality that is transcendent. The claim here, in this chapter, will be that the Bible everywhere and always presupposes that ultimate reality is supernatural. Of course, the word *supernatural* has many meanings in contemporary culture, many of them completely inappropriate here. Go into any major secular bookstore and you will probably see a section called "The Supernatural." It may also, or alternatively, be called "Metaphysical." The books in that section will probably, almost certainly, be about the *occult*. Somehow bookstores, and much of popular culture, have come to equate *supernatural* and *metaphysical* with *esoteric* and *occult*. *Esoteric* means "hidden" and usually refers to religious-spiritual beliefs and practices known only by a spiritual elite and possibly those who read their books! *Occult* also means "hidden," possibly even "secret," and usually refers to some form of divination—communication with and manipulation of supernatural powers.

Supernatural need not mean either of those, however, and it is a word with a long history often ignored by popular culture. Many people in popular culture, ignorant of that philosophical-theological history, automatically think of *supernatural* as either occultism or miracles or both. *Metaphysical*, of course, as already explained, does not mean only occult or esoteric. Those may have metaphysical visions of reality; they often do. But *metaphysical* itself is not tied to esoteric beliefs or occult practices. It is extremely unfortunate that these good words have come to be so closely tied to esotericism and occultism.

Another word popularly misunderstood and misused is *personal*. The majority of people, like the computer science professor, tend to equate *personal* with *human*, and they tend to individualize it—especially in Western cultures. If something is "personal" it is automatically pictured as human, and a "person" is an individual human self. Again, however, there is a long history of belief, especially among religious people, of personal beings who are not human: angels, demons, even mythical creatures such as goblins and fairies. To be "personal" does not necessarily mean "human"— except perhaps to a secular humanist, a person whose metaphysical view of reality is *naturalism*—that nature is all there is and humans are simply nature become conscious and free (self-transcending).

These terms are really quite unavoidable. Many times when good words become widely misused people call for new words to replace them. That's not always possible. It certainly should not be necessary. It is important and helpful, however, to explain what one means when using words that are widely misused and misunderstood.

The Bible depicts ultimate reality—the highest, best, final, eternal reality upon which all else is dependent—as *supernatural* and *personal* but *not human*. Here *supernatural* simply means "beyond nature," *not bound to nature and nature's laws*, free over nature, not controlled by nature. Some people would prefer the word *transcendent* for all that, but this writer judges it not strong enough to do justice to the Bible's vision of ultimate reality. Yes, ultimate reality, according to the Bible, *is* transcendent, which means "over nature," but *supernatural* adds a special oomph to transcendent, emphasizing that it is free from nature and cannot be regarded as a special higher dimension or depth dimension of nature itself (as some people use the word).

So much for now for *supernatural*. What about *personal*? The Bible depicts ultimate reality as *personal,* which here means *having intelligence, thought, intentions, actions, and some degree of self-determination*. It also means "relational"—being in relation to others, drawing one's identity partly, at least, from relations with others. From this definition of *personal* it should be obvious that some humans are *not* fully personal and yet are humans. One thinks, for example, of people in a vegetative state as a result of illness or accident. According to the Bible, *personal* in the sense described above is not limited to human beings. Most importantly here, according to the Bible, ultimate reality is *both* supernatural *and* personal—something scandalous to many secular and pagan belief systems that tend to deny anything supernatural and view being personal as a defect of finitude, creatureliness, and mortality.

That which is ultimate, they say, cannot be personal because personal implies limitations, growth, others, perhaps even time!

Problems immediately appear here. If personal does not necessarily mean human, what do we know about it that is not based on humanity? The specter of projection looms over this whole discussion of ultimate reality as personal. Are we not, as atheist philosopher Ludwig Feuerbach (1804–72) argued, simply projecting ourselves, humanity, onto ultimate reality? After all, what do we know about the category "person" except human personhood? And before Feuerbach, another German philosopher named Johann Fichte (1762–1814) argued that calling ultimate reality *personal* is fraught with problems especially since *personal* implies, as with humans, limitation. Even a nonhuman person, according to Fichte, would be limited, finite, because to be personal is to be in relation to others.

These are philosophical problems that have caused many people, including not a few Christians, to shy away from regarding ultimate reality as personal. Theologian Tillich, for example, responded by referring to ultimate reality, which he called "Being Itself," and which he equated with God, as "suprapersonal."

Be all that as it may, nothing could be clearer to the unbiased Bible reader than that it depicts ultimate reality as *not* a *thing* or *object* or mere *force* or *power* but as *someone* who *thinks, deliberates, acts, enters into relationships with others, responds to others,* and *has freedom to determine himself.* And it depicts ultimate reality—that which is beyond appearance, upon which all else depends, the source of all that is—as *more than nature, not part of nature,* even *the author of nature who is free to intervene in it.* What words are better suited to describe such an ultimate reality than *personal* and *supernatural*—even if they are inadequate and problematic?

What *Supernatural* Means (And Does Not Mean)

Let's take a critical look at the alleged problems with describing ultimate reality and see if they are insuperable obstacles after all.

We begin with *supernatural*. As already suggested, many people, including many Christians, shy away from the word itself for a variety of reasons. Many of those reasons can easily be satisfied by carefully defining the term. Christian philosophical theologian John Oman (1860–1939), who taught at Cambridge University in England, defined it thus: "The Supernatural means the world which manifests more than natural values, the world which has values which stir the sense of the holy and demand to be esteemed as sacred."[1] He went on to describe the supernatural as the "higher environment" that provokes a sense of sacredness in people, "the holy," that grounds everything absolute: "All absoluteness, without which truth is mere useful information, morals mere expedient actions, beauty mere pleasing of the senses, is from . . . the Supernatural."[2]

Clearly, then, *supernatural* does not necessarily mean anything like "occult" or even "miraculous" in the common, ordinary sense. Nor, however, does it mean merely "transcendent," a word with much less meaning, a more abstract term than *supernatural*. Nor does *supernatural* necessarily demean "natural." As Oman said, "The two [supernatural and natural] are not in opposition, but are so constantly interwoven that nothing may be wholly natural or wholly supernatural."[3] Still, and nevertheless, *supernatural* does contrast with *natural* in pointing to something beyond nature, even if it pervades and upholds and interacts with nature. The ultimate reality of the Bible is constantly interacting with nature and is nature's source and sustainer, not nature's enemy. More about that (viz., the Bible's view of the supernatural) later.

All that is simply to say that calling the ultimate reality of the biblical story "supernatural" does not imply what many people might assume, if they are going by the popular images of what is supernatural. The biblical story depicts ultimate reality as *more*

---

1   John Oman, *The Natural and the Supernatural* (New York: Macmillan, 1931), 71.
2   Ibid., 310.
3   Ibid., 72.

than, above, or the source and sustainer of nature. In fact, the implication is that nature itself is that ultimate reality's "work," as it were.

What *Personal* Means (And Does Not Mean)

Now, back to the category *personal*. Philosophical metaphysics has always had trouble calling ultimate reality "personal" for the reasons mentioned and more reasons. In fact, the long history of philosophical metaphysics, from Plato in ancient Greece to Hegel in nineteenth-century Germany, has *tended* to *depersonalize* ultimate reality, to represent ultimate reality as *impersonal*, a power, force, or principle behind appearances. If ultimate reality is the *source* of all that is in the universe, so the argument goes, it must be *limitless, perfect, infinite, not subject to change and decay*. Personhood, so the argument goes, necessarily implies the opposite of all that. Personhood is necessarily *dependent*; ultimate reality as the source of finite reality that appears must be *nondependent* and therefore *impersonal* or suprapersonal.

The Bible presents a different picture of ultimate reality than extrabiblical, rational, speculative metaphysics. It elevates *personhood* (as described earlier) to ultimacy; the source of all finite reality, of nature and all it contains, is revealed as irreducibly *personal* and not just an impersonal (or even suprapersonal) force, power, or principle. Can reason alone establish this? Perhaps not. But one deleterious effect of depicting ultimate reality as impersonal is the demeaning of personal reality, of relationship and community, and a tendency to elevate as "like the ultimate" the isolated, static, unchangeable individual.

Is depicting ultimate reality as personal mere projection, as Feuerbach and other atheists have claimed? Not necessarily. In fact, from a biblical-Christian perspective, not at all. One simple answer to that challenge is offered by, among others, Karl Barth, who never tired of emphasizing that human persons are *copies* of ultimate personhood, the God of the Bible. God himself projects, as it were, his own personhood onto human creatures in creating them in his image and likeness. Catholic thinkers such as twentieth-century Polish theologian Erich Przywara (1889–1972), whom Barth loved to debate, have argued for an "analogy of being" between ultimate reality, the God of the Bible, and human persons based on the image of God.[4] Barth's alternative was what he called the "analogy of faith." In either case, both Protestants and Catholics agree, the ultimate reality of the Bible, Yahweh, God the Lord, is *personal* in the primary, supreme sense, the pattern of true personhood, while human beings are *personal* in the secondary sense, copies of the pattern of true personhood. Calling the God of the Bible, the Bible's ultimate reality, "personal" is not projection; calling human beings "personal" is rather projection downward, as it were, saying that human persons, at their best, reflect something crucial about ultimate reality itself.

All of the above is a necessary clearing away of the underbrush. It is cutting a path through the dense growth of philosophical and cultural objections and confusions about important points of the biblical-Christian worldview. And much more could be done in that regard. So very much confusion surrounds the concepts we are dealing with here—all of it coming from popular and philosophical misconceptions about concepts like *personal* and *supernatural.*

What, then, about the third part of the thesis with which this chapter began—that the Bible's ultimate reality, although *personal,* is *not human?* Well, that has already been touched on in the

---

4   The issue of the "analogy of being" (*analogia entis*) is far too complicated to get into here. Suffice it to say that Barth may have misunderstood it; he certainly did if his sympathetic Catholic conversation partner Hans Urs von Balthasar (1905–88) is correct. For a thorough discussion of the twentieth-century debate over the concept of the "analogy of being," see Keith L. Johnson, *Karl Barth and the Analogia Entis* (London and New York: T & T Clark, 2010). Protestant theologian Emil Brunner, Barth's contemporary and counterpart in Switzerland, also a proponent of so-called "dialectical theology," disagreed with Barth's strong rejection of an "analogy of being" between God and humanity. He affirmed it while cautioning, in very Protestant fashion, that due to sin the analogy is broken and difficult to see without faith. Yet, *ontologically*, Brunner affirmed that God and humanity share being. Brunner stood between Barth and his Catholic debate partners (Pryzwara and Balthasar) about this. See Brunner, "Nature and Grace," 55.

foregoing discussion of why many people object to calling ultimate reality—which must be in some sense *perfect*, free of the decaying limitations of nature—"personal." The objection should *not* be that; it should, however, be focused on viewing personal ultimate reality, Israel's God, the God of Jesus Christ, human *in and of himself.* Being human is being finite, limited, mortal, composed of parts, subject to determination by what is outside of the self. Ultimate reality cannot be that, and the Bible marks a deep line between ultimate reality, God, and the human while connecting them as original pattern and copy. That connection is *the personal.* Humans, though finite and limited, subject to dependency and decay, are also personal, like God, the ultimate reality on which they depend, their source and sustainer. This will be explored more fully in a later chapter on biblical humanism. Suffice it to say here and now that the view the Bible takes, and that all of Christian tradition has held to, is that God—ultimate reality—is not a human being (in spite of what some sectarian groups calling themselves Christian say) but is personal.

Naturally, some readers will be asking at this point, "But didn't God become human in Jesus Christ?" They will be thinking about and raising the question of the *incarnation*—a key Christian doctrine. However, the doctrine of the incarnation has never been that God is *in and of himself human*; the doctrine of the incarnation is that *in Jesus Christ God took on humanity*—adding a human nature to his divine nature so that Jesus Christ was one person with two natures—one human and one divine. This preserves the biblical distinctness between God and creation while admitting that *humanness* is in some sense above the rest of creation, a proper vehicle for God's indwelling. The ground for that is *personhood.* God and humans share it, although in different ways and to different degrees.

Now it is time to turn to the biblical narrative itself to discover its own ways of expressing that ultimate reality is *supernatural and personal but not human.*

How the Biblical Narrative Depicts Ultimate Reality

According to the biblical narrative ultimate reality, the supernatural source of everything upon which all finite being depends, is God, a being above and beyond the world, yet abiding in and with it, who speaks, acts, and freely enters into reciprocal relationships with creatures by responding to their acts and pleas. The clearest revelation of him in Hebrew literature is found in the writings of the prophet who wrote under the name Isaiah.[5] Isaiah begins by speaking on behalf of God who calls his Hebrew people, his chosen people, to reason with him (1:18 KJV); he warns them of judgment for disobedience (idolatry and injustice), and promises them forgiveness for repentance and renewed faithfulness to the covenant he established with them. Yahweh God, the Creator and Lord of all the earth, the Holy (separated, above) One, enters into negotiations with his people, threatening and promising them—based on their response to his call. Isaiah's vision (6:1–9) is a classical biblical text pointing to God's ultimacy, God's supernatural existence as high and lofty. God's personal nature is expressed through his emotional outbursts of anger at the people's unfaithfulness and injustice and his compassion if they will repent and turn around. This supernatural being, this holy one, this creator of all and covenant maker, is passionate. Many philosophically minded interpreters have treated such divine emotions in Hebrew narratives as anthropomorphisms, figures of speech attributing to God humanlike characteristics, who as ultimate reality, is supposedly incapable of emotions because such are allegedly too limiting. We will return to this later; suffice it to say for now that Isaiah's revelation of God cannot so easily be interpreted figuratively. And Isaiah was not alone in this; the book of the prophet Hosea, among others, reveals God as emotional, showing grief, anger, and compassion.

---

5   I am well aware of the scholarly distinction between first and second Isaiah and the belief of many biblical scholars in a third Isaiah. That is, many scholars believe, and it is well-established, that the Old Testament book of Isaiah was actually penned by two or three individuals. Here, however, Isaiah will be used to refer to the book as it stands in the Christian canon.

A recurring theme throughout Isaiah is God's steadfast love for his people. Through the prophet God promises the people blessing because of his steadfast love, but on the condition that they return to him in faithfulness to their covenant (16:4–5). A most interesting narrative in Isaiah is about God's responsiveness to a king's plea to extend his life (chapter 38). God sends the prophet to inform King Hezekiah of his impending death. The king begs God for more years of life and God listens and relents, changing what he decreed would happen, giving Hezekiah fifteen more years to live (38:5). Again, this is often chalked up to anthropomorphic speech by philosophically minded interpreters who bring *to* the text baggage borrowed from extrabiblical philosophies. According to most extrabiblical metaphysical schemes, ultimate reality cannot be affected by finite beings. Plato's "Form of the Good," Aristotle's "Unmoved Mover" and "Thought thinking itself," Hegel's "Absolute Spirit"—all are incapable of changing his (or its) mind in response to events in time, space, and history. But God, the ultimate being, the absolute person of biblical revelation, is intensely personal, self-limiting, and self-determining, and can voluntarily change his mind in response to his covenant partners' pleas.

But is the Yahweh God of Isaiah really ultimate? Does he deserve such an exalted metaphysical title? Again, Isaiah answers (or God answers through Isaiah): "'To whom will you compare me? Or who is my equal?' says the Holy One. 'Lift up your eyes and look to the heavens: Who created all these? He who brings out the starry host one by one and calls forth each of them by name. Because of his great power and mighty strength, not one of them is missing'" (40:25–26). Thus Isaiah leaves no doubt about Yahweh God's ultimacy as the sole source of all things upon whom everything is dependent. "This is what God the LORD says—the Creator of the heavens, who stretches them out, who spreads out the earth with all that springs from it, who gives breath to its people, and life to those who walk on it" (42:5). And yet, this same supernatural, all-powerful God upon whom everything depends for its existence makes covenant with people: "I, the LORD, have called you in righteousness; I will take hold of your hand. I will keep you and will make you to be a covenant for the people and a light for the Gentiles, to open eyes that are blind" (42:6–7). Lest anyone think this creator and covenant-making God of steadfast love and judgment, this ethically minded Lord over all, is one of many, he speaks through Isaiah, declaring, "I am the LORD, the maker of all things, who stretches out the heavens, who spreads out the earth by myself" (44:24). Also lest anyone think other beings beside him determine the outcome of things, the course of history, Yahweh declares through Isaiah his absolute sovereignty: "I am the LORD, and there is no other. I form the light and create darkness, I bring prosperity and create disaster; I, the LORD, do all these things" (45:6–7).

Clearly the God who reveals himself through Isaiah is both *supernatural* and *personal* in the senses described above. And this God, Yahweh, reveals himself as *ultimate reality*—the sole source of all that is, above whom there is no other. This God holds all power, even if he delegates some to his creatures, and at the same time is free to use that power however he wishes to, even to the extent of holding it back and not using it as he threatened to. And this ultimate reality, Yahweh, is by nature loving-kindness, a long-suffering and compassionate God who also cares about justice and will not forever withhold judgment. These are all major themes of Isaiah as well as the rest of the Hebrew Bible.

The New Testament Underscores Ultimate Reality as Supernatural and Personal

The New Testament, considered by Christians a further revelation of God, builds on the Hebrew idea of ultimate reality—as one, supernatural, personal (but not human) God upon which everything else is dependent. A clear example of that is given in Acts. Paul, the Hebrew convert to Christianity, travels to Athens and engages Greek Gentiles in conversation about ultimate reality (Acts 17).

Some of Paul's interlocutors in Athens were Epicurean and Stoic philosophers whose visions of ultimate reality differed radically from the Hebrew one. Stoics, for example, considered nature itself ultimate; their ultimate reality was impersonal. Other Athenians believed in no one ultimate reality but in many deities. Paul, in complete agreement with Isaiah, tells the Athenians, "The God who made the world and everything in it is the Lord of heaven and earth and does not live in temples built by human hands. And he is not served by human hands, as if he needed anything. Rather, he himself gives everyone life and breath and everything else" (17:24–25). Then Paul adds a dimension completely consistent with the Hebrew idea of God and perhaps drawn from the Psalms (e.g., Psalm 139):

> "From one man he made all the nations, that they should inhabit the whole earth; and he marked out their appointed times in history and the boundaries of their lands. God did this so that they would seek him and perhaps reach out for him and find him, though he is not far from any of us. 'For in him we live and move and have our being.' As some of your own poets have said, 'We are his offspring.'" (Acts 17:26–28)

In Athens Paul articulated concisely what later Christian thinkers came to refer to as God's *transcendence* and *immanence*—that God is *both* present within creation and exalted above creation as its source and sustainer who needs nothing. (Psalm 139 also emphasizes God's transcendence and immanence—as does the whole Hebrew narrative of God.)

Clearly, the whole biblical narrative identifies ultimate reality, that upon which everything is dependent, as both *supernatural* (in the sense described above) and *personal* (in the sense described above) and yet *not human* (except in and through the incarnation). This reality identifies himself by giving his name to his people: "I AM" (Exodus 3:14), which came to be expressed by the name *YHWH* or *Yahweh* (translated as *Jehovah* in many English translations of the Bible). (Hebrews and early Christians often substituted *Adonai*, Lord, for the holy name of God out of reverence for God's holiness.) Christian theologian Brunner, among others, made much of God's giving of his name. According to him, this signaled that ultimate reality is personal and not an impersonal power, force, or principle—as rational metaphysics, not based on revelation, has often implied.[6] That God has a name and gives it to people points to his supernatural aspect as well as his personal aspect. The fullness of *who* God is cannot be discovered by mere mortals on their own; God must enter into their sphere of life and relate to them—and that God did and does.

Summing up, the biblical view of ultimate reality is that it is not an *it* but a *he*.[7] According to the biblical narrative, which Christians believe to be God's own story about himself and the world—including especially his covenant people—ultimate, final, eternal, all-powerful, all-determining reality is a personal being both beyond the natural world and dynamically present within it. This metaphysical vision has variously been labeled "personalistic theism" and "biblical theistic personalism." At the heart of ultimate reality, the one unifying source behind and within everything, is an intelligence, free agency, and independent will marked by loving-kindness and justice.

Nonbiblical Philosophies and the God of the Bible

Throughout the centuries after the Bible was written, many people, including many Christians, have thought, with Whitehead, that

---

6   Emil Brunner, *Dogmatics I: The Christian Doctrine of God*, trans. Olive Wyon (Philadelphia: Westminster, 1950), 128–36.

7   This writer is well aware that many contemporary people are offended by referring to God as "he" because, to them, it implies that God is male. One leading feminist thinker said that "if God is male, then the male is God." This saying is so common and so widely discussed (e.g., on the internet) that no specific source need be cited. It has entered into the stream of common discourse and religion and feminism. However, there is a problem with the English language here. There is no personal pronoun that is gender neutral. Many scholars and others have attempted to substitute *Godself* for him, but that, in this writer's opinion, is awkward at best and, like *it*, implies that God is *in himself* impersonal. The solution to the problem is to emphasize, as nearly all modern and contemporary Jewish and Christian writers do, that, although the Bible refers to God as *he* and as *Father* (etc.), this should not be taken to mean that God is male, and it certainly does not mean that the male is God! This writer will continue to use the personal pronoun *he* for the Hebrew-Christian ultimate reality because nearly all English Bibles do so.

Christianity needs to borrow its metaphysic from some other source than the Bible. The assumption has often been that the Bible, because it is a religious narrative and not a book of philosophy, needs supplementation by a speculative, rational philosophy to fill in the gaps or undergird its story about God. Beginning in the first century after Christ (the second century AD) and continuing for two millennia afterward, even Christian thinkers have searched for and found extrabiblical metaphysical visions to help Christianity explain itself. The first such interpretive metaphysical framework used by Christians was Middle Platonism—a Greek philosophy widely respected among educated people in the Roman Empire. A precedent for this had been set by the Jewish scholar Philo (20 BC–AD 50), who, in Alexandria, Egypt, had borrowed from Plato and his disciples to interpret and explain the true meaning of the Hebrew Scriptures. Church fathers known as "Apologists," such as Justin Martyr and Origen (second and third centuries), interpreted the Bible through the lens of Platonic philosophy. Beginning with Origen and continuing through fifth-century theologian Augustine of Hippo and hitting its pinnacle with an anonymous Christian writer known as Pseudo-Dionysius the Areopagite (late fifth to early sixth century), a new type of Greek philosophy known as Neoplatonism was used by Christian thinkers as the metaphysical framework for interpreting Scripture and explaining Christian theology to educated, intellectually minded Roman people.

During the great age of Christendom, the union of church and empires in Europe, many Christian thinkers such as Thomas Aquinas (1225–74) turned to Aristotle's philosophy as a new lens for interpreting the Bible and explaining Christianity to the educated elite of culture. Through Thomas, dubbed the "Angelic Doctor" by the Catholic Church, Aristotelianism became the semiofficial metaphysical vision attached to the Bible and Christian theology. Both Platonism and Aristotelianism *tended* to portray ultimate reality as impersonal or at least nonrelated in any way that might affect it. The "logic of perfection" lay at their roots. The idea was that the *Arché* —the source of all finite, mortal reality including time and space, nature itself—must be free of whatever qualities impaired creatureliness. And so God, the *Arché*, was regarded by many church fathers and medieval theologians as incapable of any kind of change or suffering, free of the limitations of time and space. The tendency grew and became firmly entrenched to regard all the biblical references to God's intimate interactions with creatures— especially where God is affected by them, provoked to emotions, or where God changes his mind or plans because of them—as anthropomorphisms, figures of speech and not realistic descriptions of anything happening within or to God who, as ultimate reality, the *Arché* of all things, must be totally invulnerable.[8]

Of course, Christian thinkers from Justin Martyr to Aquinas and beyond, who used Greek philosophical metaphysics to interpret the Bible and explain Christianity, did not accept or endorse all of it lock, stock, and barrel. No, as numerous historical theologians have pointed out, they adopted and adapted them, as much Christianizing them as Hellenizing Christianity. However, as German theologian Wolfhart Pannenberg (1928–2014) often argued, "The living God of the Bible . . . can be distinguished from the idea of God that is found in Greek philosophy by the fact that he is seen to be free to act powerfully in the world."[9] Unfortunately, many Christian theologians who relied heavily on Greek philosophy, who thought the Bible did not have its own metaphysical vision of ultimate reality and who borrowed Greek ones, *tended* to water down, if not implicitly deny, God's *personal* nature as *relational* and *living* and *active*. The stress fell instead on the Greek idea of ultimate reality as

---

8   This account of the Greek idea of ultimate reality as the Arché and its influence on early and medieval Christian thought is influenced by this writer's theology professor Wolfhart Pannenberg. Pannenberg discussed this issue as a problem for Christian theology throughout his writings including, for example, in *Faith and Reality*, trans. John Maxwell (Philadelphia: Westminster, 1977) and in various articles contained in the collections published in English under the title *Basic Questions in Theology* (Minneapolis: Fortress, 1970).

9   Pannenberg, *Faith and Reality*, 10–11.

self-sufficient, moving but unmoved, incapable of having emotions or being affected by creatures. The *living* God of the Bible, supernatural and personal, gradually came to be regarded as *static* and *untouched* by the world with all its alleged metaphysical messiness of time, chaos, struggle, and evil.

Nineteenth-and twentieth-century Protestant philosophers and theologians discovered new and quite different metaphysical visions for interpreting the Bible and Christianity. Discarding Greek philosophy, many liberal Protestants turned instead to various forms of *idealism*—a type of philosophy that emphasized ultimate reality as *mind* and *thought*. The German philosopher G. W. F. Hegel (1770–1831) interpreted ultimate reality as "absolute spirit" or "absolute mind" and created an amalgam of Christianity with his own unique, modern, rationalist metaphysic. Many Protestant theologians latched onto Hegel's philosophical theology which depicted ultimate reality, God, Absolute Spirit or Mind, as inseparably tied to human history. Hegel and his followers created a Christianized form of pan*en*theism in which God and the world are eternally interdependent such that "without a world God is not God."[10] God, for them, became dependent on the world for his full self-actualization. God's *supernatural* aspect began to disappear.

During the twentieth century certain Protestant theologians known as "process theologians" began to borrow heavily from Whitehead's metaphysical vision of ultimate reality that, like Hegel's, made God a prisoner of the world (panentheism): "It is as true to say that God creates the world as that the world creates God."[11] God and the world are, in that metaphysic, locked together inseparably in an eternal process of evolution with God as the superior partner. For process thought, God is personal but ultimate only in the sense that he is universally related, exercising persuasive power but unable to cause anything to happen. Process thought tends to naturalize

---

10   Quentin Lauer, *Hegel's Concept of God* (Albany, N.Y.: SUNY Press, 1982), 272.
11   Whitehead, *Process and Reality*, corrected ed. (New York: Free Press, 1978), 348.

God such that nature, interpreted broadly enough, includes God. God becomes for it a depth dimension to nature, not a supernatural being creating and determining the world. It might be fair to say that for it, there *is no* ultimate reality, at least nothing *absolute* or *infinite* and certainly nothing *supernatural*.[12]

These are just a few of the major extrabiblical, metaphysical visions of ultimate reality, or reality beyond appearance, that Christian thinkers have adopted and adapted to help interpret and explain the biblical story of God and the world. *The assumption behind all of these projects is that the Bible itself does not have a philosophy, a metaphysic, and stands in need of one borrowed from elsewhere.*

Illustrating the Problem (Syncretism) with Ethics

An analogy from Christian ethics might help explain this situation. During the 1970s and 1980s American Mennonite theologian John Howard Yoder (1927–97) argued very strongly that Christian ethics, especially Christian *social ethics*, was in trouble. His foil was leading Christian ethicist Reinhold Niebuhr (1892–1971) of Union Theological Seminary, author of numerous influential books promoting Christian realism—a type of theological ethics that supported just war and Christian involvement in the harsh realities of government, including the military. According to Yoder, in his very influential book *The Politics of Jesus* (1972) and elsewhere, Niebuhr and other Christian ethicists, both Catholic and Protestant,

---

12   Process thought and the theology it has inspired (process theology) is one major reason why this writer chooses to use the much maligned word *supernatural* for the ultimate reality of the biblical narrative rather than *transcendent*. Certainly the God of biblical-Christian metaphysics *is* transcendent; he transcends the world. But *transcendent* is insufficient in light of process thought and process theology, where God is described as transcendent but not supernatural. According to Whitehead and his theological disciples, God is one among many, he is limited and finite, and he is incapable of controlling the process of the world, which is controlled by the free choices of creatures who can either embody or resist God's ideal will. God is interpreted as transcendent *in the sense* of being *universally related*. God's job, as it were, *within nature*, is to present to each actual occasion coming into existence (not created by him) with an ideal aim and to persuade it to accept and live out that ideal aim for harmony. But every actual occasion has freedom to resist God's ideal aim. For Whitehead and process thinkers, including process theologians, God is necessary and transcendent but not supernatural, personal but not absolute or sovereign.

had wrongly assumed that the Bible itself contained no workable ethic for public life, only an ethic for private life. Niebuhr and
others, so Yoder cogently explained, had turned to extrabiblical,
philosophical ethics for Christian social ethics. Yoder claimed that
the Bible, including especially the New Testament, and particularly
the teachings of Jesus, *do in fact* contain *and* promote a workable
Christian social ethic. It was ignored, he argued, because Christians
like Niebuhr wanted to correlate Christianity with non-Christian
culture, including war. But since Jesus and the New Testament
promote an ethic absolutely opposed to war, Niebuhr and others
like him (including the whole Catholic tradition going back at least
to Augustine) had supplemented the ethic of Jesus with an extrabiblical ethic that, in the end, set aside Jesus's teachings about
violence and peace. After Yoder died, his friend theologian Stanley
Hauerwas of Duke University picked up where he left off, making
the same argument against all attempts by Christians to draw on
philosophical ethics that ignore or override the ethics of Jesus and
the New Testament. Hauerwas has been especially hard on Niebuhr
in that regard.[13]

Some modern Christian thinkers have come to believe something similar about metaphysics and the Bible. Like Yoder objecting
to Niebuhr (and implicitly the whole long tradition of Christian
social ethics going back to Augustine), these modern Christian
thinkers argue that *most* of Christian theology has been wrong
about the Bible needing to be interpreted through the lens of some
extrabiblical, philosophical metaphysical vision. For the most part,
anyway, they do not object to Christian theology *borrowing* from
extrabiblical philosophies to *supplement* biblical metaphysics, but
they object to any wholesale *imposition* of extrabiblical philosophy

---

13   The literature about this controversy is vast. For Niebuhr's position see *An Interpretation of Christian Ethics*, reprint ed. (Philadelphia: Westminster, 2013). For Yoder see *The Politics of Jesus*, 2d ed. (Grand Rapids, Mich.: Eerdmans, 1994). For Hauerwas see *With the Grain of the Universe: The Church's Witness and Natural Theology*, reprint ed. (Grand Rapids, Mich.: Baker Academic, 2013).

onto the Bible *as if* the Bible itself is devoid of one or *as if* its metaphysical vision is so weak as to be worthy of ignoring.

As will be seen in the next chapter, these theologians, especially Tresmontant and Cherbonnier, claimed about the Bible and philosophy exactly the same as Yoder (and Hauerwas) claimed about the Bible and social ethics. That is, that throughout the centuries and yet today Christian thinkers have succumbed to the temptation to *replace* the thinking of the Bible with *alien* philosophies under the wrong assumption that the Bible is a bunch of stories from which no reasonable, workable metaphysical vision (or ethic) can be drawn for later cultures and their Christians.

These back-to-the-Bible Christian theologians who wish to *retrieve* biblical metaphysics, disentangling it from the accretions of later centuries of philosophical theology, should not be confused with fundamentalism. The early church father Tertullian (160–220) is famous, or infamous, for rejecting philosophy, asking, "What has Athens to do with Jerusalem?" and answering, "Nothing." Tertullian, like modern fundamentalists, was vehemently antiphilosophical and a biblical literalist. He found no good in extrabiblical philosophies such as Platonism (Athens). He was overreacting to the project of Origen, his contemporary North African Christian thinker, who blended Platonism with the Bible (Athens with Jerusalem). The irony is, of course, that even Tertullian was not free of philosophical influences; he was (perhaps unconsciously) influenced by Stoicism! Modern-day fundamentalism tends to shun philosophy altogether; many of its adherents would even deny there is any such thing as a biblical philosophy or metaphysic. Most take the Bible as literally as possible, viewing it as a not-yet-systematized system of doctrines.

The theologians of the next chapter, represented especially by Tresmontant and Cherbonnier, were not fundamentalists; they were not literalists or opponents of all philosophy. Both held earned doctorates in theology and were thoroughly familiar with intellectual history, especially philosophy as it bears on theology. Both were highly regarded, influential Christian thinkers with ecumenical influence. And yet, like Yoder (and Hauerwas), they believed that much Christian theology has been held captive to extrabiblical philosophies when, in fact, the philosophy of the Bible *can stand on its own two feet.*

Interlude 2

Before proceeding to our explication of the Bible's metaphysical vision of reality, it will be helpful, even essential, to stop and clear up some possible misconceptions.

Science and Ultimate Reality

First, readers should not assume, based on the previous discussion of epistemology, that I believe *science* is doubtful or unimportant. Some critics of science have used postfoundationalism and the fact that even science works within paradigms (bliks) to accuse science of being not factual but only a bunch of opinions. With the rise of postmodernism and fundamentalism a deep and dangerous antiscience attitude has appeared especially in America. I believe that all facts, including scientific ones, are influenced by subjectivity; all facts are someone's interpretations of reality. All facts are open to possible revision in light of further research and changing paradigms based on research. However, that should not be used to demean science or ignore its settled, material conclusions—even if they are open to revision.

It's important to make a distinction between science and scientism. The latter is an irrational commitment to science as the *only* reliable path to knowledge and as *beyond criticism* (except perhaps by scientists themselves). It is a kind of idolatry of science—at least from a religious perspective. It is putting science on a pedestal where people tend to worship it and judge all beliefs in its light. That is clearly contrary to postfoundationalism as well as to most religious beliefs. It makes the scientific method a religion and scientists its priests.

Science, however, is simply the examination and exploration of physical regularities in nature. It is always worked out from within some vision of reality; it is always influenced by scientists' nonscientific commitments. Therefore, it is not purely objective. Its conclusions are rarely absolute. There are questions it cannot answer and should not try to answer. The line between science and religion, for example, should be respected—a principle often ignored, which leads to conflicts between them. Religion should pay attention to science and avoid unnecessary conflicts with it while at the same time calling "foul" when scientists overstep their boundaries and make metaphysical claims unsupported and unsupportable by science.

The biblical-Christian worldview by no means necessarily conflicts with science itself, and its explorers and explainers should take science into account; it is always possible that a new fact of science will shed important light on metaphysics and even require a reconsideration of traditional interpretations of the Bible. That has happened in history—as with the case of Galileo.

Postfoundationalism does not undermine science; it only injects humility into science so that science can no longer be regarded as absolutely value neutral, objective, unaffected by what one philosopher of science called "myths, models, and paradigms." No scientist approaches the study of nature with a pristine, objective "view from nowhere."

Most of the conflicts between science and religion arise from scientists adopting a *naturalistic worldview*—the perspective that nature is all that is real—and from religious people approaching science with an unjustified negative view based on a totally unnecessary literalism about biblical cosmology (view of how the universe works). Freed from these two hindrances, science and religion, including biblically based Christianity, need not fear each other.

Critical Realism, Not Relativism

Second, our postfoundationalist epistemology, including our orientation toward postliberal theology, does not imply relativism of truth itself. What it requires is what philosophers call "critical realism"—belief that although "reality is out there" (outside the mind), no finite individual or group can claim to have a perfect, objective, complete grasp of reality. Relativism is the belief that there is no stable, permanent, enduring, absolute reality or truth. Some postfoundationalism may go in that direction, but postfoundationalism need not lead there. Postfoundationalism requires a certain degree of humility about truth claims, because "apodictic certainty," such as Enlightenment thinkers sought, is not available to finite minds. All knowledge is conditioned by perspectives. But that does not mean all claims to knowledge are false or equally true! It only means that all knowledge is embedded in preconceived (even if rationally justified) belief systems.

Postliberal Metaphysics

Third, some scholars and students of philosophy will object to this book's entire enterprise on the grounds that *metaphysics* and *postfoundationalism* (including postliberal theology) are incompatible. Many believe that, far from opening the door to metaphysics after its long decline in modern philosophy and theology, postfoundationalism slammed the door shut on it once and for all. That claim is based on a different meaning of *metaphysics* than this book's. Here *metaphysics* is being used as a synonym for "world perspective" and "reality-vision." It is *not* being used for a "construction of some science of 'being' (reality in general)."[1] It is, however, being used for any "picture" that seeks to "penetrate beyond 'appearance' to 'reality.'"[2]

Some critics will no doubt object that, in order for such a picture of reality beyond appearance to count as metaphysics, it must be *rational* and even *scientific* in the sense of objective as an

---

1   This is part of a definition of *metaphysics* offered by philosopher R. W. Hepburn as quoted in James Richmond, *Theology and Metaphysics*, 1.

2   This is the rest of Hepburn's definition of metaphysics cited in the previous footnote.

orderly path to knowledge. If that is the only meaning of *metaphysics*, then metaphysics is truly not only the sick man of philosophy but probably the dead man of philosophy (although there are still philosophers attempting to revive it). Suffice it to say that here, following a number of Christian thinkers such as those mentioned in the Introduction, especially Tresmontant and Cherbonnier, *metaphysics* includes any religious depiction of ultimate reality—whether that be scientific or not.

This book assumes the validity of a "revealed metaphysics," something especially secular philosophers would consider an oxymoron. And yet, it may be asked, must not any account of "reality beyond appearance" depend on some kind of revelation even if only nature revealing itself to the human mind? Be that as it may, let it be known that this book simply declines to permit the concept *metaphysics* to be owned by rationalists. This book treats metaphysics as any world perspective about the nature of reality beyond appearances. After all, even Alfred North Whitehead called Buddhism a "metaphysic generating a religion."[3] Buddhism can hardly be regarded as a science in the sense of the objectors to our use of *metaphysics* here.

A Modest Natural Theology

Fourth, some readers may fear that this project is a return to natural theology—something strongly eschewed by much modern and postmodern Protestant theology. Richmond defined natural theology as "that knowledge about God and the divine order which man's reason can acquire without the aid of (supernatural) revelation."[4] Twentieth-century Swiss theologian Barth famously condemned all natural theology—and with it metaphysics—as products of humanity's sinful pride and idolatry. As mentioned earlier, Barth even went so far as to respond with an angry "Nein!" (No!) to Brunner's idea of the existence of a "point of contact" in the natural, sinful human

---

3   Whitehead, *Religion in the Making*, 39–40.
4   Richmond, *Theology and Metaphysics*, 1.

person for the gospel. Much Protestant theology has developed a strong allergy to natural theology.

The main point that must be made about this, however, is that *metaphysics as here understood* is not natural theology. A basic presupposition of this book is that the true depiction of ultimate reality beyond appearances (metaphysics) is *revealed*, not naturally or rationally discovered. Scottish Christian thinker Neil MacDonald, author of *Metaphysics and the God of Israel* (mentioned earlier), also makes a strong distinction between biblical-Christian metaphysics and natural theology.[5] Here I am using *metaphysics* in exactly the same sense as MacDonald—as the depiction of reality beyond appearances presupposed by the Bible and primarily discovered there—via "canonical hermeneutics."[6]

Of course, if natural theology is interpreted differently than Barth, then there may be some sense in which the project undertaken in this book counts as natural theology. It corresponds closely with what Emil Brunner meant by that phrase and by *eristics* in his various writings. However, that meaning comes down to two things, neither of which amounts to what Barth condemned. For Brunner, and for me, natural theology means only (1) that the biblical-Christian worldview better answers life's ultimate questions than its competitors and alternatives, and (2) that *eyes of faith* for whom the Bible "absorbs the world" *see* the natural world *as* God's good creation—"charged with the grandeur of God"—even if eyes of unbelief cannot see it as such.

Biblical Metaphysics and "Critical Orthodoxy"

Fifth, the explication of biblical-Christian, narrative-based metaphysics here will not be particularly concerned with fitting some preconceived standard of theological orthodoxy (even though this

---

5   MacDonald, *Metaphysics and the God of Israel*, 38–40.

6   Ibid., xvi. MacDonald relies on this approach to biblical interpretation pioneered especially by Brevard Childs, a colleague of Frie's at Yale. "Canonical hermeneutics" insists that the Bible be interpreted *as a whole* and not "picked apart" with focused attention given only to units in isolation from other units.

writer considers himself orthodox doctrinally). In other words, this project seeks to "bracket out" traditional Christian orthodoxy as a doctrinal system, as much as possible, in order to look with fresh eyes at what the Bible really presupposes and says about ultimate reality beyond appearances. And yet, I stand within the Christian tradition-community and cannot claim to be able to escape that perspective. I cannot claim to climb to some objective mountain peak of thought, some "view from nowhere," independent of my own identity conditioned by the Protestant Christian heritage, to interpret the Bible. No one can totally escape his or her own narrative skin, so to speak. However, I do believe it is possible to at least attempt to bracket out orthodox ideas of what the Bible means in order to look at it again with fresh and faithful eyes.

I have already mentioned two guides in this attempt at biblical-metaphysical map making—Edmond La Beaume Cherbonnier and Claude Tresmontant—both of whom made valiant attempts in the 1950s and 1960s to bracket out church orthodoxies in order to discover what the Bible itself really implies about ultimate reality—God and the universe—beyond appearances. Both were examples of what might be called "critical orthodoxy." That is, they were faithful adherents of Christian traditions—one Protestant (Anglican) and the other Catholic—but both were willing, when forced by the Bible itself, to revise common Christian beliefs about God and reality.

A feeble analogy might help illustrate this approach called "critical orthodoxy." Years ago I purchased a detailed, government-created map of the Black Hills of South Dakota—one of my favorite landscapes. Then I traveled there and, using the map, explored parts of that region where tourists usually do not go. I had never gone to them before. On foot and by car I explored parts of the Black Hills, presupposing the map to be valid but open to discovering its flaws should there be any. The terrain before and around me was my ultimate authority, as it were, but the map functioned as a secondary guide through the territories I traversed. Lo and behold! I found a flaw. The map showed a mountain road where there certainly was not one. I went back and forth several times looking for the road, which was shown on the map as branching off a highway. It simply was not there and never had been. The entire stretch where the road should have been was densely forested with tall pine trees with not a footpath between them.

This explorer had to revise the map in light of the terrain. Did that make the map useless or entirely unreliable? Not at all. For the most part it matched the territory, but it was not the territory. So "Christian orthodoxy" is here presumed to be generally accurate but not infallible; it is open to revision in light of fresh exploration of the territory that (at least for Protestants) it is supposed to map out.

In fact, I, along with Tresmontant, Cherbonnier and others, *have indeed* found aspects of common Christian belief *not* consistent with the Bible itself. None of these touch the *heart of Christian orthodoxy* and certainly not *the gospel itself*, but some may shock conservative Christians who have always taken for granted that the Bible teaches certain things it does not. In some cases the Bible strongly implies realities quite contrary to what the majority of Christians have come to believe—especially, for example, about *God and time*.

The chapters that follow will take up themes of metaphysics implied by the biblical narrative and explore what that narrative, as a whole, has to say about them. The aim will be to show that the Bible does, in fact, contain and communicate a universal perspective, "picture," of ultimate reality including God and the universe (creation), and *does not require an extrabiblical metaphysic* as Whitehead suggested. None of that is to say that Christian thought cannot benefit from extrabiblical metaphysical pictures; it is only to say that it contains its own metaphysical vision of reality, and Christians should start with that and only supplement it from extrabiblical ones when they are helpful and do not conflict with the Bible's own.

CHAPTER 3

The Biblical Vision of Ultimate Reality Retrieved

Against all who would borrow an extrabiblical metaphysic to impose on the Bible and Christianity, as if they had no distinctive metaphysical vision that is uniquely Christian, Catholic theologian-philosopher Tresmontant asserted that "there exists . . . a metaphysical structure, original, inherent in Christian theology as in biblical theology. There exists a Christian metaphysic."[1] Because Tresmontant was Catholic some knowledgeable critics might think he was talking about the Platonized or Aristotelianized Christian philosophy of Augustine or Thomas Aquinas. While he did not outrightly reject those, he did argue that there is in the Bible itself a holistic philosophy of a metaphysical and even ontological (having to do with the nature of being) nature that is unique to it and stands in contrast to all other, especially Greek-inspired philosophies.

Retrieving Biblical Metaphysics

Tresmontant pressed his thesis strongly. Speaking of the Hebrew worldview presupposed and indirectly expressed in the Bible, he averred that there a definite "revolution" in metaphysics may be found.[2] For him, "Christian metaphysics carry on the metaphysics contained in biblical theology. Biblical metaphysics and Christian

---

1   Claude Tresmontant, *The Origins of Christian Philosophy*, trans. Mark Pontifex (New York: Hawthorne Books, 1963), 20.
2   Ibid., 27.

metaphysics in outline are the same."[3] He called the biblical-Christian metaphysic a "homogeneous system"[4] and said that a careful analysis of the structure of biblical revelation yields a definite, if not detailed, vision of ultimate reality.[5] He meant that the Bible reveals a distinct conception of God that also includes God and the world, man, matter, time, human freedom, human nature, and reason.[6] He contrasted this biblical perspective on reality with others that even Christians have sometimes confused with biblical-Christian thought: Indian philosophy, Plato, Neoplatonism (Plotinus), Baruch Spinoza's (1632–77) pantheism, Hegel's panentheism. Without denying points of contact and similarity, Tresmontant argued that the tension between these and the biblical view of reality—both absolute and relative—is greater than their commonalities. His whole project was to separate them and warn Christians against relying heavily on extrabiblical metaphysical worldviews.

Again, yet in a different book, Tresmontant strongly asserted the independence of biblical-Christian metaphysics over against alternative visions of reality: "There is a Christian metaphysic, as there is a Newtonian or an Einsteinian physics."[7] According to him, there is one and only one "Christian philosophy" and it includes an "original metaphysic."[8]

Tresmontant denied that this unique Christian philosophy is a school of philosophy like the ancient Greek schools (e.g., Neoplatonism); rather it is a "synthetic" and "synoptic" account of reality grounded in the Bible itself of which Christianity gradually became aware as it reflected on the biblical narrative over time. According to him, the Bible is *not* a book of philosophy, but, he averred, biblical revelation implies an organic system of beliefs

---

3   Ibid., 23.
4   Ibid., 33.
5   Ibid., 32.
6   Ibid., 40.
7   Claude Tresmontant, *Christian Metaphysics*, trans. Gerard Slevin (New York: Sheed and Ward, 1965), 8.
8   Ibid., 20.

about reality.[9] "A Christian philosophy exists from the moment in which Christian thought reflects, technically and rationally, upon the metaphysical conditions of its own content, taken from Scripture."[10]

Tresmontant's main concern was to distinguish this unique, organic, synthetic, synoptic biblical-Christian metaphysic from all others. According to him, "For well-defined organic reasons any metaphysic whatever is not compatible with any theology whatever. Any cosmology whatever, any anthropology whatever is not compatible with any metaphysic."[11] His other main concern was to argue that "Christian metaphysics has its legitimate and rightful place among the other existing metaphysics in the world."[12] In other words, Christians should neither be embarrassed by the worldview of the Bible, including its openness to the supernatural,[13] nor fall into syncretism, inappropriately mixing the biblical worldview with incompatible ones. For Tresmontant the main alternatives to the biblical-Christian view of reality are many: Platonism (especially Neoplatonism), Gnosticism, emanationism, dualism (Manicheism), Spinoza's pantheism, Hegel's idealism. According to him, the biblical-Christian metaphysic stands in stark contrast with all these and more on two fundamental principles: (1) God has created all things but himself, and (2) Everything that God has created is very good.[14]

Greek Philosophy and the Biblical Picture of Ultimate Reality

For example, according to Tresmontant, ancient Greek philosophy, which he believed is still influential in Western culture, denied that absolute reality, the ultimately and really real, could manifest

---

9   Tresmontant, *A Study of Hebrew Thought*, trans. Michael Francis Gibson (New York: Desclee, 1960), 146.

10   Tresmontant, *Christian Metaphysics*, 30.

11   Ibid., 65.

12   Ibid., 111.

13   Ibid., 108–9.

14   Tresmontant, *The Origins of Christian Philosophy*, 101.

universal truth in and through the temporal, or that the temporal could be meaningful, good, and a vehicle of the absolute and ultimate. The Bible, however, and both Hebrew and Christian thought, when they are faithful to the Bible, reveals the particular, the finite, the sensible as meaningful and good and proper vehicles for the ultimate, the really real. This shows in God's choice of Israel and in the Incarnation. This is what some biblical scholars and theologians have referred to as "the scandal of particularity" and Tresmontant recognized it as the greatest stumbling block for Greeks' acceptance of biblical religion.[15] Not only ancient Greek philosophy, but also modern Western philosophy struggles against this biblical emphasis on the particular and on the sensible world as objects of God's love and as vehicles of God's revelation of himself. The rationalist philosopher Spinoza, a pantheist, and Hegel, a rationalist and panentheist, both rejected this biblical emphasis.[16]

Similarly, according to Tresmontant, ancient Greek philosophy, which has never died out entirely in Western thought,[17] denied the real, ontological distinction between ultimate reality and souls (emanationism) while pitting souls against bodies (dualism). Tresmontant rightly pointed out that for biblical thought the line is drawn primarily between the creator and his creation rather than between bodies and souls as in Greek thought.[18] For biblical-Christian thought, in contrast with Greek philosophy, souls are *created* by God, they are not emanations, offshoots, of God's own substance. On at least this one crucial issue there can be no "conciliation" between Neoplatonism, the ultimate in Greek thought, and biblical metaphysics which grows naturally and organically out of biblical revelation.[19]

For Tresmontant, the very rock-bottom difference between the biblical view of reality and other myths and philosophies is

---

15   Tresmontant, *A Study of Hebrew Thought*, 64.
16   Ibid., 81.
17   Ibid., 97.
18   Ibid., 95.
19   Ibid., 97.

the difference-in-relation between God, ultimate reality, and the universe, creation. The biblical metaphysic is unique in positing non-ultimate reality (the universe and all it contains) as created.[20] Yet, also in contrast to other worldviews, the alienation between God, ultimate reality, and creation is not built into matter or ontological distance (difference) between God and it, but instead the alienation is a result of misuse of God-granted free will. Sin and stupidity, spiritual alienation, result from "hardening of the heart," not from a "fall" of souls into bodies or entrapment of the divine "sparks" in the sensible world.[21]

All of these points anticipate the rest of this book, which will unfold the biblical-Christian metaphysic in contrast with alternative philosophies—following, in part anyway, Tresmontant, who I believe was largely right. The biblical narrative holds within itself an original, organic, synoptic worldview that answers life's ultimate questions *differently* than numerous alternatives—most of which are still swimming around in our pluralistic culture and too often being soaked in by Christians and inappropriately mixed and mingled eclectically with their own native, biblical-Christian worldview.

An American Protestant Guide to Retrieving the Bible's Philosophy

At about the same time that Catholic thinker Tresmontant was retrieving the original and unique biblical-Christian metaphysic and asserting its independence and power, an American Protestant theologian named Cherbonnier was making the same case, even if in a different way. Cherbonnier criticized Protestant theology for usually taking a generally negative view of philosophy. In his opinion the Reformers were right to be somewhat suspicious of the ontological and metaphysical systems adopted by medieval Catholic

---

20   Ibid., 117.
21   Ibid., 123.

theology.[22] Thus, they and most of their Protestant followers have tended to eschew philosophy in theology. However, Cherbonnier rightly noted, even theologians like the notoriously antiphilosophical Karl Barth, could not and cannot escape philosophy altogether— insofar as they reason.[23] "It is impossible to avoid philosophy; and the attempt to do so only betrays the theologian into the very position he seeks to avoid."[24] In other words, Cherbonnier was saying, even antiphilosophical theologians such as Tertullian in the ancient church and Barth in the modern church rely on philosophical modes of reasoning whether or not they are aware of it.

However, like Tresmontant, Cherbonnier reserved his strongest criticisms for Christian theologians such as Augustine and Tillich, his constant nemeses and foils, who, at least in his eyes, corrupted Christian theology by relying on extrabiblical metaphysical visions of reality that conflict with the biblical one. Augustine, he argued, relied on what he, Augustine, called "the books of the Platonists," which meant Neoplatonism. According to Cherbonnier, and I agree, that philosophy, though often used by ancient Christian thinkers to fill the alleged gap Whitehead observed (viz., that Christianity is a religion in search of a metaphysic), was inadequate to protect the basic Christian beliefs.[25] Similarly, Tillich's ontological philosophy, an amalgam of Platonism and existentialism, created in his theology an unbiblical doctrine of God as "Being Itself." In the Bible, Cherbonnier incisively noted, "God certainly is conceived as 'a being besides other beings.' To the complaint that this implies that God is *related*, and therefore *conditioned*, the answer is that of course God is related."[26]

Like Tresmontant, Cherbonnier did not reject philosophy itself or the many extrabiblical philosophies Christians have used in

---

22   Cherbonnier, "Biblical Metaphysic and Christian Philosophy," 365.
23   Ibid., 365.
24   Ibid., 366.
25   Ibid., 361.
26   Ibid., 363.

their theological systems—at least not totally. Many of these philosophies, he admitted, provide some help to Christian theology in its attempt to understand and explain biblical revelation. However, they all also sometimes undermine important aspects of Christian truth.[27] We will come back to what those other important aspects are later. One has already been mentioned: Nearly all extra-biblical philosophies struggle with the idea of a *personal, related, vulnerable ultimate reality capable of being influenced by what creatures do.*[28] Also like Tresmontant, Cherbonnier argued most insistently that (1) The Bible contains its own, unique, independent metaphysic, and (2) This metaphysic has been largely overlooked even by Christian theologians, who have opted to borrow their "Christian" visions of reality from elsewhere.

Cherbonnier defined *metaphysics* with a question it attempts to answer: "What is true always and everywhere, regardless of time or place?"[29] That is the same as to ask about *ultimate reality* and *the connection that connects all things* and *reality beyond appearances.* In fact, he also defined metaphysics as the "quest for ultimate reality."[30] Cherbonnier labeled "absurd" objections to such an enterprise because all serious wrestling with life's ultimate questions presupposes some vision of such truth. He admitted that many people, including especially Protestant theologians, consider "biblical metaphysic" a "contradiction in terms," which is why they go searching elsewhere for one.[31] According to him, however, as for Tresmontant, there is a biblical metaphysic, vision, perspective of ultimate reality, the connection that connects all things, and the biblical metaphysic is simply the Christian answer to the questions all metaphysicians ask based on implicit assumptions found in the biblical story.[32]

---

27 Ibid., 361.
28 Ibid., 363.
29 Cherbonnier, "Is There a Biblical Metaphysic?" 454.
30 Ibid., 460.
31 Ibid., 454.
32 Ibid.

Unfortunately for the Christian search for truth, Cherbonnier complained, the implicit biblical metaphysic is often denied a fair hearing due to the dominance of Platonic metaphysics.[33] Whitehead once claimed that the entire history of philosophy has been but a series of footnotes to Plato.[34] Cherbonnier tended to agree and averred that because Christian theology borrowed so heavily from Platonic philosophy in its varieties, Christian thought has often suffered internal conflicts [35] by reading "into the Bible a metaphysic which has no place there."[36] Much Christian theology, he argued, has simply embraced contradictions, attempting to combine but ultimately leaving side by side in contrary juxtaposition Greek philosophy's ideas of god and the biblical idea of God.[37] One approach to resolving such conflicts was and is the doctrine of "double truth"— the attempt to embrace contradictory beliefs either explicitly as in some medieval philosophy and theology or implicitly as in some so-called dialectical theologies.[38]

Cherbonnier agreed entirely with Tresmontant (and even mentioned him[39]) that the solution to many of the confusions in Christian thought is a *retrieval* of the *Bible's own metaphysic*, the discovery of a unique, independent, revealed, *biblical-Christian philosophy*. What is needed, he wrote, is a "genuine *philosophia Christiania*,"[40] a respectable alternative to the Platonic metaphysic "derived from the philosophical implications of the Bible."[41] Cherbonnier boldly claimed that there is no reason why such a metaphysical hypothesis should not be given serious consideration—especially by Christians.[42] What metaphysical hypothesis? That "the Biblical

---

33   Ibid., 468.
34   Whitehead, *Process and Reality*, 39.
35   Cherbonnier, "Is There a Biblical Metaphysic?" 455.
36   Ibid., 455–56.
37   Ibid., 456–57.
38   Ibid., 457.
39   Ibid., 457–58.
40   Ibid., 456.
41   Ibid., 458.
42   Ibid., 459.

God [ultimate reality itself] is not a universal, but a particular—*a* Being, not Being Itself."[43] Cherbonnier believed an honest, straightforward reading of the biblical narrative could not escape its "bold anthropomorphism" in which ultimate, final reality is Some*one* and not some*thing*—whether a power, force, principle, or idea.[44] The ultimate reality of the Bible is the *living God*, described with *verbs* as an active agent *in time*.[45] For the Bible, the relation of God to the world is that of Creator to creation. In other words, according to Cherbonnier, biblical revelation reasonably represents ultimate reality as an agent related to his acts.[46] Greek philosophy, and all its derivatives throughout intellectual history, including much Christian theology, has tended to dissolve the "many," the particular, into the "One," the absolute. In contrast to this, the biblical metaphysic invests reality in finite free agents, creatures and their decisions, without undermining God's ultimacy. Unlike Platonic and much philosophical metaphysics, the Bible does not disparage the created world but regards it as "the best possible medium for the self-expression [not self-realization] of God."[47] According to Cherbonnier, and Tresmonant would wholeheartedly agree, only the God of the Bible can create a reality that is not a negation of himself.[48] This biblical perspective on God and the world invests human decisions and actions with metaphysical significance without making them ultimate: "The small decisions and casual interchanges of daily life are thus transmuted from a hum-drum round of tedium and trivia into a dimension of ultimate opportunity, from Plato's meaningless shadowplay into the frontier of the Kingdom of God."[49]

---

43   Ibid., 458.
44   Ibid., 459.
45   Ibid., 460–61.
46   Ibid., 462.
47   Ibid., 463.
48   Ibid.
49   Ibid.

Perennial Philosophy and the Biblical View of Reality

Lumping many Greek-inspired metaphysical philosophies together under the label "perennial philosophy," Cherbonnier laid out *six points* at which it fails to provide an adequate metaphysical framework for biblical Christian thinking about reality.[50]

First, in the Bible ultimate reality, God, is conceived as *a being* who is voluntarily *related* and *conditioned—influenced*—by his creation. And yet the Bible maintains a clear distinction between God and creation. Greek-inspired philosophies always tend to *both* blur the distinction between ultimate reality and nonultimate reality *and* depict ultimate reality as unrelated and unconditioned, absolute in the sense of incapable of being influenced by finite being. In contrast to rational philosophies deriving from Greek thought, biblical revelation represents ultimate reality, God, as voluntarily, not necessarily, conditioned by what his creatures do.[51]

Second, biblical philosophy portrays creatures' *knowledge of God* as received through communication from God or his agents.[52] In other words, there is no immediate knowledge of God, or ultimate reality, that is simply always there or automatically discoverable. Biblical thought makes human knowledge of God dependent on God. In perennial philosophy, *rational contemplation* is capable of *achieving positive knowledge* of ultimate reality; such knowledge is never made dependent on revelation. This points toward God's *supernatural* nature, the *supernatural* nature of ultimate reality in biblical metaphysics.

Third, salvation is not simply a form of *self-realization*.[53] Perennial philosophy, inspired by Plato but carried on in permutations by Aristotle and Neoplatonism and many others, has always tended to imply an *identity philosophy* in which the human person's

---

50 Cherbonnier, *Biblical Metaphysic and Christian Philosophy*, 363–64.
51 Ibid., 363.
52 Ibid., 363–64.
53 Ibid., 364.

soul or mind is always already *one with the absolute, the ultimate.*
In biblical reality, salvation is not simply an unveiling of identity but
a restoring of relationship, not through reason or mystical contemplation but through grace and faith.

Fourth, the biblical narrative emphasizes *communal relationship with the ultimate*, God, in place of individual "flight of the alone
to the alone" (Plotinus).[54] In the Bible, one's relationship with the
absolute—God—is inseparable from one's relationship with other
persons. The vertical and horizontal dimensions are united; the
emphasis is on community. Perennial philosophy tends to emphasize individuality in relating to the infinite, the ultimate. In Plato's
allegory of the cave, it is the isolated individual who crawls out of
the cave of illusion into the light of reality; he has no need to bring
others with him. In the biblical worldview, no person is an island
and God—ultimate reality—makes covenants with people, and
people relate to God in and through relationships with each other.

Fifth, biblical metaphysics is a metaphysics of *love—agape—*
not *union.* It requires *relationship* and not *identity.*[55] Love of this
kind, that regards the *other as other* and does not regard or respect
the other for likeness—union—is scandalous to reason. The perennial philosophy, according to Cherbonnier, contrasts with biblical
philosophy in viewing love as union, even identity, rather than personal relationship.

Sixth, the perennial philosophy elevates rational *knowing* as
primary; to *know* the good is to *do* the good—a basic principle of all
Platonic-inspired philosophy and ethics. Biblical philosophy emphasizes the *heart* and the *will* in relationship with ultimate reality and
the good. "Knowing" with the mind is not primary; what is primary
is the *orientation of the heart, the will* of the knower.

According to Cherbonnier, these and other aspects of extrabiblical philosophy have crept into and corrupted Christian theology

---

54   Ibid.
55   Ibid.

over the centuries and still does so today. While he specifically listed these six in one place, throughout his articles (and his book *Hardness of Heart: A Contemporary Interpretation of the Doctrine of Sin* [1955]) he contrasted biblical metaphysics with extrabiblical philosophies at almost every conceivable point while admitting there may be some service the latter can offer here and there to Christian thought.

The general topics where Cherbonnier and Tresmontant find biblical thought and extrabiblical philosophies conflicting are: knowledge of ultimate reality (reason, revelation, and heart), the nature of ultimate reality itself (impersonal absolute versus personal yet supernatural God), creation (fallen emanation or unreality versus good but dependent), humanity (dualism between body and soul versus whole good but fallen creation loved by God), time (unreal versus created framework for relatedness), freedom (illusion versus gift), history (meaningless return of the same versus meaningful and teleological), and salvation (realization of identity versus restored relationship). According to them, much Christian theology has been heavily infected by extrabiblical philosophies in these areas with the result that the Christian view of reality has become syncretized, eclectic, at war with itself, or even deviant from biblical reality.

Dispelling the Myth of Harnack as Founder of De-Hellenizing Christianity

It would be wrong to suggest that Tresmontant and Cherbonnier were absolute pioneers in this endeavor to retrieve biblical metaphysics and disentangle it from alien philosophies. At the same time, however, it would be wrong to suppose that they were merely repeating the infamous "de-Hellenizing" project of early twentieth-century liberal Protestant thinker Adolf Harnack (1851–1930). Unfortunately, some Christian scholars who hear anyone criticizing the influence of Greek thought on Christianity immediately assume the influence of Harnack, the great church historian and theologian who produced a massive, three-volume history of Christian theology and a very popular manifesto of classical liberal Protestantism entitled *What Is Christianity?* (1901). Neither Tresmontant nor Cherbonnier mention him or show any evidence of being influenced by him. Harnack took the de-Hellenizing of Christianity to an extreme, even attributing the classical, orthodox doctrine of the Trinity to Greek philosophy's allegedly pernicious influence on Christianity. Like other liberal Protestants who engaged in a naturalistic "search for the historical Jesus"—a Jesus stripped of everything supernatural, apocalyptic, and even Hebrew (!)—Harnack looked down into the deep well of history to find the "Jesus of history" and found his own countenance looking back at him.[56]

No, Tresmontant and Cherbonnier were not heirs of Harnack, but they were influenced by pioneers in retrieving biblical philosophy before them. Tresmontant frequently mentioned the great Catholic thinker Maurice Blondel (1861–1949), the father of the *Nouvelle Théologie* school of modern Catholic thought that emphasized "ressourcement" or retrieval of biblical theology and ancient Christian thought. Cherbonnier stood on the shoulders of Jewish theologian Abraham Heschel (1907–72) but also seems to have been influenced by Brunner. At least his approach to philosophy paralleled Brunner's especially in the latter's *The Philosophy of Religion*. No, Tresmontant and Cherbonnier were not following or dependent on Harnack's de-Hellenizing project; they would both have rejected it as influenced by modernism. But no claim was made by them or by me to be absolutely original. Who can claim such? However, they are informative and generally reliable guides in our own ressourcement or retrieval of biblical philosophy and separation of it from other, alien worldviews and metaphysical visions of reality.

---

56   Adolph Harnack, *History of Dogma, vol. 1*, trans. Neil Buchanan (New York: Russell and Russell, 1958), 41–57. See about Harnack's description of the "historical Jesus": George Tyrrell, *Christianity at the Crossroads* (London, UK: Longmans, Greed and Co., 1910), 44.

Two More Guides to Retrieving the Bible's Philosophy

It will be helpful to digress momentarily, at least, from our two main guides to look at the two mentioned thinkers who influenced Cherbonnier: *Heschel* and *Brunner*. Both, before Cherbonnier, also sought to discover and develop uniquely biblical philosophies dependent solely on the biblical narrative. Both believed and argued most strongly that Judaism and Christianity *need* a philosophy and that the *philosophy* they need can be found in the Bible and not elsewhere—but without rejecting truth in other sources.

Brunner is usually lumped together with Barth as another dialectical theologian. The rap on both and all of them (often called neo-orthodox) is that they absolutely rejected philosophy in Christianity and, like Tertullian, pitted them against each other. Brunner, however, did write an entire book on philosophy of religion and frequently, throughout his writings, mentioned the need for a Christian philosophy. What he meant, however, is something many philosophers, especially secular ones, would reject—an account of ultimate reality and the experienced world (metaphysics) based on *revelation,* not reason alone. He believed that all types of philosophy *not* based on biblical revelation such as idealism, realism, critical philosophy, etc., fail to answer life's ultimate questions. According to Brunner, "Man . . . precisely in his rationalism is the most irrational, indeed anti-rational, of all beings. History affords a thousand instances of what faith declares, viz., that apart from faith, man is incapable of seeing himself as he is."[57] Note, however, that he did not reject *reason* but *rationalism*.

Brunner argued that secular philosophies—metaphysics—starting from observation and reason alone, can only raise life's ultimate questions and end in "aporias" or dead ends of thought instead of satisfying answers. Creation, he argued, cannot satisfyingly be comprehended by traditional extra-biblical philosophies.[58]

---

57   Brunner, *The Philosophy of Religion*, 97.
58   Ibid., 83.

For him, the Word of God affords "the ground of reality, as well as the knowledge of the self."[59] And yet Brunner embraced what he called "eristics"—dialogue with non-Christian philosophies not grounded in God's Word; discussion with them is essential to any holistic and contemporary, culturally relevant Christian philosophy of religion.[60]

So, for Brunner, Christianity ought not to reject philosophy, but it ought not to develop one as a "universal science" out of experience and/or reason alone because the living and personal God cannot be understood solely from rational examinations of the world or humanity.[61] According to the Bible and Christian tradition generally, God is truly known only through himself. "Christian faith consists precisely in taking this peculiar view of ultimate truth."[62] But Christianity *should* develop its own, unique, particular, independent philosophy from revelation that consists not in abstract conceptions but in analysis of revelation and answers to life's ultimate questions suited to the needs of the times.[63] Eristics is the practice of developing such a culturally powerful philosophy rooted in God's revelation, the biblical narrative, and showing it to contain the most satisfying answers to life's ultimate questions in dialogue and debate with competing visions of the absolute and ultimate reality.

Much to Barth's chagrin, Brunner believed God *is* revealed in nature and to the human spirit generally (general revelation). However, such general revelation of God has two problems that make it an unreliable source for true knowledge of God and the world, including humanity. First, "from nature we know the hands and feet but not the heart of God."[64] In other words, nature and univer-

---

59   Ibid., 89.
60   Ibid., 17.
61   Ibid., 15.
62   Ibid., 16.
63   Ibid., 18.
64   Brunner, "Nature and Grace," 38.

sal human experience, general revelation, yield only a "thatness" of God but not God's "whoness," personhood, and will. What humanity needs is to know God personally, not just God's nature as ultimate reality. Second, according to Brunner, in complete agreement with most classical Protestant theology (and the Bible in Romans 1!), reason, or the use of reason, has been spoiled in humanity by sin.[65] By no means did Brunner believe, as some critics of all dialectical theology have asserted, that *reason itself* is bad or useless. He even went so far as to aver that there is no "Christian logic": "The laws of logical thought are the same for all."[66] However, he believed that sin distorts the uses of reason; autonomous reason—reason set against the moral claims inseparably connected with revelation—until liberated and elevated by faith, is incapable of true knowledge of the absolute, ultimate reality: the personal God of the Bible. According to Brunner, "the greatest riddle of all is rational man himself,"[67] *because* he misuses reason against that which is most reasonable.

Brunner refused to pit reason against revelation, at least in his *Philosophy of Religion* book.[68] For him, the problem is not reason as such but human pride in their own discoveries and achievements. The "real opponent" of faith, he argued, is not human knowledge or culture but humans' failure to recognize how inadequate these are for a full understanding of human life and reality in general. The reason the human person cannot use his own reason to arrive at a satisfying life philosophy or vision or reality is his own natural tendency to minimize evil—especially in himself.

Contrary to so many critics and even sympathizers, then, Brunner did not reject philosophy. For him, philosophy at its best is simply *any* attempt to discover the connectedness of all things, to penetrate behind everyday appearances, the naïve realism of common sense, to the really real, the absolute, the ultimate. In

65   Brunner, *The Philosophy of Religion*, 97.
66   Emil Brunner, *Revelation and Reason*, trans. Olive Wyon (Philadelphia: Westminster, 1946), 379.
67   Brunner, *The Philosophy of Religion*, 97.
68   Ibid., 187.

true postfoundationalist fashion, however, Brunner argued that "everyone who philosophizes does so from a definite starting point, upon which he, as this particular man, stands. The Christian philosophizes from that point at which God's revelation sets him."[69] In other words, as contemporary postliberal theologians are fond of saying, "There is no view from nowhere." Everyone who philosophizes has a beginning point, his or her own perspective on reality, on what counts as evidence and what's reasonable to believe in. For Brunner, a distinctively Christian philosophy is possible because revelation and faith do not escape or reject reason but lead it back to its own true purpose.[70] Thinking Christians are not wrong or engaging in special pleading or rejecting philosophy when they begin by making the revelation in Christ their presupposition.[71]

Very much like Cherbonnier, Brunner described Christian philosophy as *occupation with the problems that lie in the background of biblical revelation*.[72] In other words, it is exploration of the only indirectly expressed presuppositions of the biblical narrative that have not been explicitly worked out in systematic, propositional form.[73] Christian philosophy deals not so much with *church dogmas* as with larger, more abstract principles about reality presupposed by the biblical writers. It seeks to discern the biblical-Christian perspective on "the whole of reality and human life" implied by the biblical narrative.[74] Also like Cherbonnier, Brunner believed far too much Christian thought has been distorted by attempts to *synthesize* Christianity with particular alien types of philosophy. His main nemesis in this regard was Neoplatonism, which he believed corrupted Augustine's theology and, through him, much orthodox Christian doctrine.[75] One of Brunner's favorite whipping

---

69 Brunner, *Revelation and Reason*, 393.
70 Ibid.
71 Brunner, *The Philosophy of Religion*, 130.
72 Brunner, *Revelation and Reason*, 390.
73 Ibid., 387.
74 Ibid.
75 Ibid., 388.

boys is the unknown fifth- and sixth-century Christian mystical theologian known as Dionysius the Pseudo-Areopagite (or just "Pseudo-Dionysius"), who developed "apophatic theology" or "negative theology" out of fascination with Neoplatonism. According to him, God, as the absolute "One" wholly different from the world, can only be known by what he is *not*, so negative attributes are to be used when speaking of God. The tendency, according to Brunner, was to minimize the personal and relational nature of God and remove God from time and make God incapable of being affected by creatures. Brunner believed that Christian theology based on Greek philosophy has gone overboard in paying metaphysical compliments to God that move him farther and farther away from the irreducibly *personal* God of the Bible.

For Brunner, the God of biblical revelation is *supernatural* and *personal* but *not human*. This very well sums up Brunner's whole doctrine of God in his *Dogmatics 1: The Christian Doctrine of God* (referred to earlier). This one God, both above and beyond nature and yet intrinsically personal, not human and yet creating humanity in his own image and likeness, is ultimate reality, the absolute, that upon which everything else depends for its being and yet not "Being Itself" (as for Tillich, whom Brunner blasts as guilty of inappropriately mingling biblical-Christian metaphysics with alien philosophies). This is presupposed throughout biblical revelation and stands apart from all rationalist, pagan, and secular philosophies as the center of Christian metaphysics.

But why do philosophy at all? According to Brunner, why is Christian philosophy necessary or valuable? There are several reasons. First, Christian philosophy, such as he describes it, is necessary to help Christians avoid syncretism—the inappropriate blending of the truth about God, the world, and humanity derived from revelation with alien philosophies and worldviews. Second, Christian philosophy is necessary for the integration of Christian faith with disciplines of life, for "the co-ordination of the various spheres of life" with each other around the one connecting point of ultimate reality, the supernatural and personal God upon whom everything depends.[76] Third and finally, Christian philosophy is necessary as the foundation of culture. While Brunner did not believe in theocracy, he did believe that Christianity, the Christian life and worldview, provides the best foundation for culture. That is not to say it should be imposed on culture, on nonbelievers. However, he did believe that for culture to thrive, "we need Christian specialists in all spheres of life" and he urged educated, thoughtful Christians to become involved in and influence every area of human life.[77]

A Jewish Theologian Recognized the Bible's Own Philosophy

The second thinker who stands in the background of especially Cherbonnier's retrieval of biblical-Christian philosophy is Heschel, perhaps the twentieth century's most eminent Jewish philosopher and author of, among many other books, *Man Is Not Alone: A Philosophy of Religion* (1951). According to Heschel, what characterizes humanity is an inescapable "sense of the ineffable"—what has earlier here been labeled "the supernatural." (I am well aware that *ineffable* and *supernatural* are not exactly synonyms, but as used here they overlap if not correspond.) According to Heschel, "what is intelligible to our mind is but a thin surface of the profoundly undisclosed [to the senses]"[78] and "it is the ineffable from which we draw the taste of the sacred, the joy of the imperishable."[79] Heschel was not exactly a mystic in any usual sense of the word, but he did reject Enlightenment rationalism and naturalism in favor of a universal encounter with the "ultimate mysteriousness of being" and "spiritual suggestiveness of reality" which is not merely "subjective" but is hinted at in everything experienced with "radical amazement"

---

76   Ibid., 395.
77   Ibid.
78   Abraham Joshua Heschel, *Man Is Not Alone: A Philosophy of Religion* (New York: Farrar, Straus and Young, 1951), 6.
79   Ibid., 9.

and "wonder."[80] According to him, everything deeply experienced "hints at something that transcends it."[81] And "trying to pierce the mystery [of being] with our categories is like trying to bite a wall."[82]

For Heschel, as for Brunner, what reveals itself to us from beyond the sensible world is beyond reason but not unreasonable. It is the basis and foundation of all that is really important.[83] Ultimately, human experience includes a pre-conscious awareness of something (or someone) transcendent and spiritual that questions us.[84] "What gives birth to religion is not intellectual curiosity, but the fact and experience of our being asked."[85] Our sense of being "asked," "questioned," being held accountable by something, someone, beyond ourselves and nature, leads to God. God, for Heschel, is not an explanation of the mysteries of life but an eternal call and even demand.[86]

But who is this God who questions and demands? According to Heschel, drawing on the Hebrew prophets, God means "holy otherness" but also "togetherness of all being."[87] In other words, God is, as Brunner stated, the connection that connects all things and yet is beyond them all (supernatural). Like Brunner and Cherbonnier, Heschel was harshly critical of the influence of Greek philosophy on theology—in his case Jewish theology. For him, the prophetic idea of God was not of "perfect being"—an idea of ultimate reality rooted in Greek philosophy.[88] God is one but "the One" [of Neoplatonism] is not God.[89] Furthermore, the God of the Hebrew prophetic tradition, the God who calls and demands, is *supernatural* but not *outside of nature*. The natural and supernatural are not detached realms;

---

80 Ibid., 22–30.
81 Ibid., 31.
82 Ibid., 30.
83 Ibid., 11.
84 Ibid., 64, 69.
85 Ibid., 76.
86 Ibid., 92.
87 Ibid., 109.
88 Ibid., 101.
89 Ibid., 107.

God is personally with us but not ontologically identical with us. God is both ontologically beyond and personally present.[90] And yet, according to Heschel, God's personal presence does not mean God and the world are always already united as one. Heschel expressed very succinctly the biblical-Christian view of God and the world which is identical with the basic Jewish view:

> The world is *not* one with God, and this is why His power does not surge unhampered throughout all stages of being. Creature is detached from the Creator, and the universe is in a state of spiritual disorder. Yet God has not withdrawn entirely from this world. The spirit of this unity hovers over the face of all plurality.[91]

It would be difficult to find a clearer, more concise expression of the biblical-Christian worldview! But, as Heschel notes, completely in agreement with Brunner and Cherbonnier, this truth comes not from extrabiblical philosophy and cannot be found in it. For biblical metaphysics, both Jewish and Christian, ultimate reality, called "God" but self-named "Yahweh," is not an abstract principle of unity or an object but a "unique, living being." "He is not the Unknown, He is the Father, the God of Abraham."[92] As Christian thinker Blaise Pascal (1623–62) so beautifully expressed it, "The God of the philosophers is not the God of Abraham, Isaac and Jacob."[93]

The Point of All This

For Heschel, as for Brunner and Cherbonnier and even Tresmontant, there is an implicit metaphysic embedded in the biblical narrative. It is radically different from all other metaphysics even if, at certain

---

90   Ibid., 122.
91   Ibid., 112.
92   Ibid., 133.
93   This is a paraphrase of a sentence found in a famous set of statements found sewn inside Pascal's tunic after his death. It is so well known and so often quoted and always attributed to Pascal as to need no definite documentation here.

points, it touches truth with them. None of these thinkers denies the old aphorism (attributed to third-century church father Clement of Alexandria) that "all truth is God's truth" wherever it is found. But they all agree that extrabiblical philosophies and metaphysical systems built on reason alone without recourse to revelation are alternatives to the biblical vision of ultimate reality. Heschel, in complete agreement with the others, emphasized that the ultimate reality of the biblical narrative is *compassionate*—something no other metaphysic envisions. And for that alone, many metaphysicians have rejected the Bible as lacking a metaphysic *or* have deliteralized the Bible to the point that its God is not truly compassionate. One representative example of the latter is the great medieval Christian theologian-philosopher Anselm of Canterbury (1033–1109) who, under the influence of Platonism, denied that God feels compassion because that would be an imperfection.[94] Against all extrabiblical, speculative metaphysics, Heschel rightly declared that the God of the Bible is passionately concerned with the suffering people of his world; he is purely interested in their plights and not untouched by them.[95]

The *point* of this entire chapter is that *there is a biblical, narrative-based metaphysic that contrasts with other metaphysical visions of ultimate reality, is not irrational, lies at the foundation of Christianity itself, and is being retrieved by Jewish and Christian scholars who are also separating it from extrabiblical philosophies that conflict with it.* The next chapter will explore what those extrabiblical philosophies are and why they conflict with Christianity.

---

94   Charles Hartshorne and William Reese, *Philosophers Speak of God* (Chicago: The University of Chicago Press, 1976), 99.
95   Heschel, *Man Is Not Alone*, 143–44.

Interlude 3

So much misunderstanding could arise from the foregoing chapters that it is important to stop to consider and clear up the most predictable ones. I beg the reader's indulgence and patience while I make some very important clarifications.

No Christian Antipathy toward Philosophy

First, nothing written before or after should indicate any antipathy toward philosophy per se on the part of the Jewish or Christian thinkers named as "guides" or on the part of this writer. In fact, exactly the opposite is the case. They and I highly value philosophy, including metaphysics. That is why this book is being written! What the guides mentioned and quoted and I share in common is no antipathy or hostility to philosophy; what we share in common is belief that philosophy *alone*, divorced from revelation, cannot satisfactorily answer life's ultimate questions and that *there is* an independent, unique *biblical philosophy*, worldview if you like, that can stand on its own two feet and that Christians should know about and live by.

Many scholars tend to define the difference between philosophy and theology as revelation—theology uses it and philosophy does not. There are, however, exceptions. "Natural theology" is the rational exploration of the evidence of God in nature and universal human experience. "Philosophical theology" is philosophy that explores reasons for belief in God or at least spiritual realities and may analyze the nature of revelation and truth claims based on revelation. So the line of revelation—that theology uses it and philosophy does not—is not quite as clear as many people think.

Historically, among Christian thinkers especially in the Middle Ages, philosophy and theology were inseparable. The so-called "scholastic thinkers" of the medieval universities such as Aquinas were *both* philosophers and theologians. Hardly anyone would deny it. In the early twentieth century many philosophers are returning to theology and theologians to philosophy. British philosophers Keith Ward (b. 1938) and Richard Swineburne (b. 1934) and American philosophers Nicholas Wolterstorff (b. 1932) and Alvin Plantinga (b. 1932) are well-known philosophers who do not eschew revelation, although their approaches to revelation are critical and analytical. Similarly, German theologian Wolfhart Pannenberg (1928–2014) and American theologian Langdon Gilkey (1919–2004) were Protestant thinkers who relied heavily on philosophy. Both Catholic and Anglican theologians have tended to engage in philosophy without eschewing revelation.

It is generally true, however, that philosophy alone, using reason and experience of the sensible world alone, is generally agreed by all to be incapable of discovering or establishing ultimate reality, the "absolute," as *personal* and *supernatural*. But that does not mean that belief in an ultimate reality that is personal and supernatural, based on revelation, cannot be philosophical in its own right insofar as it uses the intellect in the service of revelation, to understand that self-revealing ultimate reality. And philosophy by itself *reaches toward* the ultimate, the absolute,[1] even if it cannot get there on its own; it inevitably raises the *question* of the ultimate reality, whether named as "God" or not, *unless* it limits itself to *logical analysis of language* (which much twentieth-century philosophy has done, especially in English-speaking cultures).

Here, in this book, there is no bias intended against philosophy, nor is philosophy being elevated above revelation. Here philosophy is simply being treated as "love of wisdom" translated into a method—discerning the underlying metaphysical structure of the

---

1   Wolfhart Pannenberg, *Metaphysics and the Idea of God*, trans. Philip Clayton (Grand Rapids, Mich.: Eerdmans, 1990), 16–17.

biblical narrative—and a way of life—knowing and revering ultimate reality as *personal* and *supernatural* and integrating all of life with that reality, bringing all thought into captivity to him.[2]

Tensions and (Unnecessary) Conflicts between Philosophy and Theology

The relation between philosophy and religion/theology is one fraught with conflicts from both sides—in spite of the fact that for much of history they were virtually inseparable even if distinct disciplines. In general, not uncritically, I follow the approach to relating philosophy to religion/theology outlined by my professor Pannenberg. According to him, philosophy and religious inquiry, theology, are interdependent especially when the inquiry in view is metaphysics—the nature of ultimate reality, the really real beyond appearances, the absolute. The key question, Pannenberg suggested, is:

> Can the metaphysical ascent toward the concept of the One fully grasp the reality of the Absolute on the basis of independent philosophical reflection, and can it sufficiently establish its conclusions? Or is philosophy capable only of formulating criteria which every conception of the absolute One must satisfy, while being unable to grasp the reality of the Absolute fully or sufficiently to justify its acceptance?[3]

The German theologian argued that whenever philosophy has claimed to be able to establish the true conception of God by philosophical reflection alone, using autonomous reasoning alone, as has been the case in much metaphysics, it has claimed to stand in the place of revelation. He rightly stated (and spoke for me), "I hold that such claims were exaggerated and have been justly criticized."[4]

---

2   Of course some philosophers and some devout Christian believers will still demur at calling this project *philosophy*, but here this writer is relying on the definition provided by W. H. V. Reade in *The Christian Challenge to Philosophy* (London: S.P.C.K., 1958), 168.

3   Pannenberg, *Metaphysics*, 18.

4   Ibid., 19.

Pannenberg concluded that philosophy *as philosophy*, not theology, working with reason alone and not depending on revelation, makes a genuine contribution to a metaphysical doctrine of ultimate reality, even of God, but *cannot replace* religion, which depends on revelation, in arriving at a true conception of God.[5] What is that genuine contribution? It is a corrective function of laying down universal *rules of thought* that even religion, when it is being critical and reflective, must not abuse.[6] For Pannenberg, as for Brunner (a strange pair!), Christian thought and discourse must be *reasonable* and *not irrational*. That is, its universal truth claims about reality, even ones based solely on revelation, must not be *esoteric* or *absurd*. Christian philosophy must be intersubjective even if its starting point is personal, intuitive, and faith based.

That is *not to say* that Christianity's vision of ultimate reality must be dragged before some bar of reason set up in nowhere land—as if there is any neutral philosophy, worldview, or vision of reality that is not itself perspectival. All that Pannenberg (and Brunner at his best) insist on is that Christian thought, explicating the metaphysical vision of revelation, abide by the universal rules of all thought and persuasion such as the law of noncontradiction. Two truth claims cannot stand in absolute contradiction and both be true. That is not a rule derived from some non-Christian philosophy; it is a universal rule of thought Christians attribute to the *Logos*—the mind, reason, and communication of God himself through whom all things were created.

Mystery, Paradox, and Contradiction Differentiated

Second, the question naturally arises, whenever this is said among Christians especially, about *paradox* and *mystery*. Let's clear up some common confusions. Even Pannenberg admitted the realities of *mystery* and *paradox* in thinking about God, about ultimate

---

5   Ibid.
6   Ibid., 19–20.

reality, the absolute. But "mystery" is not "contradiction"; it is what is beyond human comprehension fully to understand or explain. The absolute, ultimate reality, even when revealed as *personal* and *supernatural*, remains, in a sense, incomprehensible. But *every person* is, in a sense, incomprehensible, mysterious, insofar as they are incapable of being completely predicted. No one can read another person's private thoughts; therefore, in that regard, persons are *mysterious*. But that is not to say they are contradictions. In fact, it is doubtful that two absolutely contradictory ideas can be believed by anyone at the same time. One idea can be believed at one moment and its absolute contrary believed in the next moment, but they cannot be believed together at the same moment.

For example, light, physicists say, is mysterious in that it displays characteristics of both particles and waves. *How* it can be both at the same time is not fully understood; that remains a mystery. That is a paradox but not a contradiction. It would only become a contradiction, and be impossible to think or believe, *if* a physicist said that light is *exclusively particles* and *exclusively waves* at the same time. But no physicist, or anyone, says that about light! The claim is being made here, following Pannenberg (but not only him!) that all metaphysics, which is the ultimate goal of all philosophy, its pinnacle, as it were, points to mystery. Even Christian metaphysics does because God is believed to be *personal*, not a thing or object that can be examined and fully comprehended. It is part of God's *supernaturalness* that he, God, transcends human thought—as God himself said through the prophet Isaiah in 55:8–9: "'For my thoughts are not your thoughts, neither are your ways my ways,' declares the LORD. 'As the heavens are higher than the earth, so are my ways higher than your ways and my thoughts than your thoughts.'" By *no means*, however, does this mean that *our beliefs and truth claims about God may be irrational or totally contradictory*. This prophetic saying points to *mystery*, not contradiction, and justifies *paradox* (like light being both particle and wave), not absurdity.

To sum up, then, "Christian philosophy" is not an oxymoron even though many secularists and Christians think and say so. Everything depends on the meaning of *philosophy*. One cannot simply look it up in a dictionary. As it is being used here it does not rule out consideration of revelation or faith. Also, philosophy using reason alone is incapable of reaching its own ultimate destination—the absolute, ultimate reality, God. It can posit and perhaps establish that such must exist, but it cannot know or describe it except using abstract terms such as *infinite*. In the end, if the ultimate, the absolute, is to be known as more than an abstract *something* it, he, must self-disclose. The answers to life's ultimate questions depend on such. But also, and equally important, "Christian philosophy," the exploration and explication of ultimate reality as self-revealed, cannot be anti-intellectual, irrational, or absurd by reveling in contradictions. Philosophy comes into play by helping Christian thought purify itself of such.

Understanding Christian Apologetics Rightly

Third, and finally (for this interlude), the question of *Christian apologetics* needs review and consideration. Can the Christian account of ultimate reality, Christian metaphysics, be *proven*? The simple answer has to be no. Can it be *defended*? Yes. This is not a book of apologetics; it is simply an attempt to explain and clarify the metaphysical vision of the biblical narrative. Inquiring minds will want to know, however, whether that vision is capable of being established as true intersubjectively or whether it is a matter of a leap of faith.

Protestant theology has been deeply divided over this issue. Modernity, stemming from the Enlightenment launched by Descartes and other rationalist philosophers, set the standard of proof so high that very little of any real importance, outside of mathematics and physics, can meet it. The Christian mathematician and philosopher Pascal asked the rationalists, who insisted that knowledge consists only of what cannot be doubted, "Do you love by reason?" For him, great intellectual that he was, the truth of Christianity is mystical, apprehended by faith rather than comprehended by reason. On the other hand, many rationalist Christians of the modern age attempted to use autonomous reason, the scientific method (broadly defined), to demonstrate the truth of Christianity. The Danish Christian writer, philosopher, poet, and theologian (and prophet!) Søren Kierkegaard (1813–55) vehemently rejected all such attempts as treating God as an object rather than as the subject of his own revelation. Karl Barth, the most influential Protestant theologian of the twentieth century, also rejected rational apologetics as a betrayal of faith and of the freedom of God's Word.

On the other hand, Pannenberg stood out from the modern pack of antiapologetic orthodox Protestants by insisting that, overall and in general, Christianity is intersubjectively verifiable if not provable. He staked his entire career and reputation on arguing that the resurrection of Jesus Christ was a verifiable historical event and proof of Jesus's deity. He plumbed the depths of human existence, using secular as well as religious sources, to show that human existence itself presupposes God as the infinite horizon of all human thought.[7] Basically, what Pannenberg argued was that *revelation,* as understood and believed by historical, classical Christianity, better answers life's ultimate questions than all competitors, although he admitted that ultimate verification is eschatological.

Brunner's eristics is a type of apologetics. The Swiss theologian, who long struggled under the shadow of his better-known Swiss counterpart Barth, is enjoying something of a rediscovery in the second decade of the twentieth century. Brunner coined the term *eristics* for his own belief that, when set alongside alternative worldviews, Christian philosophy is superior. He did not think that could be proven in any kind of knock-down, drag-out way—as if

---

7   For Pannenberg's apologetic, which he called "fundamental theology" (*not* "fundamental*ism*"!), see his *Anthropology in Theological Perspective*, trans. Matthew J. O'Connell (Philadelphia: Westminster, 1985).

someone who does not see it is simply stupid or perverse. He did believe it, however, and this is mentioned in several of his books, including his first major work, *The Mediator* (1934). It is a largely overlooked aspect of Brunner's theology which has wrongly come to be identified with Barth's dialectical theology except for the quirk of their debate over natural theology in the 1930s. Brunner's eristics was very Wittgensteinian before Wittgenstein! He believed that *seeing* reality *as* God-centered requires eyes of faith, a work of the Holy Spirit, but he also believed it was possible to help a person not yet possessing eyes of faith to begin to *see* life and the world *as* the Bible reveals it by showing him the pattern in reality that Christians see. Ultimately, however, *if* a person comes to faith and really sees reality as God-centered, that will be attributed to the Holy Spirit who can work through dialogue.

I believe Christian apologetics has *one major function*. It cannot prove Christianity true to minds closed to it. It can, however, help people deceived by virulent unbelief to overcome the false stumbling blocks put in their way—secular worldviews and arguments based on them—and show that, contrary to what they have been told, Christianity is *not irrational*.

The purpose of this book, however, as already said, is *not* Christian apologetics but simply explanation of the implicit metaphysical worldview presupposed by biblical revelation *and* clear separation of it from radically alternative, competing metaphysical worldviews. The purpose is *exposition* and *therapy*—to help Christians clarify their own belief system about ultimate reality and avoid harmful syncretism.

CHAPTER 4

Non-Biblical, Non-Christian
Views of Reality

I grew up in a very large, religiously variegated, extended family. Family reunions, large and small, were almost guaranteed to include some discussions of religion. One aunt was a passionately devoted member of the Presbyterian church; she was, in fact, a ruling elder in her own Presbyterian congregation. However, sometime during her life she had adopted what is known as "cosmic" or "metaphysical dualism"—belief that evil exists because there are *two ultimate realities*—the God of Israel, the Father of Jesus Christ, perfectly good in every way, creator of the world and all that is in it, except evil—and an equally powerful and equally eternal, opposing evil force. I do not remember whether she named this anti-god Satan, but she believed, as she explained to my father (her brother, an evangelical pastor), that evil is the result of an eternal struggle in the universe between the "good God" and the "evil force."

This writer's aunt was one of the sweetest, most intelligent and devout Christian women he has ever had the privilege to know, and he stayed in her home many times while growing up. And yet, whether she was aware of it or not, her worldview, her metaphysical vision of ultimate reality, was radically contrary to that of the Bible and Christianity. It was, however, her *blik* and there seemed no possibility of talking her out of it. It was her version of what has been labeled by most philosophers, including Christian ones, *cosmic dualism* and even *Manicheism*—after a popular religion of the

Roman Empire that held just such a metaphysical vision of ultimate reality as its core doctrine.

Metaphysical Dualism (Manicheism)

Manicheism has gradually, over the centuries, become the common term used to label any such dualist metaphysic because *dualism* can mean other things as well. It is very doubtful that my aunt was influenced by Manicheism, which doesn't exist as a religion anymore. However, the metaphysical dualism of the Manichean religion preexisted it and still exists—at least in some people's minds. (An ancient Middle Eastern religion called Zoroastrianism was dualistic and may have influenced Manicheism, which arose later.) The essence of Manicheism is belief in two equally powerful, equally eternal opposing ultimate realities—one good and one evil. The Manichees themselves also taught a dualism between spirit and matter, with the former being good and created by the good god and the latter being evil and created by the bad god. Although the Manichean religion considered these opposite ultimate realities personal, many dualists do not. Insofar as they believe in morally opposed absolutes, however, they are usually labeled *Manicheism* in terms of their worldview.

Two considerations often support Manichean dualism. First, it *seems* to explain the reality of evil in a world that is also good. That is probably how many people arrive at it for themselves; it's a hunch about the background reason for the apparently endless struggle everywhere and at all times between good and evil. This is what first attracted Augustine to Manicheism—before his conversion to Christianity. Many inquiring minds searching for a metaphysical answer to the problem of evil arrive at some form of metaphysical dualism whether they've ever heard of Manicheism or not.

In fact, popular culture often portrays ultimate reality this way. A very popular children's television cartoon series during the 1980s (and afterward in syndication and computer gaming) was

He-Man and the Masters of the Universe, which portrayed the world as a battleground between two equally powerful, eternal, opposite forces—Greyskull and Skeletor. He-Man is the hero who leads the battle for Greyskull's honor against Skeletor and his evil minions; every episode ends with a temporary victory for He-Man and a defeat for Skeletor, but with the promise of another round of conflict to come. Apparently, for the show's writers, Skeletor could only be defeated temporarily, never fully or finally. Like the later movie series *Star Wars*, He-Man presented a popularized and mythical version of Manicheism for the masses.

Second, many Christians fall unconsciously into Manichean dualism by thinking of God and Satan as two equal powers, one good and the other evil. This is usually a very qualified Manicheism, because most such Christians also believe Satan will ultimately be defeated by God in the eschatological apocalypse described in Revelation. At least within history, however, since the archangel Lucifer's expulsion from heaven, Lucifer is God's equal challenger, independently wreaking chaos and havoc in the universe. This is not pure Manichean dualism, of course, but as soon as Christians (or others) elevate Satan to equal status with God, even temporally, Manichean dualism is on the horizon and God's sole supremacy and sovereignty, as revealed in Isaiah and throughout the biblical story, are compromised.[1]

Exactly why Manichean dualism and all the other metaphysical visions of ultimate reality described in this chapter are wrong from a biblical-Christian point of view will become clearer as later chapters examine and explain in more detail the biblical-Christian view of ultimate reality. Here, in this chapter, only a few basic reasons will be given why each worldview is false and to be avoided by Christians.

---

1   For an excellent Christian biblical-theological account of Satan that avoids dualism but acknowledges Satan's power and influence in human history see Michael Green, *I Believe in Satan's Downfall* (Grand Rapids, Mich.: Eerdmans, 1981).

Although Augustine, the father of Western Christian thought, toyed with Manicheism for several years as a young man, he finally left it behind even before his Christian conversion. For months he looked forward to meeting the leading Manichean philosopher-theologian, a man named Faustus, hoping to get some of his questions answered. According to his own *Confessions*, however, Augustine was severely disappointed in Faustus's answers and left Manicheism behind, spending many years of his life as a Christian bishop and theologian arguing against it and its dualistic view of ultimate reality. The main question Augustine needed answered is the one about metaphysical dualism C. S. Lewis said is *unanswerable* in *Mere Christianity*. The question is simply this: *If there are two ultimate, absolute powers—forces equal in being, power, and eternity—what makes one of them good and the other one evil?* One does not have to be Christian to see the problem. Even Plato recognized why metaphysical dualism is logically impossible. Somehow, Plato knew and argued, "the good" and "being" must be connected; if ultimate being is not goodness itself, then "the good" is not absolute. In other words, as Lewis and many others have pointed out, *if* metaphysical dualism is true, then there must be *another being above* the two—the "good one" and the "evil one"—a being who decides that one is good and the other is evil!

From a biblical-Christian perspective, of course, there is only one ultimate reality, Yahweh God, the *personal, supernatural,* and *perfectly good* maker of heaven and earth and all that is in them. Admittedly, this raises the problem of evil—of how evil came to be in God's good creation (a basic element of the biblical-Christian metaphysic to be fleshed out in a later chapter but already touched on earlier). The Bible itself does not explain that metaphysically; it only requires that evil be subordinated to God and not be God's doing. Early Christian thinkers such as Gregory of Nyssa (335–94) and Augustine presented part of what came to be the main Christian answer: that evil is *not* a substance but is instead the "absence of the good." If it were a substance, they cogently argued, God would have to be its creator as, according to the Bible, God created everything that has being and pronounced it good (Genesis 1:31). Evil, then, is not like a germ but like a broken bone; it is not a some*thing* but a *condition*—a privation, a lack, a brokenness within creation brought about by creatures' rebellion and disobedience. *How* and *why* it came about is another question, and Christian philosophers and theologians have posited various *theodicies*—explanations of the reason for evil, the absence of the good, in God's good creation. To that we will return later.

Suffice it to say for now that *Manichean dualism*, or just metaphysical dualism, is one perspective on ultimate reality that has floated around in the ancient and modern worlds. In the ancient world it was the formal metaphysic of at least two organized religions; in the modern world it tends to exist primarily in popular culture and in individuals' private belief systems. It is a competitor to the biblical-Christian metaphysical perspective on ultimate reality and ought to be avoided and expunged from Christian thinking. It dishonors God as the sole supreme ultimate reality, the source, moral standard, and sovereign ruler of creation.

Metaphysical Monism: Pantheism, Emanationism, and Absolute Idealism

Many well-meaning, sincere inquiring minds, including many Christians, turn to a metaphysical vision *opposite* of dualism in terms of evil. Concern about evil seems to drive many thoughtful people, including many Christians, into the arms, as it were, of unbiblical and non-Christian worldviews. Metaphysical dualism is untenable rationally and biblically. So many modern people have turned to *metaphysical monisms* of various kinds—including that evil is not only a privation of the good but an *illusion*.

Monism is a flexible word used to label any view of *all reality* as *one substance*. Monism denies not only dualism but also *duality*—except in appearance. Reality *behind* the appearances is *one being.* Usually, along with monism comes the idea that this metaphysical *one*, this *universal substance or being*, is good and evil and is, like duality and multiplicity, unreal. There are and always have been varieties of monism. A popular one in both the ancient world and contemporary Western society is *emanationism*, belief that ultimate reality is *one substance* and all reality is *that substance*; in addition, finite, physical beings are emanations from that substance who have forgotten their ultimate, metaphysical *oneness* with *the One.* Sometimes emanationism is treated as a separate metaphysical perspective on ultimate reality, but in terms of its view of the "one and the many," the "infinite and finite," it is essentially monistic.

Perhaps the most consistent version of metaphysical monism is "Advaita Vedanta," an especially philosophical form of Hinduism popular in the West. The main popularizer of Vedanta in Western societies was Swami Vivekananda (1863–1902), a Hindu philosopher who spoke about Vedanta at the first World Parliament of Religions in Chicago in 1893. Vivekananda founded the first Vedanta Society in America in the 1890s. Today, in the twenty-first century, independent branches can be found in most large American cities. They are usually affiliated with a distinct Hindu sect in India known as the Ramakrishna Mission. One goal of both is to promote *non-duality*, another name for monism—the oneness of all being with Brahman, the divine being that unites everything and of which everything is a manifestation. The New Age movement of the 1980s largely embraced Vedanta philosophy, combining it with distinctly American and European esoteric beliefs and practices such as spiritualism and magic.

Vedanta, however, is hardly the only form of metaphysical monism. Ancient Neoplatonism was essentially monistic and emanationist. Neoplatonism is usually associated with the philosopher Plotinus (204–70) of Egypt, who created a new version of Plato's philosophy with a religious flair. In other words, Neoplatonism was as much a spirituality as a philosophy, which was not always the case in Middle Platonism, the main form of Platonic philosophy taught at the Athenian Academy in the centuries just before and after Jesus. Whatever exactly Plotinus taught, Neoplatonism has come to designate the idea that ultimate reality is "the One," a transcendent being of absolute unity, the source of everything that has being, pure and perfect in every way, and untouched and untouchable by corrupt matter. Souls are offshoots, emanations, of the One, and they long to return to their source. An analogy is the sun and its rays; the farther the sun's light rays get away from the sun, the less heat and energy they contain. In Neoplatonism *everything* is an *emanation* from the One, and souls know, but may have forgotten, their belonging to the One. Contemplation, mystical and/or rational, can help lead souls back to original unity with the One which already exists but has been forgotten.

Early Christians such as Origen, Gregory of Nyssa, and Augustine were influenced by Neoplatonism.[2] However, none accepted Neoplatonism uncritically. They rejected its absolute monism and its emanationism as too close to earlier Gnosticism—a second-century heresy that, like Neoplatonism later, believed souls are emanations, "sparks," of the divine One which can have no immediate contact with the material world and did not create it. Gnosticism and Neoplatonism have, throughout two millennia of Western, especially Jewish and Christian philosophy and theology, been combined and conflated—both by adherents and critics. That's simply because both are *monistic* and *emanationist*. Both believe ultimate reality is an absolute One of Being Itself of which finite souls, if not everything that is, are offshoots destined somehow to return into their original source.

---

2   I am aware that Origen was not directly influenced by Plotinus, but he knew Plotinus's own teacher Ammonius Saccus in Alexandria, Egypt, and much of Origen's metaphysical speculation in *On First Principles* smacks of Neoplatonism. For a general discussion of Neoplatonism in early Christianity see Harry Austryn Wolfson, *The Philosophy of the Church Fathers,* rev. ed. (Cambridge, Mass.: Harvard University Press, 1970).

Surface similarities between biblical thought and Gnostic and Neoplatonist monistic emanationism are obvious, but they are shallow. Gnosticism and Neoplatonism both were radically *monotheistic*—believing in *one ultimate reality*, God, and souls that are above nature. Both believed in a fall of creation and salvation as reunion with God. But these concepts had radically different meanings in Gnosticism and Neoplatonism from biblical thought. That will come out clearly in our exposition of the biblical view of reality. However, throughout the history of Western philosophical and religious thought and practice, both Gnosticism and Neoplatonism have appeared and reappeared frequently in various permutations. The underlying conflict with biblical-Christian metaphysics is *monism*—the belief that God, or "the One," the "Ocean of Light and Love" (as some New Agers have dubbed it), is all that has being with no ontological gulf fixed between God and creation. Usually, also, in all forms of monism, ultimate reality, even if called "God," is usually impersonal.

A final form of monism (at least to be discussed here) is *Absolute Idealism*—a modern form of monism that arose primarily in Germany (although one of its main precursors, Spinoza, was Dutch). Absolute Idealism is pantheistic—identifying God with the universe—with the twist that all reality, God and the universe, is mind or thought. That everything is a thought in the mind of God is one form of Absolute Idealism. Absolute Idealism in philosophy is usually associated with philosophers Fichte, Friedrich Schelling (1775–1854), and Hegel. Perhaps the best-known religious exponent, however, was Mary Baker Eddy (1821–1910), who founded the Church of Christ, Scientist, popularly known as "Christian Science." But she was just the best-known and most influential exponent of a larger American religious movement influenced by Absolute Idealism known as New Thought. According to all New Thought, God is the mind of the universe, the only thing that is really real, and matter is an extension of the divine mind. According to New Thought, human minds are always already part of the divine mind, God, and capable of manipulating matter. It is a mind-over-matter philosophy and religion rooted in the metaphysics of Absolute Idealism.[3]

Absolute Idealism, through New Thought, has entered into American culture with tremendous influence even among Christians, who are often unaware of its philosophical and metaphysical origins and implications. Hegel, for example, believed ultimate reality is what he called "Absolute Spirit," although the German word translated *Spirit* and that he used for God is "Geist," which has no exact English equivalent. It is usually translated into English as either *mind* or *spirit* or both. For Hegel, God is the transcendent-immanent spirit, mind, of the universe coming to self-actualization and self-realization in history.[4] But Hegel's emphasis fell on ultimate reality's, absolute spirit's, immanence in history and humanity's oneness with it. Hegel was not an absolute monist; he was more dialectical than that—emphasizing paradox moving toward synthesis (opposites coinciding). However, many of his British and American followers did adopt monism and identified humanity with God—pantheism. New Thought and especially Christian Science came to identify matter and the entire universe as an extension of the Divine Mind of the universe—pantheism. Ultimately, beyond appearances, reality is *one substance*—mind. In popular New Thought, as it filtered into American religion, positive thinking can heal, bring financial prosperity, and even overcome death. A particularly vulgarized version of this is the gospel of health and wealth founded on the New Thought-influenced teachings of evangelist E. W. Kenyon (1867–1948).[5]

All types of monism—from Neoplatonism to Advaita Vedanta

---

3   For a comprehensive and critical history of the New Thought movement see Charles S. Braden, *Spirits in Rebellion: The Rise and Development of New Thought* (Dallas: Southern Methodist University Press, 1963).

4   For Hegel's philosophy as it bears on God and metaphysics see Quentin Lauer, *Hegel's Concept of God* (Albany, N.Y.: State University of New York Press, 1982).

5   See D. R. McConnell, *A Different Gospel: A Historical and Biblical Analysis of the Modern Faith Movement* (Peabody, Mass.: Hendrickson, 1988).

to Absolute Idealism to American New Thought—implicitly if not explicitly deny the biblical idea of God as *supernatural* and *personal*. All deny the fixed gulf evident in biblical revelation between God and creation. All overemphasize the biblical idea of God as *immanent*—present with his creation—the point of letting go entirely of God's holy transcendence. They also all implicitly if not explicitly deny the biblical idea of creation—especially *creation out of nothing*—an idea implicit in the Bible and drawn out explicitly by the early church fathers in contrast to Greek metaphysics. All monisms have the *tendency* to deify humanity by asserting an underlying oneness between ultimate reality and the human soul or mind.

And yet, in spite of the stark contrast between monism of all kinds and the biblical-Christian metaphysic, various monistic philosophies have worked their way into Christian thought—both popular and scholarly. But this is syncretism at its worst and to be avoided and corrected wherever it rears its ugly head in churches and church-related institutions.

Panentheism: Almost Monism (But Not Quite)

A variation on monism, a kind of halfway metaphysical view between biblical-Christian personalist theism and monism, is *panentheism*. It is not sheer *pantheism* because the latter, on the back of monism, identifies God with the universe. Panentheism is any view that denies there is any ultimate reality except *God and the universe—together*. In panentheism, God and the universe are inseparable and interdependent. Like monism, panentheism denies the supernatural aspect of God, but it usually affirms God's personal nature. Ultimate reality is self-sufficient, supernatural, omnipotent, and personal but not free. Creation, nonultimate reality, is necessary for God.[6]

---

6   For an exhaustive explanation of all varieties of panentheism see Hartshorne and Reese, *Philosophers Speak of God*. For a more contemporary exploration and even recommendation of panentheism

Process thought, mentioned earlier, is based on a panentheistic metaphysic, for God depends on the world for his self-actualization and enjoyment. And this is not due to some voluntary self-limitation of God; it is necessary for God and, as Hegel affirmed, "Without a world God is not God." Process theology is a type of liberal Christian thought that builds on a panentheistic metaphysic in which God has no being apart from the world and is not supernatural or omnipotent. This is attractive to many people because it solves the problem of evil; if panentheism is true, then God cannot be responsible for evil because he could not stop it. His only power is the power of persuasion. But this solution to the problem of evil is bought at great cost—a radical denial of the biblical-Christian metaphysic of the biblical narrative in which God is supernatural, omnipotent, sovereign, and self-sufficient.[7]

Anglican philosopher-theologian Austin Farrer (1904–68) rightly spoke of the "prior actuality of God" in biblical-Christian thought.[8] That means that, contrary to monism, pantheism, and panentheism, the biblical narrative *requires* belief that God's existence precedes the world's not only temporally but ontologically. That is, the world is dependent on God, not vice versa. Nowhere in biblical revelation is God's being dependent on the world; "Christian" panentheism is based on sheer speculation and is contrary to the biblical perspective on ultimate reality and creation. One obvious reason this is so is *eschatology*. The biblical narrative is forward-looking, filled with promise and hope. Panentheism undermines all realistic confidence in God's ultimate victory over evil.

So far we have here explored and critiqued *three major metaphysical visions of ultimate reality that are radically alternative*

---

see *In Whom We Live and Move and Have Our Being: Panentheistic Reflections on God's Presence in a Scientific World*, eds. Philip Clayton and Arthur Peacocke (Grand Rapids, Mich.: Eerdmans, 2004). For a Christian critique of panentheism see John W. Cooper, *Panentheism: The Other God of the Philosophers* (Grand Rapids, Mich.: Baker Academic, 2006).

7   For a good Christian critique of process theology see David Basinger, *Divine Power in Process Theism: A Philosophical Critique* (Albany, N.Y.: State University of New York Press, 1988).

8   Austin Farrer, *Essays in Reflective Faith* (Grand Rapids, Mich.: Eerdmans, 1974).

to the intrinsic biblical-Christian one: dualism (Manicheism), monism (including emanationism and pantheism), and panentheism. Each one has many historical variations. Each one contains *some truth*; none is totally, one hundred percent false. Christians have borrowed each one, or some version of each one, at times to attempt to fill Whitehead's alleged gap of a Christian metaphysic. Each one stands in stark contrast to the biblical vision of ultimate reality. Each one is speculative, not provable, or more rational than the biblical-Christian metaphysic.

Naturalism: The Worldview of Atheism

A fourth rival metaphysical vision to the biblical-Christian worldview is *naturalism*. Naturalism is any belief that nature—a closed causal network *in principle* completely understandable by science—is all that exists. Naturalism is necessarily *atheistic*; it denies any divine reality beyond or outside of nature.[9] A naturalist *might* admit some kind of spiritual depth dimension within nature itself, but, if so, it is considered part of nature not yet fully understood by science. A popular expression of naturalism is the quote often attributed to scientist Carl Sagan: "The cosmos is all there is, all there ever was, and all there ever will be."[10] A major problem is that many people hear or read such statements of naturalism uttered by scientists and assume science and naturalism are inseparable if not identical. "The cosmos is all there is, all there ever was, and all there ever will be," however, is *not* a scientific claim; it is a philosophical and even speculative metaphysical claim. It is the expression of a blik—but a very popular one because it is so widely considered essential to the progress of science.

Naturalism, like the other metaphysical schemes under review here, takes many different forms, but underlying them all is that *nature, understood as mathematically describable laws and phenomena ruled*

---

9   For much on naturalism and why it is internally incoherent, see Alvin Plantinga, *Where the Conflict Really Lies: Science, Religion and Naturalism* (Oxford and New York: Oxford University Press, 2011).

10   This, or something very close to it, is the opening line of Sagan's film series *The Cosmos*.

by them, is all that is real. Methodological naturalism is essential to the progress of modern science; that is simply the assumption in scientific research that nature is predictable. The key term there is "in scientific research." Methodological naturalism is not metaphysical naturalism, although many modern scientifically minded people, and those influenced by them, confuse the two. A theist, someone who believes in a *supernatural* and *personal God*, can practice science using methodological naturalism in the field and in the laboratory. To extrapolate that into metaphysical naturalism is not warranted or justified by methodological naturalism or natural science.

Atheism is really not a metaphysical worldview; it is simply denial of the reality of any God. Underlying atheism is normally, perhaps always, *naturalism.* Naturalism is the metaphysic of atheism—at least in modern Western culture. (Some forms of Buddhism are atheistic but not naturalistic.) Religious people who attack atheism often make a mistake; what they should do is criticize, point out the flaws in, naturalism. If naturalism is untenable philosophically, as some philosophers believe and argue, then atheism crumbles with it. Atheism is just naturalism in disguise, and if nature is all there is, then there can be no moral absolutes and life has no ultimate meaning—only whatever meanings people invest in it (e.g., happiness). The main argument against naturalism is that it necessarily requires nihilism, which most naturalists do not wish to embrace. (Nihilism is belief that life is absurd, meaningless. Its main problem is that it undermines what psychologists call "basic trust," which is a basic human need.)[11]

Naturalism's conflict with the biblical-Christian vision of ultimate reality is obvious. If naturalism is true, humans are truly alone in the universe and are nothing more than highly evolved animals, products of blind evolutionary forces. There is no God, no intelligence or will or love behind appearance, no guiding power to

---

11   For a devastating critique of both atheism and naturalism, insofar as they do not end up in nihilism, see Hans Küng, *Does God Exist? An Answer for Today* (New York: Doubleday, 1979).

guarantee that, in the end, all will be well. But naturalism also has some logical challenges it cannot meet or overcome.

First, if naturalism is true, as philosopher Plantinga convincingly demonstrates, then there is no reason to believe it is true—a real conundrum! Plantinga points out that *if* naturalism is true, then there is no reason to trust our cognitive functions:

> We [all] assume that our cognitive faculties are reliable. But what I want to argue is that the naturalist has a powerful reason *against* this initial assumption, and should give it up. I don't mean to argue that this natural assumption is false; like everyone else, I believe that our cognitive functions [basic abilities to know] *are*, in fact, mostly reliable. What I do mean to argue is that the *naturalist . . .* is rationally obliged to give up this assumption.[12]

The reason is that *if* naturalism is true, then all our ideas are products of forces in nature over which we have no real control (as all is ruled by natural laws). Our very thoughts are products of chemicals in the brain. Naturalism implies that our beliefs, whatever they are, are controlled by nature, which is a closed system of mathematically describable laws and material-energy forces and phenomena. Therefore, when anyone *asserts* something as true he or she is not really saying anything other than "this is what I think and I cannot think otherwise."

Plantinga turns the tables on naturalists, who often claim that naturalist metaphysics and modern science go inseparably hand in hand. He closes his book *Where the Conflict Really Lies* (2011) with this devastating critique:

> Turning to naturalism, clearly there is superficial concord between science and naturalism—if only because so many naturalists trumpet the claim that science is a pillar in the

---

12 Plantinga, *Where the Conflict Really Lies*, 326.

temple of naturalism. As I argue in this chapter, they are mistaken: one can't rationally accept both naturalism and current evolutionary theory; that combination of beliefs is self-defeating. But then there is a deep conflict between naturalism and one of the most important claims of current science. My conclusion, therefore, is that there is superficial conflict but deep concord between science and theistic belief, but superficial concord and deep conflict between science and naturalism. Given that naturalism is at least a quasi-religion, there is indeed a science/religion conflict, all right, but it is not between science and theistic religion: it is between science and naturalism. That's where the conflict really lies.[13]

Catholic theologian Küng presents a parallel argument against naturalism in his massive *Does God Exist? An Answer for Today* (1979). According to him, atheism, naturalism, is a rational choice *but only if* the person choosing it is willing to embrace nihilism. Basic trust in the meaningfulness of reality, of life, however, is necessary for healthy human functioning, according to psychologist Erik Erickson (1902–94). If nature is all there is, then there is no real, ultimate meaning in the universe; it is simply an accident and there is no answer to the ultimate question, "Why is there something rather than nothing?" Nor is there any answer to "What is the meaning of my life?" other than to eat, drink, and be merry. Finally, there is no absolute reason why oppressing and taking advantage of people is wrong so long as it does not disadvantage the person or group doing it. "Might makes right" is the only reasonable ethic if nature is all there is.[14]

---

13   Ibid., 349–50. Obviously this implies that Plantinga is a believer in *theistic evolution*.

14   This has, of course, been disputed by many naturalists, including philosopher Kai Nielsen in *Ethics without God* (Buffalo, N.Y.: Prometheus Press, 1973). However, all such responses rely on some subjective belief in compassion and empathy as built into humanity by nature. That is disputable and unprovable. And it does nothing to contradict the person who decides to go against this mythical humanist trait of empathy and exercise power instead. Ayn Rand (1905–82) is perhaps the most consistent naturalist; she embraced and promoted not empathy but self-interest if not sheer power.

Secular Humanism Is Also Naturalism

Many people talk about *secular humanism* as a worldview or metaphysical belief system. Unfortunately, many people, both Christians and secular humanists, simply equate the latter with humanism when, in fact, *originally* humanism was Christian. Christian humanism predates secular humanism, which is simply one expression of naturalism. For example, the great Renaissance-Reformation Catholic thinker Desiderius Erasmus (1466–1536) was *both* Christian *and* a humanist. Humanism is simply any belief in the dignity and creativity of human persons, that human beings are unique and above nature, in some sense transcendent, capable of great cultural achievements as well as terrible destruction. It places special value on humanity. As a later chapter here will demonstrate, the *real humanism* is *Christian humanism* because of the biblical-Christian emphasis on humans as created in the image and likeness of God.

Secular humanism, however, is one very popular expression of naturalism. It is naturalism that elevates humanity over the rest of nature in terms of special dignity and worth.[15] According to secular humanism, human beings are only products of nature, but they are nature become self-aware, conscious, and free. There is no ultimate purpose for or meaning in human life other than what humans themselves create, but nature has "built into" humans, its highest and best product (so far), compassion, empathy, and desire for community. Ethics is based on this natural sense of the common good upon which every individual's personal happiness and thriving depends.

What many secular humanists do not wish to admit is that secular humanism is itself a metaphysical belief system, not a conclusion of science. Science itself cannot prove that human beings

---

15   The understanding of secular humanism offered here is drawn largely from one of secular humanism's main proponents: philosopher Paul Kurz (1925–2012), author of *In Defense of Secular Humanism* (Buffalo, N.Y.: Prometheus Press, 1983).

are "higher" or "better" than the rest of nature or that, just because (if) there is an "altruistic gene" that inclines people toward compassion for others, compassion for others is "right." The problem with all naturalistic ethics is the naturalistic fallacy—attempting to derive an "ought" from what "is." In other words, according to secular humanism, and all naturalism, there is nothing transcending nature to assign special value, dignity, or worth to human beings. That is something, then, that humans assign to themselves. Also, since there is nothing and no one above nature and nature is all there is, there can be no source or ground for what *ought to be the case*. There is simply *what is the case*. Even if it is the case that humans have a built-in compassion or empathy gene, that does not make it morally normative. It only makes it *what is the case*. A person who chooses not to live compassionately is only going against a gene, not a God. There is a difference.

The Achilles heel of secular humanism is its unsupported and unsupportable claim that, of all the species on earth, humans are higher, better, and of special dignity, value, and worth, and that they are not morally accountable to anyone or anything other than themselves. There is no *one* to whom to be accountable—outside of nature. A very good argument can be made that the real law of nature is *survival of the fittest*—a phrase coined not by Charles Darwin but by philosopher Herbert Spencer (1820–1903). Spencer, however, was simply extrapolating from Darwin's biological theory of natural selection and applying it to sociology. According to him, the father of Social Darwinism, there is no natural reason for society to help the weaker members of humanity because nature tends always to weed out weaker members of species in order to keep the population from exceeding the food supply. Compassion, then, in the sense of self-sacrificial help given to the weak, is actually *against nature*. Philosopher-novelist Ayn Rand (1905–82) popularized Spencer's Social Darwinism and took it to its logical conclusion, arguing that it is actually *immoral* to sacrifice the advantages of the strong to help the weak.[16] Of course, all talk of "moral" and "immoral" on the basis of naturalism is problematic; it can only mean "what is against what is." But "what is" cannot really yield "ought to be."

One might think that naturalism is so obviously contrary to biblical-Christian belief that it is not a threat, that syncretism between them cannot happen. One would be wrong. Denial of anything supernatural is common in modern Christianity. *Deism* is the very popular belief that, although a personal God created the universe and rules over it as its architect and moral lawgiver, he does not interact with or intervene in human affairs or nature. Some sociologists of religion have claimed that "moralistic, therapeutic deism" is the popular folk religion of most young Christians in America.[17] A good case can be made that deism of some kind, whether "moralistic" and "therapeutic" or not, is the popular religion of most Americans—usually mixed quite inconsistently with belief in the supernatural "in Bible times" (and often "in other countries"). In America, popular religion, including grassroots Christianity, has by and large adopted naturalism into Christianity, mixing and mingling the two. Of course, the belief is not *pure* naturalism—belief that nature is all that is real—but *functional* naturalism—belief that although God exists and is personal, he does not intervene in history or human lives, which are ruled by natural laws and explainable by science.

Some forms of *liberal Protestant theology* have claimed to have discovered something called "naturalistic theism"—belief that God is personal and real but that nature, as described by science and as believed in by naturalism, is, using an analogy, the "glove on God's hand." That is, God's agency in the world works only and

---

16   This writer heard her say this to talk show host Phil Donahue on *The Donahue Show* in 1979. The interview can be seen and heard on YouTube. Rand's Social Darwinism is the theme of many of her novels, including the ever-popular *Atlas Shrugged* (New York: Plume, 1999).

17   See Christian Smith and Melinda Lundquist Denton, *Soul Searching: The Religious and Spiritual Lives of American Teenagers*, reprint ed. (Oxford and New York: Oxford University Press, 2009).

always through natural laws.[18] This is one very popular approach to "concordism" between science and religion, but, of course, it requires that the Christian function with something like Thomas Jefferson's truncated Bible that cut out everything he considered unreasonable.[19]

The "Two Truths" Solution Not a Real Solution

Science teachers in high schools and universities have often mixed and mingled naturalism with their teaching of biology, physics, and astronomy. The two—science and naturalism—have become almost inseparable in many people's minds. One way religious people handle the problem is to adopt a "two truths" approach— believing in naturalism in classrooms and laboratories and believing in the personal, supernatural God and miracles of the Bible (e.g., the resurrection of Jesus) in church and home. This approach to relating philosophy to religion was recommended by medieval Christian thinker Siger of Brabant (1240–84). He could find no way to reconcile the increasingly popular and influential philosophy of Aristotle—then becoming the basis of much teaching in medieval universities—with classical Christianity. So, instead of reconciling them, he suggested believing in *both*. For example, according to Aristotle the universe is eternal—without beginning. According to the biblical-Christian worldview the universe was created by God "in the beginning" and only God is eternal. Siger taught that a Christian should believe both even though they contradict each other. This has become known as the "two truths theory," which was condemned by the Catholic Church in 1277.[20] Siger's contemporary, Thomas Aquinas, attempted to reconcile and

---

18   See, for example, Lutheran theologian Philip Hefner, "Why I Don't Believe in Miracles," *Newsweek* (May 1, 2000): 61.

19   See Thomas Jefferson, *The Life and Morals of Jesus of Nazareth* (also known popularly as "The Jefferson Bible") (Boston, Mass.: Beacon Press, 2001).

20   I know there is some debate about whether Siger actually taught the "double truths" theory, but I choose to go with tradition which says he did.

integrate Aristotle's philosophy with Christianity. How successful he was, or whether he permitted Aristotle's philosophy to master biblical-Christianity in terms of metaphysics, is a much debated issue especially among Protestants, who are not devoted to him as the "Angelic Doctor."

The alternatives to personalist theism's metaphysical vision of ultimate reality discussed in this chapter pretty much exhaust the possibilities—excluding odd combinations and idiosyncratic belief systems most of which, when pushed to logical consistency, boil down to one of these: dualism (Manicheism), monism (nonduality, emanationism), panentheism, or naturalism. Of course, many people carry around in their minds eclectic mixtures of two or more of these, but, again, these are the several and perhaps only somewhat consistent metaphysical visions of ultimate reality prominent in the West and impinging on Christianity and Euro-American societies. (Animism and polytheism have been intentionally left aside here because of their lack of influence in Western cultures.)

Interlude 4

The metaphysical visions of ultimate reality discussed in the preceding chapter do not exhaust the possibilities. One more must be described and discussed although mention has been made of it before—the generic Greek philosophy of the educated elite of the Roman Empire. This is the metaphysical philosophy that has *most often and most profoundly* influenced Christian thought—especially the Greek and Latin church fathers and, through them, the entire history of what can be called classical Christian theism.

Classical Christian Theism

In 1646 a group of British divines—church leaders—met in what was called the Westminster Assembly to establish the basis for a new British national church. The model was the Presbyterian Church (the Kirk) of Scotland. One product of the gathering was the Westminster Confession of Faith—a rather detailed exposition of Protestant Christian doctrine heavily informed by Reformed theology (Calvinism). The Confession states that God is "without body, parts or passions" and "immutable" (unchangeable). The Confession is just one example of classical Christian theism, what is taken by many conservative Christians of all branches of Christianity to be *orthodox doctrine* and a necessary part of the Christian worldview.

However, many Christian critics have asked what *biblical warrant* there is for declaring God to be "without parts or passions" and "immutable." They know that Scripture can be cherry-picked for proof texts to support such ideas of God, but they are not satisfied that *Scripture as a whole* supports them. In fact, many critics of classical Christian theism believe it is actually an amalgam of

Greek metaphysics with *biblical metaphysics* and that, in many cases, it has permitted the former to control the latter. Among those critics is Cherbonnier. Others include Brunner and, to a certain extent, Barth. A chorus of Christian voices began to be raised throughout the nineteenth and twentieth centuries arguing that classical Christian theism, the typical doctrine of God, is an unacceptable and ultimately incoherent blending of Greek philosophy with biblical revelation. One of the first to claim this was the great German Lutheran denominational leader and theologian I. A. Dorner (1809–84), who wrote a groundbreaking essay about God's immutability,[1] claiming that it should be stripped of Greek influences and interpreted only as referring to God's stability of character. Throughout the following century numerous Christian thinkers attempted to purify Christian belief in God from the influences of Greek philosophy.

The particular Greek philosophy most critics of classical Christian theism are talking about—as corrupting the biblical concept of God—has been mentioned several times already: Middle Platonism. However, another type of Greek philosophy the critics include is Aristotle's philosophy, which became such a prominent part of especially Catholic thought through Thomas Aquinas. Both Middle Platonism—prominent among the educated elite of the Roman Empire around the time of Jesus and for a long time afterward—and Aristotelianism emphasize *ethical monotheism*—belief in one God only who is the very standard of goodness. Later, Neoplatonism built on Middle Platonism its idea of creation as emanation and souls as stray sparks of the divine being. Such ideas could already be found implicit in Middle Platonism.

It's easily understandable why early Christian thinkers adopted Greek philosophy as a metaphysical framework for explaining Christianity as a *respectable religion and philosophy* to educated

---

1   Part of Dorner's essay may be found in *God and Incarnation in Mid-Nineteenth Century German Theology,* ed. Claude Welch (New York: Oxford University Press, 1965).

people in the Roman Empire—including emperors. First, the most prominent Jewish thinker of the Roman Empire, Philo, had already in the first century "discovered in Greek philosophy rudimental truths of the teachings of Scripture"[2] and used Greek philosophy to interpret Scripture using the allegorical method. Philo had already created a "philosophized Judaism" on the back of which certain second- and third-century Christian Gentile thinkers created a "philosophized Christianity."[3] Second, there really were significant similarities between Judaism and Christianity, on the one hand, and the best of Greek philosophy (e.g., Middle Platonism), on the other hand, such as *ethical monotheism*, and highlighting these similarities helped second- and third-century Christians called "Apologists" defend Christianity to emperors and other leaders of the empire. Critics maintain, however, that they, like Philo earlier, swallowed too much Greek philosophy with good intentions and ended up with a syncretized metaphysical vision—half biblical and half Greek philosophical.

Third, as H. A. Wolfson pointed out in *The Philosophy of the Church Fathers*, Greek philosophy was useful in the Christian struggle against heresies such as Gnosticism.[4] Gnosticism, like the many mystery cults of the Roman Empire, was highly esoteric, occult, and mythical. Second- and third-century Christian thinkers wanted to distinguish Christianity from all of that as many people were prone to lump Christianity together with the mystery cults as just another one of them.

Greek Philosophy and Christian Theism

All that is to say: creating a *philosophized Christianity* using Greek philosophy was useful as a means of making Christianity *respectable* in the ancient world. Wolfson noted that "once philosophy was

---

2   Wolfson, *The Philosophy of the Church Fathers*, 3.
3   Ibid., 11.
4   Ibid., 13–14.

introduced into Christianity in the second century, it had a continuous history among both the Greek Fathers and the Latin Fathers."[5] Wolfson rightly noted also that this history was not without controversy among Christians and that even the most philosophically minded Christian church fathers such as Clement of Alexandria, who referred to Christianity as "the true philosophy," saw dangers and shortcomings in Greek philosophy. None embraced it uncritically.[6] The most outspoken opponent of this philosophized Christianity was North African church father Tertullian, who declared in his *Prescription Against Heresies* that philosophy is the cause of all heresies and urged Christians to avoid it. Yet, as Wolfson also points out, Tertullian himself was knowledgeable about Greek philosophy and made some use of it.[7] For example, even the most pro-Greek philosophy church fathers rejected the typical Greek philosophical idea of the eternity of the world and emphasized instead something scandalous to most Greek philosophers—the creation of the world out of nothing. Also, they all emphasized the resurrection of bodies—both Jesus's in the past and all humanity's in the future—something absolutely anathema to Greek philosophers, who denigrated bodies as prisons or tombs of souls.

So in what *negative ways* did Greek philosophy influence Christian metaphysics—according to critics such as Dorner, Brunner, Cherbonnier, and others? Remember medieval theologian Anselm of Canterbury's claim, mentioned earlier, that God cannot actually have compassion? And the Westminster Confession's later description of God as "without passions"? Many critics of Greek philosophy's influence on Christian thought have focused on "divine impassibility"—the idea that God, as ultimate reality, cannot suffer—as the perfect example of Greek philosophy's pernicious influence on Christian thought, leading it away from biblical

---

5   Ibid., 14.
6   Ibid., 15–16.
7   Ibid., 102–6.

revelation about God as passionate. Anselm, the lead bishop of the Catholic Church of England in the eleventh century and a highly revered theologian, claimed that it would be inconsistent for God to have passions, including *feeling sympathy for the wretched*, and at the same time be the highest of all beings, the being greater than which none can be conceived. Therefore, according to Anselm, when we attribute compassion to God we are only describing our own feelings when contemplating God's great mercy.[8]

Classical Christian theism, born in the cauldron of philosophized Christianity in the second and third centuries in the Roman Empire, reached its zenith in Anselm and Aquinas. Aquinas agreed that God, being absolute and ultimate in terms of reality, cannot change in any way and therefore cannot suffer—including feeling emotions such as compassion and sympathy. But classical Christian theism is not limited to early or medieval Christian thought; it still has its defenders in the twenty-first century in spite of being embattled.[9] Very few Christian theologians except out-and-out liberal Protestants (e.g., process theologians) reject classical Christian theism entirely. Rather, following Dorner—a pioneer in attempting to return the Christian doctrine of God to biblical thought, separating it from Greek metaphysics that conflicts with that—many simply want to adjust Christian metaphysics "back to the Bible." Most, this writer included, gladly affirm broad areas of agreement between the best of Greek philosophical theology and biblical revelation of God. At the same time, however, together with Dorner, Brunner, Cherbonnier, and other Christian critics of classical theism, I believe it important to base Christian metaphysics on the biblical narrative and not allow Greek or any other metaphysical thought to draw it away into extrabiblical speculation.

---

8   Hartshorne and Reese, *Philosophers Speak of God,* 99.
9   See Stephen E. Parrish, *God and Necessity: A Defense of Classical Theism* (Lanham, Md.: UPA, 2001).

Middle Platonism and Christian Theology

Middle Platonism is an artificial name given to a kind of generic Greek metaphysical philosophy that prevailed at the Athenian Academy during and around the lifetime of Christ. There is no single philosopher who stands out as its most eminent representative, but many historians name Plutarch (45–120) as one of its most formative thinkers. However, Plutarch's distinctive idea of God should not be regarded as typical of all Middle Platonism. The key to all Middle Platonism's attraction for Jews and Christians in the Roman Empire lies in its *ethical monotheism*—a belief that ultimate reality is *one* and *the substance and source of all goodness*. Middle Platonism rejected literal interpretations of the Greek and Roman myths and legends of the gods and goddesses. It looked down on popular polytheism and the mystery cults that populated the Roman Empire. It claimed to be based solely on reason and universal experience, although it did not reject divine oracles.

For Middle Platonists, drawing on Plato himself, ultimate reality is divine, one, perfect, self-sufficient, incapable of change or suffering, outside of time (nontemporal), and a simple substance. This God is the antithesis of all that is wrong with finite reality and is free of evil, which is the product of matter. God relates to the world through his Logos, a semidivine emanation, and the world, especially humans, relate to God through their rational minds. According to Middle Platonism, God, ultimate reality, is the very embodiment and standard of justice, absolutely free of all wickedness of every kind. But he is not identified as love or loving. Whether and to what extent Middle Platonism's absolute and highest reality, God, was personal is debated. The general consensus is that he was conceived by most Middle Platonists as personal in some sense but very different from human persons in being free of all limitations and evil.

Here is how Plutarch described God around the time of Christ:

God exists . . . and he exists for no fixed time but for the everlasting ages which are immovable, timeless, and undeviating, in which there is no earlier or later, no future or past, no older or younger. He being one has completely filled "forever" with one "now"; and being is really being only when it is after his pattern, without having been or about to be, without a beginning and not coming to an end. Therefore in our worship we ought to hail him and address him with the words "Thou art."[10]

A later Middle Platonist named Albinus (dates unknown but second century) believed in two gods—a "First God" who is highest and best and a "Second God" who creates—a mediator between the First God and the world. According to Albinus, writing around the same time as the second-century Christian Apologists,

The First God is eternal, ineffable, self-sufficient—that is, without needs, ever-sufficient—that is, always perfect, all-sufficient—that is, completely perfect: Deity, Substantiality, Truth, Symmetry, Good. I mention these aspects not as providing definitions but as naming aspects in every respect characteristic of the one under consideration. And he is Good because he benefits all things as he is able, being the cause of every good thing; beautiful because his form is by nature perfect and symmetrical; Truth, because he is the source of all truth as the sun is of all light; he is Father because he is the cause of all and sets in order the heavenly Mind and the soul of the universe toward himself and toward his own thoughts.[11]

Clearly, then, there were points of similarity between the biblical depiction of God and Middle Platonism's depiction of "God." It was

---

10   Quoted in Robert M. Grant, *Gods and the One God* (Philadelphia: Westminster, 1986), 76.
11   Quoted in ibid., 80.

natural and understandable for early Christians, following Philo, to make use of Middle Platonism's metaphysics as a framework for explaining Christianity to emperors and other influential, intellectually inclined Greeks and Romans. And yet, one has to wonder if *some* of them went too far in adopting Middle Platonism and later Neoplatonism and yet later Aristotelianism—using *them* instead of the biblical narrative as their Christian metaphysic.

Speaking of second-century Christian Apologists, historical theologian Robert Grant said, "As the first Christian philosophical theologian, Justin went well beyond Aristides and juxtaposed his special interpretation of divine transcendence (based on Middle Platonic philosophy) with biblical and traditional Jewish and Christian ideas of God."[12] Aristides (dates unknown except second century) was one of the first of the Christian Apologists; he used Middle Platonism to explain Christianity to Roman emperor Hadrian when he visited Athens. Justin Martyr (100–165) was a Greek philosopher from Palestine who converted to Christianity and remained a philosopher, interpreting Christianity as the fulfillment of Greek philosophy. Of Plato and Christ he declared: "I confess that I both boast and with all my strength strive to be found a Christian; not because the teachings of Plato are different from those of Christ, but because they are not in all respects similar, as neither are those of the others, Stoics, and poets and historians."[13] He went on to declare that "whatever things were rightly said among all men, are the property of us Christians"[14] because the Logos of God, the Christ who became incarnate in Jesus, was the seed of truth in all people. Thus, according to Justin, insofar as the Greek philosophers, especially Plato, spoke truth, and they did, the source of that truth was the Logos, Christ.

---

12 Robert M. Grant, *Greek Apologists of the Second Century* (Philadelphia: Westminster, 1988), 59.

13 "The Second Apology of Justin" in *The Apostolic Fathers with Justin Martyr and Irenaeus: Volume I, The Ante-Nicene Fathers*, eds. Alexander Roberts and James Donaldson (Grand Rapids, Mich.: Eerdmans, 1985), 192–93.

14 Ibid., 193.

It would not be too far off the mark to consider Justin Martyr and some of the other second-century Christian Apologists Middle Platonists. Certainly in a formal sense Justin was one; he continued to wear his philosopher's distinctive garb even after converting to Christianity, and he taught Christianity, as he understood it, as true philosophy, not the absolute contradiction to Greek metaphysics but its fulfillment. He borrowed Middle Platonic language for God to describe the Christian God to the Roman senate and emperor.

Another second-century Christian Apologist was also a philosopher—Athenagoras of Athens (133–90), who wrote a defense of Christianity addressed to Roman Emperor Marcus Aurelius (emperor from 161–80). The emperor was also a philosopher and, according to Grant,

> Athenagoras' theology was deeply influenced by the popular Platonism which he knew well. Like Albinus he conveniently summarizes: God is "uncreated, eternal, invisible, impassible, incomprehensible, and infinite." He "can be apprehended by mind and reason alone." He is "encompassed by light, beauty, spirit, and indescribable power."[15]

Still another second-century Christian Apologist who drew heavily on Middle Platonism to describe Christianity's ultimate reality, God, was Theophilus of Antioch, who also described the God of Christianity using negative theology—what God is *not* more than what God *is*.

Slightly later Christian thinkers in Alexandria, Egypt—Clement and Origen—philosophized Christianity further, borrowing heavily but not uncritically from Platonism. Gradually, Christians began to envision ultimate reality, God, along the lines of Platonic metaphysics—including the idea that God, being metaphysically complete and perfect in every way imaginable, cannot suffer or be affected by temporal events or creatures. The word for this was and is *impassibility*.

---

15   Grant, *Greek Apologists*, 106.

Medieval Catholic thinker Thomas Aquinas envisioned God, borrowing from Aristotle, as *Actus Purus*—pure actuality without potentiality with the result that God cannot change in any way or become anything he is not already. Aquinas also described God as so self-sufficient as to be incapable of being affected inwardly, emotionally, by the world.

Classical Christian theism is, then, a combination of Greek philosophy with biblical revelation. Some Christian critics, even ones concerned to retrieve and preserve the biblical revelation of God, suspect that much classical Christian theism has tended to move God away from being fully personal toward being so remote and unmoved as to be quite different from the passionate Yahweh of the Bible. The suspicion is that, over the Christian centuries, beginning in the second century, Christian theologians tended to adopt and adapt Greek metaphysics, setting aside biblical metaphysics—or, perhaps more often, mixing the two in a syncretistic and eclectic blend that is unbalanced.

A Vulnerable God?

Perhaps the deepest point of controversy in this debate about the influence of Greek philosophy in Christian metaphysics is *whether it is appropriate biblically and in terms of Christian thought to describe God as vulnerable*. Certainly Greek philosophical theology would reject that idea as absurd. The highest and best being, the being greater than which none can be conceived, the being of all perfection, infinite, immutable, and impassible, cannot be vulnerable. And yet, many modern Christian thinkers have said, the God of the Bible, the God of Israel and of Jesus Christ, is revealed in the biblical narrative as very vulnerable—voluntarily open to being angered, grieved, blessed, made happy, or satisfied by creatures. Reformed theologian James Daane wrote that "those who define the God of the Bible as the Unconditioned Absolute have lingered too long at the waterholes of Western rationalism."[16] By "Western rationalism"

---

16   James Daane, "Can a Man Bless God?" in *God and the Good*, eds. Clifton Orlebeke and Lewis B. Smedes (Grand Rapids, Mich.: Eerdmans, 1975), 172.

Daane meant the whole stream of philosophical theology stemming from Middle Platonism, not just the Enlightenment rationalism of the modern world. He concluded his essay "Can a Man Bless God?"—which was meant to correct classical theism—by describing the God of the Bible thus:

> In freedom God *became* Creator and re-Creator, a God who both creates conditions and overcomes sinful conditions, a God who responds to conditional, contingent reality in judgment and in grace. In the biblical view God hears and responds to the cries of the needy, and is indeed so involved in conditional, contingent reality that he can be both sinned against and, no less, blessed by man in such a way that it makes a difference to God himself. But a God who is unconditional [absolute] because he himself accounts for all conditions by virtue of his essence or decree is a God who cannot hear, let alone answer prayer.[17]

So, a great debate rages and has raged within especially scholarly Christian circles for more than a century about Christianity's metaphysical vision especially as it relates to *ultimate reality*—God. There is agreement that God is *supernatural, personal,* but *not human* (except in the incarnation), but great disagreement about whether Greek philosophy's influence on classical Christian theism and especially ideas about God's attributes has been overall helpful or pernicious. The turning point, the point of great controversy, to boil it down to one word, is *vulnerability.* Can, should, Christian metaphysics interpret the ultimate reality of the Bible and of Christian religion as voluntarily *truly vulnerable*—to the point of being open to being affected inwardly by what creatures do? Or should all that be interpreted as anthropomorphism under the influence (many would say) of Greek philosophy?

For one party, the defenders of classical Christian theism, what

---

17   Ibid., 173.

is at stake is *God's transcendence*. For the other party, the critics of classical Christian theism, especially those who want to retrieve the biblical view of God separated from the influence of Greek metaphysics, what is at stake is *God's personal nature* and *accessibility*. Is it possible that there is real truth on both sides? And yet, it seems, on the turning point of *divine vulnerability* one has to decide.

This book takes the side of those Christian thinkers who wish to retrieve a genuinely biblical metaphysic even if that means sometimes discarding some traditional attributes of ultimate reality, God, in favor of more biblical ones. However, this book will *not* go so far as Hegel or Whitehead in stripping God of being supernatural— above and free from nature and nature's laws and able to intervene powerfully within nature and history. The key to this middle way, if it is truly a middle way between extremes, is *divine self-limitation*— the idea that the God of the Bible is vulnerable *because* he makes himself so out of love.[18]

---

18   A book that especially well lays out the basis for this metaphysical vision of God as voluntarily vulnerable and yet in himself transcendent is *The Work of Love: Creation as Kenosis*, ed. John Polkinghorne (Grand Rapids, Mich.: Eerdmans, 2001). This book contains essays by Christian thinkers critical of traditional Greek-inspired classical theism and yet holding to God's transcendence over the world. The key to all their essays (with one or two exceptions where process thought seems to intrude) is divine voluntary self-limitation or "kenosis."

CHAPTER 5

The Biblical-Christian View
of Ultimate Reality: God

At the heart of every metaphysic, every vision of ultimate reality, lies something absolute, something believed to be the source and/or connecting center of all that is. By *absolute*, here is meant only *"unsurpassable"* in terms of explanatory power; it is whatever sustains, controls, governs, or connects everything else. To reject such an absolute, ultimate reality is to reject metaphysics entirely. Even strict *pluralists*—people who believe all reality is but a collection of individual things without any absolute or ultimate reality connecting them—believe in some force or principle such as "creativity" or just "energy." The reason metaphysics is ultimately unavoidable is due to the persistent pressing questions of all inquiring minds: "Why is there something rather than nothing?" and "What is the meaning of existence?" Only a nihilist can answer with a firm denial of *source* or *purpose*.

A Brief Review

We saw in the previous chapter and interlude that over the centuries and across cultures people have used reason and experience to speculate about the one great answer to life's ultimate questions. Metaphysicians have traditionally referred to this particular central issue of metaphysics as the problem of the "one and the many"—what is the "one" that underlies the "many"? Is it one eternal substance that is all that really exists such that the many are just manifestations of it, ultimately unreal in and of themselves (monism)? Is it nature, a set of mathematically describable laws controlling eternal matter and energy (naturalism)? Is it two ultimate realities, beings, principles, powers, one good and one evil, locked in eternal conflict (dualism)? Is it a finite, nonabsolute being related to everything else, giving them their aim, their purpose, but struggling to bring unity out of chaos and harmony out of conflict (panentheism)? Is it a powerful but remote deity, creator of all but uninvolved or unaffected by the world of finite things and persons (deism, Greek philosophical theism)?

Whitehead said that Christianity is a religion searching for a metaphysic; it has at times borrowed these and other metaphysical visions and attempted to synthesize them with biblical Christianity. Christians living in pluralistic cultures where these and perhaps other visions of ultimate reality swim around in popular culture or in "the universe next door"[1] often confusedly borrow aspects of extrabiblical metaphysical visions and combine them with their Christian faith. Throughout Christian history Christian philosophers and theologians have frequently used Greek philosophy and metaphysics as a theoretical framework for Christianity.

The thesis of this book is that, while philosophy can be helpful for answering questions the Bible does not answer, two considerations must be made. First, the Bible is not devoid of any metaphysical vision of ultimate reality; it implies one and that is easily discernable if one does not approach the Bible with a wrong assumption (e.g., that narrative cannot imply a metaphysic). Second, discerning that biblical metaphysic is a matter of looking behind the narrative at what it *assumes* about ultimate reality. There a clear vision of ultimate reality is apparent to any discerning reader looking for it.

That clear biblical vision of ultimate reality is, as already expressed, the *supernatural, personal (but not human) God of Israel*

---

1   James Sire, *The Universe Next Door: A Basic Worldview Catalog,* 5th *ed.* (Downers Grove, Ill.: InterVarsity, 2009).

and of Jesus Christ. Brunner rightly stated that, in biblical revelation and therefore in Christian philosophy, the "metaphysical background" of every atom is God: "In order that I may know what it is that holds the world together in its inmost being—this means no less than the knowledge of the Creator Himself."[2] Also, according to Scripture, ultimate reality, God, is "one personal spirit" and "the one true reality" behind all else who can be known only as he reveals himself.[3] Finally, the same Christian thinker declared that the personal God of the Bible is revealed there as the one "principle of all things," "both cause and reason" for everything else's existence.[4] Brunner also rightly emphasized that for the Christian this is no "theory of the world," no rational, speculative hypothesis, but revealed truth of the "one word of God."[5] On the other hand, the biblical-Christian vision of God as ultimate reality answers life's ultimate questions better, more satisfactorily, than all types of extrabiblical philosophy.[6]

God-World Duality without Dualism

The concern of this chapter is to elucidate the biblical vision of this ultimate reality—God, the sole absolute, the metaphysical source and sustainer of all that has being. Every effort will be made to follow the examples of Tresmontant, Cherbonnier, Brunner, Heschel, and other Christian and Jewish thinkers who were determined to take the biblical narrative seriously and not interpret it through the lens of an extrabiblical philosophy or metaphysic. Extrabiblical, philosophical language must be used at times, but it will be filled with biblical content as opposed to content drawn from Neoplatonic, Aristotelian, or other extrabiblical philosophies that have been used to say what the Bible must really mean when it is assumed it cannot mean what it says.

---

2   Brunner, *Revelation and Reason*, 382.
3   Brunner, *The Philosophy of Religion*, 82.
4   Ibid., 83.
5   Ibid., 84, 86.
6   Ibid., 81.

At the most basic level, in contrast to some other worldviews and metaphysical visions of ultimate reality, the Bible assumes a *fundamental duality* in reality as opposed to *dualism* and *nonduality*. That is, the Bible everywhere presupposes an *irreducible ontological interval* between God, the source and sustainer of everything, and himself. And yet, both sides of the interval are real—one ultimately so and one penultimately so; one independently real and the other dependently real.

Whether or not one takes the Genesis narratives of creation literally, their theological meaning is obvious to anyone who approaches them without bias against personal theism: The whole world, the universe, everything outside of God, was created by God "in the beginning." If God's sole creatorship as source and sustainer of the world is not clear there, the prophet Isaiah (quoted earlier) makes it abundantly clear. So does the Psalmist; Psalm 104 is one of at least six Psalms devoted to extolling God as creator of all. Jesus asked the Father to glorify him with the glory they shared "before the world began" (John 17:5), and God's independence over against creation is emphasized by Paul in his speech to the Athenians in Acts 17.

The biblical narrative assumes and implies throughout that *both* creator and creation are real, but also that the relationship between them is *asymmetrical*. There is an irreducible interval, gap, between them. Not a gap that keeps them *apart* but a gap of *quality of being* that is signified by *dependence* of one on the other—the world, creation, on God. The world is full of meaning, value, and purpose *because* it was created by God and is sustained by God. The fact that it is *not* God, or made of "God stuff" (divine emanations or divine substance), is the reason all worship of created things is condemned in Scripture as *idolatry*. However, the fact that it is not *God*, or made of "God stuff," takes nothing away from its value. The interval, gap, between God and the world is not first of all moral. That is, God declared everything he created as *good* (1 Timothy

4:4). Nothing that has being is therefore intrinsically evil; evil is not built into creation. Evil is, however, a *possibility* built into creation (Genesis 3). The gap between God and the world is *not* due to a flaw in either God's design or creation itself but due to the creature's defection from God's design and will (Romans 1).

Basic to the biblical-Christian view of reality, then, is *duality* without *dualism*. There is *one* and *only one* ultimate reality—God—so the world, creation, is not ultimate or absolute. Only God is absolute in the sense of *not dependent on anything else*. The world, although *not absolute*, although *dependent*, is both real and good. Nowhere does the biblical narrative imply that evil is intrinsic to matter, for example, or that creatureliness—dependence on God, lack of absolute being—is the source of evil. Nor is there any hint of any evil being alongside of God, equally absolute, eternal, and full of being.

This naturally raises the question of Satan. Doesn't the biblical narrative treat Satan as God's equal, a kind of evil divine twin? That would be dualism, something foreign to the biblical narrative, which places emphasis on God's uniqueness, glory, holy transcendence, and sovereignty. The Bible does not explain Satan's origin; many (such as poet John Milton) have speculated that Satan was originally "Lucifer," an archangel in heaven who led a rebellion of angels against God. Belief in that myth is not entirely without biblical support, but it is speculative. The point is that the biblical narrative throughout keeps Satan *subordinate* to God. Jesus had power over Satan and talked how he saw Satan "fall like lightning from heaven" (Luke 10:18). The context makes clear the vision was not about an original fall (Milton's rebellion described poetically in *Paradise Lost*) but a divine defeat of Satan in the future.

Without doubt Satan is an enigmatic figure in the Bible, and Christian theology has struggled mightily with him. The point here, however, is that neither Scripture nor historical, classical Christianity has ever implied that Satan or anyone or anything else is God's equal.

The biblical vision of reality, encompassing everything, is *duality* without *dualism* and excluding *monism*. The world is not God; the world is God's good but dependent creation.[7] Classical Greek metaphysics, and perhaps every metaphysic, wrestled with the issue of the *one and the many*—"many-ness" being obvious, an inescapable aspect of the world of experienced appearances. The question is whether there is anything, any power, for example, that connects the many? If not, then how can reality be a "uni-verse" and comprehensible as anything? If not, what holds it all together? Why, for example, has entropy not yet resulted in total dissolution? While the Greeks did not know about the second law of thermodynamics, they did realize that the multiplicity of the world without any unifying being behind or within it all would make it incoherent. They speculated, as already noted, that the unifying reality was "Mind." The Bible depicts the unifying reality as "Spirit"—the Spirit that is *supernatural* and *personal (but not human)* called God, the Lord. And, yes, God *has* mind, intelligence, thought, purpose, but his essence is not "Mind" (*Nous*) as Greek philosophy conceived it.

According to the biblical narrative, then, there are two basic categories of reality—*God's,* which is *supernatural* and *personal (but not human)*, eternal, independent, self-sufficient; and *the world's*, which is dependent but good, filled with purpose and value and governed as well as sustained by God.[8] The world belongs to God, but the world also has a *relative autonomy.* "The earth is the Lord's, and everything in it, the world, and all who live in it" (Psalm 24:1). It is his handiwork, to do with as he pleases, but it also stands on the other side of that gap with its own reality. This duality is implied by the whole biblical narrative, much of which tells the story of creation's corruption, permitted but not caused by God (Romans 8:18–21; Genesis 3).

---

7   For a classical modern exposition of the biblical-Christian idea of God and creation see Langdon Gilkey, *Maker of Heaven and Earth: A Study of the Christian Doctrine of Creation* (Garden City, N.Y.: Doubleday, 1959).

8   Tresmontant, *The Origins of Christian Philosophy*, 96: The two "fundamental principles of Christian metaphysics" are (1) God has created everything, and (2) Everything that God has created is very good.

God "a Being," Not "Being Itself"

A second, closely related, metaphysical assumption of the biblical narrative is that ultimate reality is not *"being itself"* but *a being.* Extrabiblical, rational, and speculative metaphysical thought struggles with this. It seems to the rational, speculative mind that this would be an oxymoron: *the source of all being that is also a being.* And yet the Bible clearly reveals God—the absolute (in himself unconditioned), the source and sustainer of all other reality—as the *fullness of being* and yet *a being.* Cherbonnier emphasized this against a long train of speculative metaphysical theism from Augustine to Tillich that pays God the metaphysical compliment of being "Being Itself." Against that, Cherbonnier insisted that "in the Bible, God certainly is conceived as 'a being besides other beings.'" The living God of the Bible, he averred, against the "perennial philosophy," is "a Being beside others," singular, not "Absolute" in the speculative metaphysical sense of including everything in himself or itself. Hegel is an example of what Cherbonnier was protesting. The German philosopher spoke of God, the Absolute Spirit, as the "true infinite" (*warhaft Unendliche*) that *includes the finite in himself.*[9]

Cherbonnier was both right and wrong. He was right to emphasize God's singularity and particularity as *a being* against all monistic and pantheistic attempts to portray God as *the only being* or *the being within everything that has being.* Rational, speculative philosophy, especially the "perennial philosophy," has tended to assume that the "absolute" must be all-inclusive, must not be limited or conditioned by anything outside itself. Often, the philosophically conceived "Being Itself" inclines toward a depersonalizing of God (if God is in view at all). The main modern Christian thinker who insisted on describing God as "Being Itself," Tillich, referred to God as "suprapersonal"—because it would be too limiting to think of

---

9   See Lauer, *Hegel's Concept of God*, esp. 132–36.

God, Being Itself, as personal or a person. A person would be *a being*, not *Being Itself*. Cherbonnier rightly asked about the difference between super-personal and sub-personal and rightly questioned whether such a distinction makes sense.[10] Against all speculative metaphysics that thinks it necessary to subsume the world into God or God into the world, Cherbonnier wrote, "The Biblical God, alone among candidates for his title, can create a world which is not the negation of himself."[11]

The distinct, singular personhood of God, the reality of God as a being among beings, not an all-inclusive, unconditioned, absolute Being Itself, is a hallmark of the biblical portrayal of God. Much philosophical interpretation of the Bible has tended to label all that *anthropomorphism*. Tillich was not alone in attempting to pay God metaphysical compliments by deliteralizing everything and saying that the only nonsymbolic thing that can be said about God is that God is Being Itself. Cherbonnier was right to retrieve as realistic, if not literal, the biblical depiction of God as *an agent* acting *among others*, as *related* and therefore *conditioned*.

However, the above does not mean that it is entirely wrong to think *biblically* of God as *Being Itself* so long as that is not pushed to monism (even in its emanationist form). If Being Itself is attributed to God in a biblical sense, respecting biblical *duality*, maintaining the interval between God and creation, it must mean what Paul meant in Athens when quoting a Greek poet about the "unknown God." Paul, referring to the God of Israel and of Jesus Christ, Yahweh God, the Lord, said that "in him we live and move and have our being" (Acts 17:28). That means the gulf, the interval, between God and creation cannot be absolute; it is an expression of creation's *dependence on God* as its *source and sustainer*. Insofar, then, as "being itself" attributed to God does not imply "the only being" or "the being of everything that has being"—which would imply at

---

10   Cherbonnier, "Biblical Metaphysic and Christian Philosophy," 368.
11   Cherbonnier, "Is There a Biblical Metaphysic?" 463.

least a loss of God's transcendence and creation's relative autono-my—it is permissible for biblical-Christian metaphysics. It is even implied by the Bible's constant emphasis on creation's dependence on God—not just for its beginning but for its continuation and final fulfillment.

What It Means to Say that God Is Personal

As has already been said several times, the biblical narrative depicts ultimate reality as *supernatural* and *personal (but not a human)*. That was explained in some detail in chapter 2. Here, then, only brief attention will be given again to this seeming paradox. Rational and mystical metaphysics have often struggled with the idea of ultimate reality as *personal* because to be personal is to be *related* and to be *related* is to be *conditioned*—even when *human personhood* is not in view. Again, Cherbonnier argued strongly against any nonpersonal, impersonal, or even suprapersonal view of ultimate reality—whether Christian or otherwise. In a very pithy but pregnant saying he rightly declared, "The category of the personal is the north pole of human thought."[12] Going past it, he said, means going beneath it. In other words, to depersonalize ultimate reality is to demean personhood. The very idea of the inviolable dignity and value of human persons *depends* on ultimate reality being personal. To him, as to Heschel, this is one of Hebrew-Christian thought's greatest contributions to humanity.

But what about the challenge that *if* ultimate reality is *intrinsically personal* (that is, does not just "take on" personal *form* occasionally), it/he is *related* and therefore *conditioned* and therefore not absolute? Cherbonnier responded simply that "of course" God is related—as he is portrayed in biblical thought.[13] He went on to remind us that in the Bible God is *voluntarily* influenced by

---

12   Cherbonnier, "The Logic of Biblical Anthropomorphism," *The Harvard Theological Review* 55, no. 3 (July 1962), 190.

13   Cherbonnier, "Biblical Metaphysic and Christian Philosophy," 363.

what creatures do, not necessarily influenced by them as if he were dependent on them. The God of the Bible, he rightly asserted, can be as related or absolute as he wants to be; he can even take the *risk* of endowing creatures with freedom to resist him![14] By the free act of creation, by creating something outside of himself with limited autonomy, the God of the Bible has become a being beside other beings[15] and limited by them in a limited way. In what sense, then, is God "holy other"—different from creatures? Cherbonnier correctly asserted that the biblical sense in which God is unlimited is that he can do anything—even create something outside himself.[16] Does that mean, then, that God *became personal*? Not at all. As Cherbonnier also rightly noted, to *decide to create* and then *create based on a free decision*, both basic assumptions of the biblical narrative, God had to already be personal in and of himself.[17]

Cherbonnier railed against those philosophers, theologians, and mystics who would claim that God's personal attributes in the biblical narrative, such as emotions provoked by creatures, are "mere anthropomorphisms." For support he turned to the Hebrew prophet Hosea. "Hosea is one of the most daringly anthropomorphic authors of the Bible."[18] According to the story, God called the prophet to marry a prostitute who then is unfaithful to him, to convince the prophet, and God's people through him, how grieved he is by their idolatry, their unfaithfulness. Cherbonnier's point can be put in a question: "If that is mere anthropomorphism, what is it *of*?" In other words, what is it saying about God *if not* that God can be grieved and provoked to anger by creatures? Cherbonnier was quite right that the biblical narrative, contrary to much philosophical theism, assumes throughout that the *difference* between God and humans is *character*, not *personhood*.

---

14   Cherbonnier, "The Logic of Biblical Anthropomorphism," 195.
15   Ibid.
16   Ibid., 195.
17   Ibid., 193.
18   Ibid., 188.

What It Means to Say God Is Supernatural

What about *supernatural*? Again, as stated before in chapter 2, that is a much maligned and misused word. The correction of that explained there will not be repeated here. Suffice it to say that there is no equivalent and alternative word that does justice to the point that, according to the biblical story, ultimate reality— the personal God of Israel and Jesus Christ, the God of Abraham, Isaac, Jacob, and the apostles—is not limited by nature. Nature is created; it has a degree of autonomy on the other side of the God-world interval. But that gap is not spatial; it is ontological—having to do with dependence versus nondependence. Nature is dependent on God, not vice versa. In one sense, *supernatural* simply means God's quality of ultimacy over against nature. God is not a prisoner of nature—either locked into it or out of it. As Tresmontant boldly declared, "Christian metaphysics is characterized by an opening to the supernatural."[19]

There is no escaping the fact that the biblical narrative contains numerous miracles—events beyond the natural. Most of them are attributed to God—either acting directly or through human beings. Two especially stand out as crucial to the biblical narrative's identification of God: the exodus and the resurrection. In both cases God is recorded as acting in ways not even in principle explainable by science. Both are events of revelation and salvation. Scholars and others determined to deny anything supernatural or miraculous have gone out of their way to explain both events as myths, legends, or explainable in terms of natural law. What really happened, in other words, was not supernatural at all but only took on that appearance in the retelling.

Especially in the modern world, since the Enlightenment and scientific revolution, even many Christians have attempted to demythologize the Bible. That is, they have attempted to interpret

---

19   Tresmontant, *Christian Metaphysics*, 108.

its miracle stories as nonliteral accounts, usually referring to and expressing the rise of faith in God by God's people—Israel and the apostles. This is, of course, evidence of *naturalism* overruling the Bible's plain meaning—just as, in the ancient world, Platonism often overruled the Bible's plain meaning with allegorical interpretation. In both cases Christians brought an extrabiblical metaphysical belief system to the Bible and used it to determine what the Bible can and cannot really mean. But unless one buys into the truth of naturalism, an alien, extrabiblical metaphysical perspective on ultimate reality that in effect makes nature ultimate, there is no good reason to demythologize the great miracles of the Bible such as the exodus and Jesus's resurrection.

Many people have confused *science* with *naturalism*, but, as explained earlier, science itself does not require naturalism and, in fact, is actually undermined by naturalism. As philosopher Plantinga explained, the scientific search for truth assumes nature is not all there is. If nature is all there is, then truth itself is a chimera and our human faculties for discovering and knowing it are unreliable.

However, many modern Christians have become confused by the very idea of divine *interventions* in the course of nature and history: Why would God, the creator of nature and sovereign ruler of history, interrupt, violate, and "break into" the natural course of things he himself set in motion and governs? The whole idea of miracles as "violations" of natural laws, as God "breaking" the course of nature, as divine interruptions of history, rests on a false set of assumptions—false from a biblical-Christian metaphysical perspective.

As already explained, according to the biblical view of God and the world, the world has a *relative autonomy* over against God—by God's own design. Yet neither nature nor history are *independent* processes operating entirely under their own laws and powers. Although God is transcendent, he is also *immanent*—the sustaining, creative presence upholding all things and holding them all together: "He is before all things, and in him all things hold together" (Colossians 1:17). Modern Christian thinkers such as Scottish philosopher Thomas Reid (1710–96), Horace Bushnell (1802–76) and C. S. Lewis, among many others, went out of their way to explode the myth that a miracle must be a divine interruption of nature—as if, in order to act in special ways, God must "break into" a world that operates like a machine alongside of, over against, and independently of God's immanent, continuing creative activity. The biblical-Christian view of nature and history is that *both are in some sense always already the activity of God.* That is not to say that everything that happens in them is the direct, antecedent will of God; it is only to say that, from a biblical and Christian perspective, the very laws of nature are, in some sense, simply *regularities* of God's general providential activity. And history is always being guided, directed, and governed by God—even when God's human creatures, endowed with free will, rebel and act against God's perfect will. According to a biblical-Christian worldview, God's *agency* is always the *principle* and *power* underlying everything. Which, again, is not the same as saying everything that happens is designed or willed by God. It is simply to say that whatever happens is *at least permitted by God* and *concurred* with by God.

That means, then, that a miracle is never a "breaking" of nature's laws, a "violation" of nature, or a "disruption" of history's story as if nature and history were normally operating under their own power and overcome by God "from the outside." That is the myth about the supernatural and miracles imposed by modern naturalism. They are actually *deist* ideas, not biblical ideas. According to the Bible God is always at work in and through all things—even when they are not developing as he designed or desired. To suppose otherwise is to make God nonultimate and to elevate nature and history to ultimacy. Deism was just a halfway stage on the road to atheism.

Rather, from a biblical-Christian perspective, a miracle is simply *an event in which God acts through nature in an unusual way.* Since the laws of nature are nothing more, metaphysically, than *regularities* of God's activity in the world, ways through which God *normally* upholds and sustains the world in order (general providence), there is no need for God to violate or break them. A miracle is simply when God *suspends* their normal use and uses them differently—for his own purposes.

Theologian Bushnell rightly argued that there is an analogy to this idea of God's agency in the world in the human mind and body. Many bodily functions are *automatic* and yet under the ultimate control of the mind. An example is the heart beating. And yet, a person can slow or even speed up the beating of his or her heart by concentration (e.g., in meditation or intense alarm). There is no question of the mind "violating" the body; all the body's functions are always being regulated by the mind, even unconsciously, even while the person sleeps. Yet, at times, the body acts differently when directed to by the mind—without any implication of the mind "violating" the body or "interrupting" it— as if a power outside the person forced itself on it.

So it is, Bushnell argued throughout *Nature and the Supernatural: As Together Constituting the One System of God* (1869). God's supernatural activity in the world, events often referred to as *miracles*, must not be understood as violations or interruptions of nature but as unusual operations of God who is always already at work in and through the laws of nature, which are simply regularities of his general providence. C. S. Lewis completely concurred in *Miracles*, his modern classic about the subject (originally published in 1947 and revised in 1960). He declared that in a miracle God simply suspends the ordinary use of his own regularities of general providence (laws of nature), speeding them up or slowing them down, etc. By no means does belief in a miracle require picturing God as breaking or violating anything. As Scottish theologian Neil MacDonald expressed it, "God can certainly observe the laws of nature he has created, but he is not in any way bound by them."[20]

---

20   MacDonald, *Metaphysics and the God of Israel*, 131.

This may be the *one primary* example of an alien, extrabiblical metaphysical perspective confusing even conservative, Bible-believing Christians who wish to let the Bible absorb the world. Many have unwittingly adopted a modern, naturalistic picture of nature as independent of God, ruled by ironclad laws built into it and operating like a machine, and miracles as God having to stop the machine or break or violate it. "Throw a monkey wrench into it," as popular expression would have it. That does make both miracle and supernatural problematic, but it is a view based entirely on an extrabiblical story about nature and God—one invented by deists in the sixteenth and seventeenth centuries.

The ultimate reality of the biblical narrative is not one who must break into the world to act in it. Neither is he limited by the world to have to act only through its laws (the hand-in-the-glove analogy mentioned earlier). The ultimate reality of the Bible is a God who is *personal* but *not human*, a free agent, intelligent and purposeful, but omnipotent and eternal. The ultimate reality of the Bible is a God who is *supernatural* but *not locked out of the world*, the creative, sustaining, governing ruler who can manipulate nature and history for his own good purposes while respecting the *relative* autonomy he granted them.

What It Means to Say God Is Vulnerable

The ultimate reality of the biblical narrative, God, is *self-sufficient* but also *vulnerable*. He is not dependent on anything outside himself and yet, at the same time, opens himself to influence by his own creatures. That is, without in any way *needing* to, the God of the Bible risked creating other creative powers, cocreators, in his own image and likeness but able to resist him and cause him blessedness or grief and anger.[21] God's self-sufficiency is his *freedom*; his vulnerability is the product of his *love*. Theologian Neil MacDonald, in *Metaphysics and the God of Israel*, emphasizes God's *self-*

---

21   Tresmontant, *A Study of Hebrew Thought*, 149–53.

determination as the biblical account of God's self-sufficiency—in place of Platonic and other rational-speculative metaphysical ideas of God's self-sufficiency that exclude vulnerability. God's *first* and *most basic* action is that "God determines himself to be the creator of all things."[22] According to MacDonald, drawing on the theology of Robert Jenson (who, in turn was influenced by Barth), this self-determination of God to be the creator is not a merely external, exterior, act of God. Rather "God *is* his own decision."[23] This is simply another way of expressing the biblical paradox of God's self-sufficiency and yet vulnerability. God's self-determination to be the creator of all things (and one might add "covenant-maker" with people) is *absolutely free and unrestricted*, not compelled or coerced.[24] And God's free self-determination, biblically, includes creating beings "with whom God could be in personal relationship,"[25] coexisting with them in a "historical experience . . . spatially located in the world."[26] This is the basis of God's vulnerability.

Perhaps no modern Christian thinker has expressed the idea of God's vulnerability more powerfully than Scottish theologian Thomas F. Torrance (1913–2007) in *Space, Time and Incarnation* (1969). According to him the biblical story of God with Israel and Jesus Christ must mean the *"openness of God"* which means, in turn, "that space and time are affirmed [in the biblical narrative] as real for God in the actuality of his relations with us."[27] But he didn't stop there. Torrance, no friend of liberal Protestantism or process theology, went on to declare, on the basis of the biblical narratives of a vulnerable God, that "neither we nor God can contract out of" space and time which form the framework for the relations

---

22   MacDonald, *Metaphysics and the God of Israel*, 27.

23   Ibid., 31.

24   Ibid., 47–48.

25   Ibid., 65.

26   Ibid., 89.

27   Thomas F. Torrance, *Space, Time and Incarnation* (Oxford and New York: Oxford University Press, 1969), 74.

God has determined himself for with us.[28] This is *not panentheism*, however, because, like MacDonald, Torrance bases it all on God's *self-determination*. Torrance asked rhetorically, "Does this not mean that God has so opened Himself to our world that our this-worldly experiences have import for Him in such a way . . . that we must think of Him as taking our hurt and pain into Himself?"[29] Torrance harshly criticized classical theism for denying this. Finally, Torrance pitted the biblical narratives of a vulnerable God against classical theism's much vaunted metaphysical attributes of God based on speculative reason:

> If God is merely impassible He has not made room for Himself in our agonied existence, and if He is merely immutable He has neither place nor time for frail evanescent creatures in His unchanging existence. But the God who has revealed Himself in Jesus Christ [one might add throughout the whole Bible!] as sharing our lot is the God who is really free to make Himself poor, that we through His poverty might be made rich, the God invariant in love but not impassible, constant in faithfulness but not immutable.[30]

In other words, God—quite unlike the "absolute" and "unconditioned" of rational-speculative metaphysics, including Greek philosophical theologies—*chose not to be self-sufficient* although *in himself he is self-sufficient*. God's vulnerability, openness, potentiality, and faithful changeableness are manifestations of his self-sufficient love, results of his self-determination to be for the world and with it.

What It Means to Say God Is Eternal

A great debate has opened up in modern Christian thought about God's *temporality*. Many back-to-the-Bible Christian thinkers,

---

28 Ibid.
29 Ibid.
30 Ibid., 75.

seeking to strip away the layers of Platonic thought overlaying biblical metaphysics, have discarded the notion of God's eternity as *timelessness* or *atemporality* (also known as the Boethian view of God's eternal now, in which all times are simultaneous to God). According to them, that view of God's eternity is based on Platonic metaphysics of the absolute in which ultimate reality must be free of the infections of finite existence and especially *time*. According to them, this is an extrabiblical attempt to pay a totally unnecessary and even extrabiblical (if not anti-biblical!) metaphysical compliment to God.

In the above quoted statement Torrance affirmed that God opts into time, into history, with us. MacDonald included in God's primordial self-determination his own temporality: "Timeless eternity does not seem able to cope with the event of divine self-determination."[31] According to him, the Genesis creation narrative itself implies God's entrance into time. Referring to God's resting on the seventh day, MacDonald avers that by his characteristic act of self-determination in relation to creation God enters into the time of his creatures.[32] He rightly claims that the whole biblical story of God and creation implies that "God determines *himself* [so, self-sufficiently]—posits himself—to be part of, belong, coexist with, his own creation."[33] McDonald is right that a personal relationship involving mutual action toward each other necessarily implies temporality. [34]

Catholic Tresmontant affirmed that the God of the Bible, unlike the ultimate reality of Greek philosophy, is *not* an unchanging sameness but ever active life and action.[35] For him, Hebrew thought, in contrast to Greek thought, valued time. For the latter all becoming was degradation; time itself was privation of being. Classical theism

---

31   MacDonald, *Metaphysics and the God of Israel*, 22.
32   Ibid., 67.
33   Ibid., 75.
34   Ibid., 97.
35   Tresmontant, *A Study of Hebrew Thought*, 34.

took over this overly negative view of time; a Hebrew-based and biblical view of time needs to be recovered and positively related to God. According to Tresmontant, for the biblical authors *reality* is *historical*, the coproduction of the *new* by God and his created cocreators.[36] God and creation are *together* truly inventive, and real freedom exists in that synergistic relationship.[37] Thus, time is the necessary accompaniment of creative action.[38] But Tresmontant was careful to respect the superiority of God by affirming that God's entrance into time is free.[39] However, even God is "not beyond time."[40]

Cherbonnier's project of retrieving a truly biblical metaphysic, freed from the shackles of Platonic and other extrabiblical philosophies of ultimate reality, included a strong affirmation of ultimate reality as *the living God of Israel*. According to him, the typical biblical language for describing God is that of verbs.[41] The Bible, he declared, does not look for God beyond time but looks for him within time—even though his being and action in time are always steadfast.[42] For Cherbonnier, God's immutability is simply his *faithfulness*, not his static being-ness without becoming or eternity without temporality. He argued that mystical, speculative, and rational metaphysics (read "Greek-inspired philosophical theism") always thinks that for ultimate reality, God, to be perfect it must be above time or timeless.[43] According to him, however, there is no hint in the biblical narratives of God's "timelessness" or being-without-becoming. Rather, in biblical thought, God's perfection in relation to time simply means that he outlasts all creatures. For the biblical prophets, Cherbonnier claimed, God's perfection is completely compatible with being *temporal* because it is an expression of God's

---

36   Ibid., 36.
37   Ibid., 35.
38   Ibid., 23.
39   Ibid., 35.
40   Ibid., 34.
41   Cherbonnier, "Is There a Biblical Metaphysic?" 460.
42   Ibid., 460.
43   Cherbonnier, "The Logic of Biblical Anthropomorphism," 199.

faithfulness.[44] God's *changelessness* supersedes creatures' because God is faithful as the living and acting God of perfect character. [45]

What, then, is God's eternity? The Bible clearly speaks often about God as eternal. Christian philosopher-theologian Wolterstorff argues that, biblically speaking, God's eternity is simply his "everlasting-ness."[46] In complete agreement with most of the Christian thinkers mentioned here, Wolterstorff, who is not Hegelian or a process theologian, declared that "the patterns of classical Greek thought are incompatible with the pattern of biblical thought."[47] This is especially the case, he said, with regard to God and time. Referring to the "timeless" view known as "Boethian," that God's eternity means nontemporality, that all times—past, present, and future—are simultaneous to God, Wolterstorff wrote that "every attempt to purge Christian theology of the traces of incompatible Hellenic [Greek philosophical] patterns of thought must fail unless it removes the roadblock of the God eternal tradition. Around this barricade there are no detours."[48]

In his essay "God Everlasting" Wolterstorff argued that the God of the Bible *changes*—not in terms of *who* he is or his *character*—but in terms of "changeful variations among his states."[49] In other words, the God of the Bible *reacts* to creatures, and those reactions cannot be taken seriously while being interpreted as merely figures of speech. The changes are radically integral to the storyline of the Bible:

> God, as described by the biblical writers, is a being who changes, and who accordingly is fundamentally noneternal [in the "timeless" sense]. For God is described as a being who *acts*—in creation, in providence, and for the renewal of

---

44   Ibid., 200.

45   Ibid.

46   The account of Wolterstorff's view of God's eminent temporality here is derived from his very important, ground-breaking essay "God Everlasting," which has been published in several collections of his essays. The quotations and references here are from its publication in *God and the Good: Essays in Honor of Henry Stob*, eds. Clifton Orlebeke and Lewis Smedes (Grand Rapids, Mich.: Eerdmans, 1975).

47   Ibid., 183.

48   Ibid.

49   Ibid., 182.

mankind. He is an agent, not an impassive factor in reality. And from the manner in which his acts are described, it seems obvious that many of them have beginnings and endings, that accordingly they stand in succession relations to each other, and that these successive acts are of such a sort that their presence and absence on God's time-strand constitutes changes thereon. Thus it seems obvious that God is fundamentally noneternal.[50]

And yet, Wolterstorff affirms that God *is* "eternal" *in the sense of "everlasting."* That is, biblically, God, the absolute and ultimate in terms of being and reality, is *not* "timeless" because he acts in time and is acted upon in time, but he is *without beginning or end* and time is not a threat to or limitation on him. Although Wolterstorff is trained as a professional philosopher, no one could express the biblical-Christian metaphysical view of God as eternal but temporal better than this:

> Though God is within time, yet he is Lord of time. The whole array of contingent temporal events is within his power. He is Lord of what occurs. And that, along with the specific pattern of what he does, grounds all authentically biblical worship of, and obedience to, God. It is not because he is outside of time—eternal, immutable, impassive—that we are to worship and obey God. It is because of what he can and does bring about within time that we mortals are to render him praise and obedience.[51]

What It Means to Say God Is Good

Finally, according to the biblical narrative, ultimate reality is *the very standard of goodness—the ground of ethical right and wrong.*

---

50   Ibid., 193.
51   Ibid., 203.

This was, of course, a major reason why early Christian Apologists latched onto Platonic philosophy—because, following Plato, it included ethical monotheism. That is, Platonic philosophy's ultimate being, its absolute, was either Plato's "Form of the Good," the "form of all forms," or a divinity under the moral influence of that. The point is that Platonism always closely identifies "the good," goodness itself, with being—an identification that accords closely with biblical revelation of God as the standard of goodness. The Bible always attributes evil to rebellious creatures and always identifies God with the good. It does not claim that humans can always *know* or *understand* God's goodness as God does; the God of Israel and of Jesus Christ permits evil and sometimes seems to do things that would be wrong for humans to do. Increasingly throughout the biblical narrative, however, especially in the prophets and apostles, emphasis falls on God's *good character, especially his loving-kindness* and *justice.*

Hebrew wisdom literature is filled with reminders of God's goodness and exhortations to trust him *because* he is good; Psalms 37 and 118 are just two examples. The Hebrew prophets call for the people to show mercy and love justice *because* God, the Lord, *is* mercy and justice. Throughout the Bible emphasis falls as strongly on God's good character as on God's power. As Heschel noted about the God of the Hebrew prophets compassionately cares about widows and orphans.[52] Also, according to Heschel, in biblical thought good and evil are not merely psychological concepts (and one could add not merely conventional concepts—inventions of people) but *ontological realities*—rooted in the being of God, the highest reality. Good and evil, then, Heschel argues, are real relations within creation, not mere perceptions or terms. The "good" is what God cares for and it unites creatures with God.[53] The "uniting," however, is not mystical or ontological union but *fellowship.*

---

52   Heschel, *Man Is Not Alone*, 143–44.
53   Ibid., 225.

For biblical-Christian thought, as for some philosophy (e.g., Platonism), *metaphysics* and *ethics* are interdependent. One reason for belief in an ultimate reality behind appearances is to ground objective right and wrong in something more stable than history or culture. Especially for biblical thought, ethics is necessary for metaphysics because *knowing ultimate reality* depends on *the obedience of faith*. That is, metaphysical knowledge is not theoretical but practical.

According to Cherbonnier, "The plain inference [of the Bible] is that knowledge of God depends upon the quality of one's will, that hardness of heart produces hardness of head."[54] That is, the biblical story consistently correlates *virtue* and *knowledge* but not in the Greek sense of "to know the good is to do the good." Rather, for the Bible and Christian thought generally, "doing the good," by God's grace and with faith, produces knowledge of ultimate reality as the ultimate good. This follows from the fact that, as already explained, in biblical-Christian metaphysics ultimate reality is *personal*—not "thingy" (object-like). Cherbonnier rightly noted that for the biblical writers, knowledge that matters most, knowledge of oneself, others, and ultimate reality, depends on a proper orientation of the heart and not solely or even primarily on the intellect.[55]

Brunner agreed completely with (but independently of) Cherbonnier; for him, too, true knowledge of ultimate, final reality—God—requires something other than "spectator knowledge,"[56] *because* God is *personal* and knowledge of God includes a challenge to *decision*. But also, Brunner argued, the whole idea of an objective moral law, "right" and "wrong," depends on ultimate reality being a personal God. If moral law is not to be reduced to a law we give ourselves, and therefore can transgress without consequence, it must be given by a transcendent, personal law-giver.[57] If

---

54   Cherbonnier, "Is There a Biblical Metaphysic?" 467.
55   Ibid.
56   Brunner, *The Philosophy of Religion*, 67.
57   Ibid., 72.

it is a law given by ourselves, then we can abrogate it at will. If that be the case, Brunner rightly argued, we have no serious knowledge of good or evil. However, according to him, following the entire drift of the biblical narrative, what makes us truly good or evil is not our relation to an abstract law but our relation toward God.[58]

For biblical-Christian thought, then, metaphysics and ethics are inseparable. The very existence of objective right and objective wrong depends on ultimate reality not being amoral but moral (and therefore *personal*). Platonic philosophy has always been right about being and goodness; they go together and cannot be separated. Evil, then, as Greek philosophy put it, is not being but nonbeing. Put biblically, it is brokenness, a wrong attitude of the heart toward God that produces disobedient actions. But that wrong attitude and that disobedience lead *away* from being toward nothingness. Fellowship with God strengthens being, not by obliteration of difference but by enhancement of creation. Where Greek philosophy went wrong was to assume that the heart, attitudes, and dispositions play no role in good or evil and that evil is simply ignorance of the good arising from entrapment in matter. The biblical witness throughout is that the source of all evil is, as Augustine put it, an "evil will," not matter or ignorance. It is "the mystery of iniquity," which has no rational explanation.[59]

---

58 Ibid., 89.
59 For an in depth biblical-theological exploration of evil and sin as nonrational see Bernard Ramm, *Offense to Reason: The Theology of Sin* (San Francisco: Harper and Row, 1985).

Interlude 5

Obviously much more could be said about ultimate reality, God, in biblical-Christian metaphysics than the previous chapter (or chapter 2) could say. Entire volumes and sets of volumes have been devoted to exposition of the Bible's and Christian thought's ideas of God. The purpose of the preceding chapter was to make clear the *differences* (with some *minor similarities)* between biblical revelation of ultimate reality and metaphysical ideas developed by rational-speculative and mystical philosophies.

Two questions cannot be avoided; inquiring minds want to know! *If* Yahweh God, the Lord, is ultimate, absolute reality upon which everything else, outside of God, is dependent, how can God be conditioned or limited in any way? *How can the metaphysical ultimate reality be vulnerable?* Isn't that a contradiction in terms? How can he be *personal* in the sense of *relational* and *temporal* in the sense of *becoming*? How can ultimate, final, absolute reality be *historical*? Also, secondly, *if* the God of the Bible is *goodness itself,* the source and standard of all goodness, and he is also *creator and sustainer of all that has being,* how can there be evil in his world?

Again, these are questions the posited answers to which have filled hundreds, even thousands, of volumes over the Christian centuries. They have become especially intense, however, *because of* the twentieth century—during which Christian theology came to emphasize God's *limitedness* and *conditionedness* more than before and during which events such as the *Holocaust* raised to a fever pitch the "problem of evil" for all forms of personal theism.

God's Self-Limitations

First, then, how can God, if he is ultimate reality, absolute source and sustainer of all that has being, be *limited* or *conditioned*? As we have already seen, much metaphysics, including much Christian philosophy, has denied that God is limited or conditioned. For much philosophical theism, concerned to protect God's absoluteness, otherness, unlimitedness, all of God's attributes are *negative*—what God is *not*. The chief attribute is *infinite*. The Bible nowhere says that God is infinite, and yet that attribute has crept into Christian theism from rational-speculative philosophy to head many Christian theological lists of God's attributes. As to this common list of God's attributes found in most handbooks of traditional Christian theism, Cherbonnier commented that, for the most part, they apply more to the abstract "perfect being" of philosophical theology, infected as it is by Greek thought, than to the God of biblical thought.[1] The attributes that almost unhinged Cherbonnier are those associated with "apophatic theology," also known as "negative theology," meant to protect God's holiness as *wholly otherness* but that end up making God remote, nonrelated, almost impersonal. *Infinite* is the all-inclusive, umbrella term that covers the rest as subordinate ones (e.g., immutable, impassible, etc.).[2]

The German idealist philosopher Fichte is famous for, among other things, arguing that a being, especially a personal being, cannot be infinite. The two concepts contradict each other. He preferred to call God infinite to the exclusion, as he thought necessary, of being a particular person. Before Fichte most Christian thinkers struggled with the cognitive dissonance of calling God absolutely unlimited, unconditioned, while at the same time thinking of him as in some sense personal. After Fichte much metaphysical theology, Christian or otherwise, chose to give up one or the other—either God's personal nature or God's infinity.

---

1   Cherbonnier, "The Logic of Biblical Anthropomorphism," 190.
2   Ibid., 191.

According to Cherbonnier, the solution lies in embracing a *biblical* definition of *infinite* as opposed to a speculative, philosophical one. Instead of thinking of God as infinite because he is absolutely unconditioned, without any limitations, he claimed biblical-Christian thought should think of God as infinite in the sense of "inexhaustible."[3] In other words, *if* we are to describe God as infinite at all, we should make clear to ourselves and others what we mean and do not mean. As people who see God as personal, we confess that God is not like the powerless gods of paganism or even like human persons who must die. Again, for Cherbonnier, and I wholeheartedly agree, the Christian claim that God is infinite means simply that for God all things are possible.[4] To those who would argue that *spiritual humility* requires one to confess God's *wholly otherness*, absolute unlikeness, to anything finite and mortal, Cherbonnier cautioned that "biblical humility consists in letting God be God, a determinate personality with his own integrity, not to be confused with anyone else, least of all oneself."[5]

Still, inquiring minds want to know, how can God, the creator of all that has being, be temporal, historical, resisted, provoked, influenced, etc.? And how can there be evil, that which is against God's character and will, in God's world if God is both perfectly good and the creator and sustainer of all being? The key is to understand God as *self-determining* and *self-limiting.* Cherbonnier stated that, although God is anthropomorphic throughout the Bible, his supremacy means that he is always only *voluntarily influenced* by what creatures do.[6] The God of the Bible, he argued, is *transcendent* as well as *living*, so he must have *freedom* not to be manipulated by creatures. If God is capable of being manipulated outside of his freedom, then he is an idol and not truly God.[7] For God to be truly

---

3   Ibid., 190.
4   Ibid., 195.
5   Ibid., 198.
6   Cherbonnier, "Biblical Metaphysic and Christian Philosophy," 363.
7   Ibid., 368.

God, he cannot be treated like a marionette whose strings can be pulled.[8] And yet, biblically, God *does* allow himself to be *influenced* if not manipulated. That is because of his freedom; he voluntarily creates creatures who can affect him and allows himself to be resisted by them.

Christian theologian Augustus Hopkins Strong (1836–1921), one of a few leading theologians of his time who happened to be Baptist, pointed the way out of the Fichte impasse in his essay "God's Self-Limitations." There, referring to philosophically inspired classical theism, he admitted that the biblical story of God's involvements with humanity, including especially the incarnation and cross of Jesus Christ, is "simply unintelligible to those who know only 'The Absolute' and 'The Infinite'" as God. Referring to Fichte and his followers, Strong stated, "To these modern Greeks, quite as much as to their ancient congeners [ancestors in thought], the gospel is 'foolishness.'"[9] But this is because they wrongly assume, Strong averred, that "perfection of being" must exclude limitation of every kind. In fact, he argued, perfection itself implies a limitation—not being imperfect! But more importantly and to the point, we must permit our idea of perfection to be determined by God's own self-revelation and not by speculative philosophy. "God would not be perfect if he were not a *personal* Being."[10] To be *personal*, Strong affirmed, is more perfect than to be *impersonal*. And yet being personal automatically implies a kind of limitation: "His very perfection limits him to consciousness and freedom" as opposed to unconsciousness and lack of freedom.[11]

Pushing further, Strong stated that "a God shut up within himself would be no God at all."[12] In other words, the very act of creation

---

8   Ibid.

9   Augustus Hopkins Strong, *Christ in Creation and Ethical Monism* (Philadelphia: The Roger Williams Press, 1899), 87.

10   Ibid., 88.

11   Ibid.

12   Ibid., 91.

implies both self-limitation and self-actualization of God's deity. MacDonald, no doubt, would prefer the term *self-determination*, but it implies the same as what Strong spoke of. And here is where God's self-limitations in relation to creation begin to solve the problem of evil that so preoccupies many people's minds. According to Strong, "He [God] has narrowed himself down in order to reveal himself to creatures."[13] By "narrowed himself down" he did not mean "made himself smaller" or even "gave up his power," but *made room in his reality* for other beings besides himself to exist and be creative and even resist his will:

> Let us remember that the creation of free beings involves the possibility that freedom will be abused; the development of the highest virtue is inseparable from probation, tempta-tion, a possible fall from virtue into the depths of misery and sin. For a holy being to create a universe in prospect of sin, and to administer a universe in spite of constant oppo-sition to his will, is an act and process of self-limitation, the significance of which it is difficult for us to measure.[14]

This divine self-limitation of God, then, is the solution to how God can be *absolute* and yet *vulnerable* and how there can be *evil* in God's good world. God, though absolute and unconditioned in himself (we suppose, knowing little to nothing about "God-in-and-for-himself!"), voluntarily enters into time with us *for the sake of having real, not imaginary, relationships with beings not himself* and *permits himself to be resisted and grieved* by those beings. All that, of course, out of *love* and not out of necessity or need. If we were to suggest that God's self-limitations were out of need or neces-sity, then a nonbiblical and even pagan view of God would be on the horizon if not immediately present. As Paul said to the Athenians in Acts 17, the true God, the God he knew as a Jew and a Christian,

---

13   Ibid., 92.
14   Ibid.

the God they called "the unknown God," *needs nothing*. By limiting himself, God does not make himself *dependent* on anything outside of himself but rather opens himself up to being influenced and affected by what he has created. There is a difference.

Belief in God's self-limitations has caught on in twentieth- and twenty-first-century Christian thought—as the solution to the two problems mentioned at the beginning of this interlude—but also because of theology's gradual freeing from the alien influences of Greek philosophy and modern idealism with their abstract conceptions of absoluteness. The God of the Bible, most modern Christian thinkers agree, *is* absolute *in the sense* of not being dependent but instead being the source and sustainer of all that has being. But he is not the "unconditioned" except in the absolutely abstract sense that his being conditioned is *freely chosen* and *not imposed*.

All of this presupposes something that sets biblical-Christian metaphysics radically apart from other belief-systems about ultimate reality. Tresmontant stated it most concisely: "Christianity is a metaphysic of love."[15] This is something speculative reason alone cannot know about ultimate reality—that its very *being* is *love*. And this is the reason behind and within God's self-limitations, self-determinations, and self-actualizations: God's being as *being-for-others*. Does that mean, then, that God *must* create to have "others" to love? Not at all. The Christian doctrine of the Trinity, itself rooted in biblical narrative, even necessitated by it, means that God's creative activity, including his self-limitations in relation to creatures, is a *free expression* of the *fullness* of the love between Father, Son, and Holy Spirit in eternity. *If God were not triune, however, then creation would be necessary for God insofar as God is conceived as love.*

Evil and the God of Love

To the problem of evil, then. Some have called the existence of evils such as the Holocaust "the rock of atheism." Allegedly, the fact of

---

15   Tresmontant, *Christian Metaphysics*, 48.

horrendous, seemingly gratuitous (meaningless) evils undermines the credibility of belief in God as ultimate reality. The problem of evil has been stated many ways but perhaps most succinctly by Scottish skeptical philosopher David Hume (1711–76). If God is good, he does not want evil to be part of his creation. If God is all-powerful (omnipotent), God could stop evil. Evil exists. Therefore God must either be not good, not all-powerful, or nonexistent. Few theists would want to say God is not perfectly good, but some have responded by adopting an idea of God as not omnipotent—and not only in the sense of self-limiting. A school of liberal Protestant theologians has adopted Whitehead's process thought as their metaphysical framework for post-Holocaust Christian theology and denied God's omnipotence. According to them, the only power of God is *persuasion*. God literally cannot stop evil. The God of the biblical narrative, however, can do whatever he wants to do that is consistent with his character. Process theology is a major sellout of the biblical worldview and an accommodation of Christian theism to a secular philosophy.

So how might it be possible to answer Hume from a biblical-Christian perspective on reality, including ultimate reality, God? The solution lies, as with God's vulnerability, with God's self-limitations in relation to creation. Included is God's *risk*—as one of his self-limitations or as a necessary implication of all of them. Tresmontant went out on a limb by specifically referring to God's creative action of *other* creative actions in his own image and likeness including freedom and responsibility as "God's risk."[16] Apparently, God considered it *worth the risk* to create beings other than himself, even outside himself, with the freedom and power to resist him. And yet, contrary to process theology, God maintains the ability to *intervene* in these others' affairs from time to time. So why doesn't he *supernaturally* step in to stop all or at least some evils such as the Holocaust?

The biblical narrative offers no speculative, theoretical solution

---

16   Tresmontant, *A Study of Hebrew Thought*, 151–52.

to this problem. It simply asserts God's plan ultimately to defeat evil and his omnipotent ability to do it. Why he permits evil between the times of creation and closure of history is something of a mystery. And yet Christian thinkers *have* offered *reasonable* possible explanations that shouldn't be ignored. In the end, however, all that can be said with certainty from a biblical perspective is that evil is *not God's doing* even though *God permits it*. God is perfectly good and perfectly sovereign, so his creation is good, not evil, evil being the absence of the good brought about by creatures' misuse of free will, and God is in charge of history even if not causing everything that happens. Within those parameters of the biblical-Christian worldview, there is lots of room for speculation about why God permits evil and innocent suffering in his world. But underlying all explanations must be the general one of God's *free self-limitations* in relation to creation and creation's *relative autonomy* over against God.

Having admitted that there is no perfect theodicy (solution to the problem of evil) from the perspective of personalist theism, theistic personalism, it is important to say something else to those who use evil to attempt to undermine the existence of a personal God. The very idea of *evil* as *more than what is not liked* presupposes *some moral standard beyond humanity*. When people say the Holocaust, for example, was evil, they rarely mean it was contrary to conventional beliefs about right and wrong. And yet, what else is there to morality if there is no God? As Brunner wrote (mentioned above)—it's either God's law or humanity's self-made law. If there is no God as the ultimate moral standard and lawgiver, then why call anything evil? Call it *harmful* or *repulsive*. *Evil* carries a stronger connotation; it implies a terrible violation of an objective standard of right and wrong. And yet humanity's own standards of right and wrong change and are radically different across time and space. When people condemn the Holocaust as evil, they rarely, if ever, mean "bad from my culture's perspective" or "repugnant to my society's standards of morality." They mean something that presupposes a transcendent standard of right and wrong in which genocide is always absolutely wrong. In other words, they seem to be saying that *even if Hitler and the Nazis had won World War II and eliminated all Jews, that would have been absolutely, irreducibly, bad and wrong.* But why—if there is no God? How can there be such a thing as evil *in that sense* if there is no God to declare and judge it so?

The point is, of course, that the problem of evil is *more of a problem* for atheism or naturalism than for theism. If naturalism is true, then there are no moral absolutes; there cannot be any. If naturalism is true, only feeling and intuition can argue that might does *not* make right. If monism is true, then good and evil cannot be absolute opposites because all is one. Evil is then at best an illusion, a wrong idea, a mistaken belief. If dualism is true, then there is no moral standard above the two powers or principles deciding which one of them is good and which one is evil.

This is an example of what Brunner labeled *eristics*—showing that other worldviews, metaphysical schemes, have greater problems than the biblical-Christian one. It is not done with the intention of *coercing* anyone into Christian belief; if Brunner is right (and he surely is), that isn't even possible. However, it is for the purpose of *defending Christian belief as not irrational* and *possibly attracting unbelievers to try seeing reality as the Bible and Christian thought depicts it.*

CHAPTER 6

The Biblical-Christian Perspective on the World

The world is a battleground—both literally and figuratively. Here both senses are in view. First, conflicting worldviews and metaphysical belief systems see the world as radically different things. And that can make a great difference in ethics. How we should treat nature, and all that is in it, for example, can depend very much on what we believe it is. One theory about the environmental crisis lays the blame for the rape of nature by human industry at the feet of Judeo-Christian religion; another theory lays the blame at the feet of Enlightenment secularism. Both may be to blame, but our concern here will be what the biblical-Christian view of the natural world is, not what Judeo-Christian religion has believed. Our concern is also with modern secularism, rooted in a naturalistic metaphysic, and what it implies about the natural world, as well as with other worldviews and the place of nature, the physical universe, in their perspectives.

The second sense of the world being a battleground is literal. The earth is literally littered with the debris of war, terrorism, ecological disasters, and murders. Everyone knows this, many to their great harm. But some people believe, on the basis of the biblical narrative, that there is also an invisible war raging on and around earth—not with guns and tanks and bombs but with weapons of spiritual warfare and that among the forces locked in combat are "powers of this dark world" and "spiritual forces," and that it all began and continues "in the heavenly realms" (Ephesians 6:12). Naturally, in a world increasingly dominated by secular, naturalistic thought, such talk raises suspicions of superstition, but the biblical narrative is filled with spiritual warfare as *background* to much of the battlefield on earth—both figurative and literal—that everyone knows about.

Biblical-Christian Metaphysics and Creation

Traditionally, metaphysics deals mainly with issues of *ultimate reality* such as "the absolute," if such exists, or such as whatever *one* connects the *many*. Up to here we have been exploring what the biblical story implies about that—namely, ultimate reality, the connection connecting all things, as the *supernatural* and *personal (but not human)* God, the creator of all things on which all things outside of him are dependent. But metaphysics *can* also include the study of *penultimate* reality, that which is not absolute but dependent on the absolute, especially as it *really is* behind appearances. Everyone experiences trees, for example, but *what is a tree?* Is it *only* what a botanist says it is? Certainly botany sheds much helpful light on trees. Anyone who has one in her yard knows this when a disease infects it. *But is a tree only what botany says it is?* Or is there something more to the tree than matter? What is *life* and *meaning—purpose*—even in a tree?

Some years ago I read a syndicated question and answer column in a local newspaper. It was written by a woman who many claimed to be the smartest person in the world, the person with the world's highest known IQ. An interlocutor asked her what is the most basic science of all? Her answer was physics. According to the world's smartest person, biology reduces to chemistry and chemistry to physics. Apparently (and this was borne out by her answers to other questions about reality) she did not believe *metaphysics* is a science. She has lots of company. Another interlocutor asked her, in a separate column, what makes a life worthwhile? Her answer was that a life is worthwhile if it produces more than it consumes. That is completely consistent with a worldview that believes physics has all the answers that really matter.

One purpose of this book is to equip Christians with discernment about reality, including ideas, based on *the Bible absorbing the world*. That is, as explained earlier, the Bible's perspective—often more implied than explicitly stated, at least in philosophical terms—should be the Christian's *lens* for seeing the world as *God's good but corrupted creation, dependent but real*. The Christian for whom the Bible absorbs the world reads answers like those given by the world's smartest person, quoted above, and knows immediately that something is wrong. Unfortunately, however, too many Christians, especially in modern, Western society, read them and think, "Oh, that's interesting; that makes sense." But that can only be because their *lenses are not clear*. They have adopted nonbiblical, non-Christian *plausibility structures*, often alongside their Christian beliefs, leaving the two unintegrated. That leads to confusion and accommodation to nonbiblical, non-Christian life and world perspectives.

Hopefully, even a person not committed to a biblical-Christian metaphysical perspective on reality could see some problems with the world's smartest person's responses to the two extremely important questions. Does biology really reduce to physics via chemistry? Such a belief *implies* materialism—that matter is all there is—or at least *naturalism*—that nature is all there is. However, someone might well object that the columnist was only talking about the *natural sciences* and that nothing she said necessarily ruled out *metaphysics* or even a *supernatural basis* for life. So it may be. However, *within a Christian context* her answer would be incorrect because it is insufficient. Even a physicist informed by the biblical-Christian worldview will have to say something about *life* as *more than chemistry* and *elemental nature as more than mathematically describable laws*. Christian physicist and theologian John Polkinghorne (b. 1930), who taught both subjects for many years at Cambridge University and won the Templeton Prize for integrating science and religion, referred to the world's smartest person's answer as reductionism not really compatible with the latest insights of physics.[1] But *for the Christian*, physical reality cannot be all there is and a Christian scientist, especially one teaching in a Christian school, for example, *must* think and talk about *metaphysics* even if he or she practices methodological naturalism in the laboratory.

The world's smartest person's answer to the second question proves her naturalistic perspective on reality. And it is completely consistent with claiming that all science reduces to physics and implying that physics explains (or could explain) everything. If nature is all there is, if there is no *spiritual reality* behind, beneath, within the world, then the logical conclusion *must be* that a life is worthwhile insofar as it produces more than it consumes. Even many naturalists will demur at that, but the world's smartest person was thinking absolutely clearly—assuming she was, as indicated by her answers, a thoroughgoing, consistent naturalist in her view of reality (i.e., an atheist).

The sad and shocking reality is that many confused Christians probably read the world's smartest person's answers and thought, "That makes sense." After all, she is (according to the weekly national news magazine insert in the newspaper) the person with the world's highest known IQ. The problem is that having a very high IQ does not make one an expert on metaphysics or give one a view from nowhere. Everyone has a life and world perspective; everyone sees the world as something and not something else. And that is not a matter of proof. Yet, to refer back to Brunner's eristics, for a moment, even a hardheaded physicist such as Polkinghorne

---

1   John Polkinghorne, *The Faith of a Physicist* (The Gifford Lectures, 1993–94) (Princeton, N.J.: Princeton University Press, 1994), 28–29. The problem of reductionism in science, however, is not confined to those specific pages where "A Note on Reductionism" appears. The entire book and most of Polkinghorne's writings aim at contradicting the idea that biology can be reduced to chemistry or to physics—as total explanations of life.

comments that naturalism has a problem in that it has to believe matter is "somehow sufficiently self-explanatory":

> In fact, the physical universe, by its very rational order and fruitfulness, seems to many to point beyond itself, so that there is more intellectual satisfaction in attributing its existence to the will of a self-sufficient agent [viz., God] than in treating it as a fundamental brute fact.[2]

Again, it is not a matter of proof; it is a matter of perspective. But an argument can be made (eristics) that one perspective on reality makes more sense, overall, than others. A major weakness in the world's smartest person's perspective, as revealed by her answer to the question about what makes a life worthwhile, is that it opens the door wide to considering that life that does *not* produce more than it consumes is worthless. Can a logical line be drawn from consistent naturalism-materialism, the worldview that nature, as modern science describes it, is all there is, to something like Nazi Germany's systematic killing of the mentally ill and disabled?

All of the above is simply to illustrate that *metaphysics* matter— even in areas that do not seem, on their surface, to have directly to do with the absolute, ultimate reality. Here, in this chapter, we take up the matter of the world, the universe, and all that is in it. We experience the tree, but what is it—beyond what botany says about it? We live on the planet earth in a solar system in a galaxy in a universe. What is it—beyond what natural sciences say about it? Life's ultimate questions, including ones about the world, cannot be answered in laboratories. They are questions about meaning, purpose, and hope. And those, if they have answers at all, take us back to ultimate reality.

What Is the World in Biblical-Christian Metaphysics?

So, the questions about the world, for the Christian, become "What is the world in light of ultimate reality—the God of the Bible?" And

---

2   Ibid., 56.

"What does the biblical narrative imply about the world?" Perhaps no poet has expressed the answers more beautifully than Gerard Manley Hopkins in 1877:

The world is charged with the grandeur of God.
　　It will flame out, like shining from shook foil;
　　It gathers to a greatness, like the ooze of oil
Crushed. Why do men then now not reck his rod?
Generations have trod, have trod, have trod;
　　And all is seared with trade; bleared, smeared with toil;
　　And wears man's smudge and shares man's smell: the soil
Is bare now, nor can foot feel, being shod.

And for all this, nature is never spent;
　　There lives the dearest freshness deep down things;
And though the last lights off the black West went
　　Oh, morning, at the brown brink eastward, springs—
Because the Holy Ghost over the bent
　　World broods with warm breast and with ah! bright wings.

And yet poetry is not metaphysics, although it can express metaphysical ideas wonderfully well. According to the poet, drawing on the biblical story of God and creation, the world is God's good creation crushed and corrupted by humans and yet not abandoned by God nor turned evil.

Before delineating the biblical-Christian view of the world as God's good but corrupted and yet redeemable creation, it will help to examine alternative views of the world—those generally held by the metaphysical belief systems explained before: dualism, monism (including emanationism and pantheism), naturalism, deism, idealism, and panentheism. And we will not forget Greek philosophy. Of course, there are variations of each in the history of thought and in the world of religions and philosophies. However, most developed ones, ones with public influence especially in the West, boil down to one of these.

Alternative Metaphysical Visions of the World: Greco-Roman Philosophy

The first alternative view of the world Christians encountered— outside of their own, largely borrowed from Hebrew religion—was *Greco-Roman philosophy—Middle Platonism and Stoicism*. Stoicism was an early form of naturalism but with a spiritual flair. That is, it was a philosophy, common especially among sophisticated Romans, that viewed the world as a closed system of causes and effects, determined from within by an impersonal quasi-spiritual power. The key to Stoicism, especially as it related to the world, was *nature closed and determined*. All things, without exception, happened according to nature and could not happen otherwise. The good life was one lived in accordance with nature and with wise resignation. God (called Zeus by Stoicism's main philosopher Zeno) was not personal or supernatural but for all practical purposes one with nature. Thus, Stoicism is often categorized as a form of *pantheism*. The Stoics had no idea of "creation" as such; the world, the universe, is what it is and always has been. There is nothing supernatural to have created it. It is ruled from within by itself. This is, of course, a very basic, minimal outline of generic Stoicism, but it's sufficient to explain *one idea of the world* early Christians had to contend with. And more than one early church father was at least somewhat influenced by it.

Simultaneously with Stoicism early Christians were confronted with Middle Platonism and, later, Neoplatonism. Then, in the Middle Ages, Aristotle's philosophy became influential first in Muslim universities in Spain and then in Christian European universities. Thomas Aquinas attempted to synthesize or at least reconcile Catholic Christianity with Aristotelianism. Both Platonism and Aristotelianism, for all their differences, tended to view the world as eternal and the muddled, ambiguous creation of a god who was either unaware of it (Aristotle) or created quite by accident. In both cases, the world was viewed by sophisticated Greeks influenced by Platonism and Aristotelianism as *not created out of nothing* but formed, fashioned, or fabricated out of eternally existing material. There is an element of dualism, then, in non-Stoic Greek philosophy. Although they did not think of the material world as *evil,* they did tend to think of it as a *tomb* or *prison* of good spirits who were trapped in it. All the early Christian theologians now known as church fathers rejected the eternity of the world, as did Aquinas. All emphasized, much to the dismay of sophisticated Greeks and Romans, that God created the entire world, all reality outside of God himself, *ex nihilo*, "out of nothing" and "in time" (metaphorically speaking).

All Greco-Roman philosophy and religion had a generally negative view of the world without identifying it as evil. Still, without positing a literal, historical creation or fall, educated, philosophically minded Greeks and Romans *tended* to view matter as *faulty* because it is *fallen*.[3] That is, they thought of the world as negative and therefore a source of evil because it is *not God*. They took a generally negative attitude toward space, time, and matter. The whole world, finitude itself, was viewed pessimistically, as a prison or cave (Plato's own analogy) of the soul, the mind, which seeks liberation from the sensible world into a purely soulish or spiritual reality. This generally pessimistic attitude toward the world gave rise eventually to Gnosticism, which considered matter itself evil, the creation of a demented, if not evil, god. It also gave rise eventually to Neoplatonism, which viewed the material world of nature and time, history, as lacking being because it emanated too far from its substance source—the One. Against this pattern of Greek and Roman thought about the world, Tresmontant wrote that "the metaphysics . . . implied in the biblical narratives goes quite against

---

3   Tresmontant, *A Study of Hebrew Thought*, 11.

Greek thought's most fundamental attitudes in regard to reality, time, the multiple and the becoming."[4]

Alternative Metaphysical Visions of the World: Dualisms

"The world is charged with the grandeur of God."

Manichean dualism also conflicts with the metaphysics implied in the biblical narratives insofar as it, like Gnosticism, implies that matter is evil or the source of evil. Both believe in a dualism between matter and spirit, with the former being evil and the latter being good. Many Bible readers become confused and fall into this dualism because they misunderstand the apostle Paul's use of *flesh* (*sarx* in Greek), which is used in a very negative way in some of his epistles. *Flesh* is sometimes pitted against the Spirit. But two things ought to be explained and carefully noted. When Paul used *sarx* in a negative sense, as connected with sin and evil, he clearly did not mean "body" (*soma*). After all, the "works of the flesh" listed in Galatians 5 include what many would call "sins of the spirit"! Paul occasionally used *sarx*, often translated "flesh" in English Bibles, for the fallen, sinful, corrupt human nature, and the war is not against the human spirit but the divine Spirit—God. Confusion about Paul's use of *sarx*, "flesh," has caused many English-speaking Christians (and no doubt others) to fall into Manichean or Gnostic dualism, imagining that the Bible promotes conflict between matter/body and soul/spirit. It does not.

Manicheism and Gnostic dualism both teach that the world is not only fallen and corrupted because of sin, but that matter itself is evil and souls or spirits are "sparks of the divine" trapped in material bodies. That entrapment is the cause of sin and salvation is escape from matter into a purely spiritual existence. This is a radical departure from the biblical view of creation, even though both Manicheans and Gnostics could point to passages of Scripture that seemed to support their dualism. Fighting against such dualism

---

4   Ibid., 142.

was a major project for early Christian theologians, from Irenaeus (130–202) to Augustine.

Alternative Metaphysical Visions of the World: Monisms

Monism's idea of the world deifies it, confusing the world—creation—with God or the absolute. Tresmontant rightly asserted that for both Judaism and Christianity, based on the Bible's story of God and creation, the "absolute," ultimate reality, is not the world; it is not creation but the one who created.[5] And creation is the free act of a personal creator who acted out of his own goodness. And the free, good creator created the world, the universe, *out of nothing* ("ex nihilo").[6] The metaphysical structure of the Bible is *duality* without *dualism*. The world is not God; God is not the world. And yet they are intimately related as creator to creation by God's grace, power, and self-limiting vulnerability—allowing the world to affect him.

Monism of all varieties, whether Indian (Advaita Vedanta) or Western (Spinoza's speculative pantheism), opens the door to completely unbiblical and anti-Christian idolatry of creation. The apostle Paul identified this as near the source of all sin and evil in Romans 1: worshiping the creation rather than the Creator. Identifying God with the world without clear distinction of the former as superior and the latter dependent leads inevitably to *idolatry of the self*, where the soul itself becomes one with God, as in the New Age Movement—a popular form of monism/pantheism. Again, many Christians become confused because they do not pay careful attention to another distinction in Scripture itself—that between the created spirit of the human person and the Holy Spirit of God himself. The Bible uses the Hebrew word *ruach* for both; it can also mean "wind" and "breath." The New Testament uses the Greek word *pneuma* for both. Again, it can also mean "wind" or "breath." Only a close reading of *spirit* in Scripture reveals *when* it

---

5   Tresmontant, *Christian Metaphysics*, 42.
6   Ibid., 53.

is being used of the human person's immaterial soul and *when* it is being used of the eternal Spirit of God, the breath and wind of God that creates and sustains the world and life in it. The two are separated by that interval, gulf, spoken of before, and yet the Holy Spirit of God, by grace, comes across that gulf to indwell and even "deify"[7] the person who yields his or her created spirit to God in faith.

Alternative Metaphysical Visions of the World: Naturalism and Deism

Naturalism views the world as a closed network of matter and energy controlled by mathematically describable natural laws, all *in principle* scientifically explainable. In other words, the world, the cosmos, is all there is; nothing spiritual or supernatural exists. The universe is not the creation of any God or even the "body" of a divine force (e.g., philosopher Henri Bergson's "élan vital" [vital force]). The tension, even conflict, between naturalism and biblical-Christian metaphysics with regard to the world should be obvious, and yet many modern Western Christians have adopted aspects of naturalism into their world perspective. Especially Christians influenced by liberal Protestant theology tend to view the world as closed to the supernatural and as entirely explainable by appeal to natural laws, even if those are not all yet entirely understood. Some process theologians call their view "theistic naturalism," by which they mean they understand God to be a depth dimension within nature itself and not a supernatural being with prior actuality to the world. Philosopher Plantinga's arguments against naturalism were explained earlier; here it suffices to note simply that naturalism is incompatible with the biblical narrative of a creating and

---

7   "Deification" is an English translation of theosis—Greek for "becoming God." Especially Eastern Orthodox Christian theology emphasizes this as the goal of salvation—to become a partial partaker of God's own nature through the gift of the Holy Spirit. The doctrine is based on 2 Peter 1:4, which speaks of humans, believers, participating in the divine nature through God's gifts (i.e., by grace). In Christian theology, however, this deification is never thought of as becoming one with God but as receiving the gift of immortal life, which is God's alone but his to share.

sustaining, omnipotent yet vulnerable, interventionist God upon whom the world is dependent. None of that means that *natural science* is contrary to a biblical-Christian metaphysic; it is only to say that *naturalism*, a philosophy of life and reality, is absolutely contrary to it.

Deism was simply an attempt by some Christians to juxtapose, if not integrate, modern scientific naturalism with belief in a transcendent, even supernatural God. Deism seeks to reconcile naturalism with theism by removing God from any direct involvement in the workings of nature. According to deism, the cosmos is *not* all there is, all there ever was, etc., but it is a closed network of scientifically explainable, mathematically describable causes and effects which God created and perhaps sustains but in which God does not intervene or interfere. The only way to reconcile that belief with the biblical story is Thomas Jefferson's way—by cutting out of Scripture all that conflicts with naturalism while keeping God as original architect, creator, and moral governor over the world. The result is an inaccessible God, not the Yahweh of Israel and Father of Jesus Christ, who not only created but sustains the world and intervenes in it and is intimately affected by what happens in it. Deism denies the *relational* nature of the world to God.

Alternative Metaphysical Visions of the World: Absolute Idealism

German idealism viewed God as the "Mind" of the universe and emphasized God's immanence in the world as its Absolute Spirit marching toward total harmony through the resolutions of history's conflicts (Hegel). Its trajectory was panentheism if not pantheism. Hegel, the ultimate German idealist philosopher of religion, declared that "without a world God is not God." In other words, the world is necessary for God's self-actualization; God depends on the world as much as the world depends on God. Whitehead, the formulator of process thought, agreed, even though he was not a German

idealist. For him, as for Hegel, the world and God exist always inter-
dependently. "It is as true to say that God creates the world as that
the world creates God."[8] Panentheism, whether of the Hegelian or
Whiteheadian variety, falls into conflict with the biblical-Christian
metaphysic because it turns God's *relationality* into *dependence on
the world* and elevates *the world* to an undeserved status as more
than God's creation. In panentheism, God does not create the world
ex nihilo, out of nothing, but strives to *fashion* the world, his counterpart, into his *ideal of harmony*.

All of those extrabiblical views of the world exist in the twenty-
first century and through various media seep into Christians'
thinking about reality. One way to resist them is to *know* and *understand* the biblical view of the world which is, again, that the world
is *God's good but corrupted creation, dependent on God not only for
its beginning but also for its fulfillment.*

The Biblical-Christian Metaphysical Vision of the World: God's Good Creation Corrupted

Cherbonnier expresses the basic idea of the Bible with regard to the
world by rightly beginning with God: God is related to the world as
an agent to his acts.[9] Turned around, this means that the world is
related to God as an act is related to its agent-creator. Also, "in the
Biblical metaphysic, for which free agents are central, the Creator
is related to his creation by an act of will."[10] Turned around, this
means that the world, creation, is related to God as an act of his
will. The world, then, is *not* a negation of God, *nor* ontologically
"one with God" (of God's own substance), *nor* independent of God,
nor God's eternal, equal counterpart. The biblical view of God and
the world is truly *dialectical*—two truths that seem contradictory
to the human mind's ordinary ways of thinking but are actually

---

8   Whitehead, *Process and Reality*, 348.
9   Cherbonnier, "Is There a Biblical Metaphysic?" 462.
10   Ibid., 463.

interdependent. We tend to think if something is *dependent and not God* it is thereby automatically flawed, "fallen" by nature. We tend to think if something is *closely related to God* and *essentially good* it must be somehow "one with God." Instead, the biblical view is, from beginning to end, that the world is *God's good but dependent, contingent, creation, and also God's freely chosen counterpart and yet broken and corrupted.*

The Genesis creation stories (in chapters 1 and 2) and the story of humanity's defection from God's will with the concomitant corruption or curse on the earth may be taken as saga—Barth's term for a narrative that is true but expressed with legendary features. In other words, it is *neither* straightforward history, as in a history textbook, *nor* myth. Its main purpose, like one of Jesus's parables, is to communicate a universal and spiritual truth, but it also witnesses to something that has happened. Its "witness" character, however, is not tied to every feature being literal. The serpent of Genesis 3, for example, should not be thought of as a literal snake, but neither should it be dismissed as mere symbol.

When it comes to Genesis, many people either throw the baby of theological meaning out with the bathwater of literalism or focus so much on attempting to take everything literally that they miss the points the passages are making. This is one of the great tragedies of modern Christian and secular thought about the Bible—the false polarization between literalism and myth. Genesis is the classic example. Our concern here is with the metaphysical implications of Genesis, not how literally or historically to interpret its narratives of origins. *The purpose of Genesis 1–3 is not to replace science (see the following interlude) but to supplement science with deeper, metaphysical insight.* Genesis 1–3 is not about mechanics of origins; it is primarily about the nature of the world as creation. Later narratives and wisdom literature and biblical condemnations of idolatry, etc., follow the lead of Genesis.

According to the Genesis story of creation, God is *lord* over the world and the world is *under the lordship* of God. The narrative stresses the *ontological interval* between God and creation, clearly subordinating the world to God. It does not rule out the world partially creating itself under God's empowering lordship. The earth brought forth various things—plants and animals. And yet its own creative energies and their products are all related back to God as source and origin. One of the main points of these creation narratives is to *forbid idolatry*; the lordship of God over creation and creation's dependence on God are stressed throughout. Another point, however, is to *encourage valuing and caring for the world as belonging to God*. God is said to have declared all the "works of his hands" *good*. Then God *gives* the human dominion over the world. Within the context, this clearly indicates *care* for the world under the lordship of God. The human is to be God's freely chosen *partner* in caring for the good creation.

But then, in chapter 3, a counterpoint is made: creation, the world, is under a curse because of human disobedience. The humans' eating of the fruit of the Tree of the Knowledge of Good and Evil stands for *denial of God's lordship*. As a result, the earth itself is affected negatively so that what was meant to be a harmonious relationship between God and the world and humans and the world is disrupted with tension. The world is broken due to the brokenness of the God-human relationship. Clearly the point is to trace *evil* and *innocent suffering* back to the creature rather than to the Creator even though, as Paul says in Romans 8:20, creation was "subjected to frustration" as a result of God's will.

The rest of the story witnesses to this dual relationship between God the creator and lord of the world and his creation: brokenness within overall goodness. There is no idea in the biblical narrative of creation itself being intrinsically evil; put metaphysically, *finitude* and *fallenness*, *createdness* and *corruption*, are *not* identified or even coordinated as *cause* and *effect*. Rather, creation remains good but also corrupted or broken, existing under a curse due to a broken relationship with God who remains lord over it, caring for it and seeking to redeem it. God's assignment of the human to have dominion never hints at permission to exploit, let alone ruin, nature; it remains part of the "image and likeness of God" and there is a call to care for creation and be God's created cocreator in restoring it to its original intention.

Ethically, then, the point of the creation story of Genesis and the entire Bible's witness is *the call to care for God's good creation* while *avoiding worshiping it*. Idolatry is a major theme of the biblical narrative; it is the very root of sin and evil—setting creation or some part of creation up as God and worshiping it is wrong because God alone is Lord and creation belongs to him. At the same time, denigrating nature or any part of it as evil and/or exploiting it is wrong because it belongs to God and caring for it is part of what it means to be human.

Continuity and Discontinuity in the God-World Relation

Metaphysically, then, a major theme of the biblical narrative is *both continuity and discontinuity* between God and the world.[11] The gulf between God and his world must not be emphasized too much, so that the world floats away into an evil counterpart against God or independence from God, but neither should it be closed so that God's lordship over it is lost. Continuity between God and the world lies in the *relationship* freely chosen by God and the *reflection* of God in his work. Discontinuity between God and the world lies in the *interval* or gap of *difference* and *dependence* in which God remains always the world's superior covenant partner, sovereign lord over it, and free in his relation to it. Discontinuity comes into play *after that* due to creaturely defection from God that results in God's withdrawal, absence, which is never total but nevertheless real.

Evil and innocent suffering, then, must never be regarded by the Christian as "built into" the world; they are not "of the essence"

---

11   Cherbonnier, "The Logic of Biblical Anthropomorphism," 202.

of creation itself. They are evidence not of the *ontological interval* between God and the world but of the *moral interval* brought about by humanity's fall. "Because of you the ground will be cursed," said God to the human after his defection from God's fellowship (see Genesis 3:17). Put another way in Romans 8:20, the world was "subjected to frustration." And God intends to liberate the world from this "bondage to decay," which is evidence of God's continuing care for creation. In the meantime, humans live out their likeness to God by having dominion over the world, which means *nurturing it*, not dominating and exploiting it. The ecological crisis, insofar as it is humankind's doing, which science indicates it is, is a violation of the ethical implications of the biblical narrative even if caused partly by Christians. Christianity itself, understood as *what the Bible reveals about God and the world*, forbids rape of the environment.

Christians' Confusion about God and the World

A great deal of confusion has entered into both Christians' and non-Christians' thinking because of ignorance and/or misunderstanding of the metaphysical import of the biblical story about God and creation. So-called "New Age Christians" succumbed to esoteric ideas about God and the world in the 1980s and 1990s and confused creation with God. Esoteric philosophy and esoteric Christianity equal *monistic metaphysics*. At some deep level God and the world are identified *ontologically*—as to their *being*. The ontological interval is violated in thought. The result is idolatry. The so-called New Age Movement was just one manifestation of monism, which is always in the atmosphere, so to speak, because of humanity's *refusal of finitude*—wanting to be God for themselves—the original sin underlying all evil and the curse on creation. A myth grew out of and around the environmental movement of the 1980s (also before and afterward) that identifying the world with God, regarding the world as ontologically divine, made of "God stuff," would encourage greater care for the creation. In fact, however, identifying creation

189

with God, ignoring God's transcendent lordship over creation, meant identifying *the human* with God and reinforcing humanity's mastery over the world. The best protection against human exploitation of nature is the biblical-Christian idea of "dominion-having" as part of humanity's likeness to God, that taking care of the world under God *fulfills* humanity's supernatural calling.

At the same time, much Christian fundamentalism came to demean creation, encouraging lack of environmental care on the basis of the belief that God intends to destroy it. "Lifeboat ethics" is the term used to describe this fundamentalist denigration of the world as both godless and destined for destruction by God. This has misled some fundamentalist Christians into an almost Manichean view of the material world as the source of sin and evil. Everything secular and worldly is identified with sin and evil—a clear misunderstanding of the biblical declaration that the creation itself is good.[12]

Contemporary Non-Christian Confusions about God and the World

Some contemporary religious philosophies clearly reflect Gnosticism in promising to help humans realize their forgotten divine nature and overcome matter, energy, space, and time as if those are intrinsically bad. The biblical-Christian view is that matter, energy, space, and time are good even if broken, and they are destined to be healed even if that destiny is *hope* and not *present reality*.

Contemporary secular philosophy, rooted in naturalism, ultimately also denigrates the world, reducing it to purposeless accident as opposed to a purpose-filled home for humanity (and God with humanity). Biblical metaphysics of the world is distinctly *teleological*—purpose driven. The world is given transcendent

---

12   For more about this error and the biblical truth about both creation and re-creation (eschatology) see N. T. Wright, *Surprised by Hope: Rethinking Heaven, the Resurrection, and the Mission of the Church* (San Francisco: HarperOne, 2008). Wright rightly emphasizes the biblical theme of God's intention to *renovate*, not *destroy*, the world.

meaning and purpose by being *creation* as opposed to *accident*. God's creatorship and lordship over creation fills it with meaning and purpose, value and importance. Its purpose is variegated in Scripture. It is, as Protestant theologian John Calvin (1509–64) expressed it, a "theater of God's glory." By itself, however, that neglects another aspect of its purpose; creation is also the space for God's overflowing love to express itself and for God to enjoy receiving love back from creation. The Psalms frequently express blessing to God, more than implying that the world's Creator and Lord enjoys creation's rejoicing in his goodness.

Why God Created at All

One question raised by the biblical narrative is *why* God created the world. There is no clear and distinct answer given there. Two possibilities have emerged through Christian reflection on the biblical witness to God's creatorship. One, espoused especially by Christians in the tradition of Augustine, including Calvin, is that God created the world "for his glory"—to express outwardly, toward what is not God, the fullness of his own beauty, goodness, and greatness. Puritan theologian and metaphysical thinker Jonathan Edwards (1703–58) expressed this view especially well in his "Dissertation on the End [Purpose] for Which God Created the World." According to Edwards—and no doubt church father Augustine and reformer Calvin would concur—God created the world in order to display his glory by manifesting all his attributes without prejudice to any. In other words, the Puritan theologian argued, every attribute of God is revealed in creation and its history—including his wrath.

Edwards' contemporary John Wesley (1703–91), founder of the Methodist tradition, believed that God created the world to display his love and receive love back from creatures—especially humans created in God's own image and likeness. Christians in Wesley's tradition, known as non-Calvinists or Arminians, tend to emphasize God's love more than God's glory.

Of course, the two reasons for creation are not antithetical to one another; they are fully compatible. Most thoughtful Christians, reflecting on the biblical story, would say that God's purpose for creation is *both* to display his glory *and* to display his love. However, inquiring minds *tend* to move in one direction or the other—as the controlling or main purpose. Those in the Augustinian-Calvinist tradition tend to read Scripture as emphasizing God's glory and power and the world as the place for displaying them. The result can be an interpretation of everything in the world, even evil, as purposed by God *for his glory*. Those in the Arminian-Wesleyan tradition (and also going back to the Greek church fathers before Augustine!) tend to read Scripture as emphasizing God's love and desire for relationship and the world as the place for experiencing them. The result can be a softening of God's lordship and a sentimentalizing of God as *needing* the world for his own fulfillment. The solution, of course, is to hold the two purposes of God in creation *together in tension*. "It will flame out, like shining from shook foil."

Interlude 6

Has science replaced metaphysics in the modern world? Many people believe it has; science is now believed to offer the answers to life's ultimate questions—insofar as they are answerable at all. And yet, this belief itself is rooted in a metaphysical vision of reality—naturalism. Its popular form, related to science, is *scientism*—the blik that science can, in principle, explain whatever is explainable. Whatever lies outside the purview of science is not explainable. That's *implicit naturalism* whether it wears that label or not. Of course, *science itself* cannot prove that, *and* as mentioned earlier, philosophers of science such as Plantinga have demonstrated that naturalism actually undermines science insofar as science is a search for truth.

At the other end of the spectrum of attitudes toward science lies a popular religious sentiment, common especially among Christian fundamentalists, that *science itself* is dangerous and ought always to be viewed with suspicion. Allegedly, science itself leads away from biblical-Christian faith and undermines belief in God, to say nothing of miracles and creation.

The Alleged War between Science and Religion

The classic survey of this conflict between science and religion was published by the president of Cornell University in 1896 under the title *A History of the Warfare of Science with Theology in Christendom*. Andrew D. White (1832–1918) examined the centuries of that war with a jaundiced eye toward especially Christian theology. His aim was to demonstrate that religious thought has been a drag on the progress of science and to promote absolute freedom of science from religious-theological censorship. That book had a tremendous influence on many twentieth-century intellectuals' attitudes toward religion and science.

Throughout the twentieth century, Christian fundamentalists, "maximal conservatives" with regard to doctrines and literal interpreters of the Bible including Genesis and Revelation, founded Bible colleges largely as refuges from the rising influence of science. A few fundamentalists went so far as to eschew modern medicine, but most availed themselves of modern science's discoveries while attacking its methods and especially what they perceived as its underlying note of naturalism. Fundamentalists often confused methodological naturalism with ideological or metaphysical naturalism, but many scientists also confused the two and contributed to fundamentalists' hostility toward science by placing science *and naturalism* on a pedestal as a new religion or alternative to all religion.

Most twentieth- and twenty-first-century Christians stood somewhere in the middle between these warring parties. They were and are unsure how to value science without sacrificing biblical-Christian faith, and yet, at the same time, they are sure science has value and are unwilling to reject it. *The largely unknown key lies in distinguishing between science itself and naturalism.*

Into the middle of the fray stepped several notable scientist-theologians, Christians with earned scientific credentials, to bring peace out of the totally unnecessary conflict. Stanley Jaki (1924–2009) was a Hungarian-born physicist and Christian theologian who gave the distinguished Gifford Lectures in natural theology in 1974–76. In 1987 he received the Templeton Prize for integrating religion and science. He published many books arguing very cogently that, contrary to the sentiment encouraged by White that Christianity is endemically antiscientific, the roots of modern science lie in Christian theology.[1] According to Jaki, biblical religion

---

1   See especially his final book which sums up his life's work on this project of tracing modern

demystifies nature, making it available for human investigation. Science should thank biblical-Christian thought and Christians should thank science, insofar as it sticks to its intrinsic limits, for many of the great humanitarian achievements it has brought about.

Earlier mention was made of another Christian physicist and theologian who has promoted *coordination* and *correlation* between science and Christian belief and demonstrated the absolute non-necessity of conflict between them: John Polkinghorne. Alongside him stands Francis Collins (b. 1950), a widely recognized expert in genetics who has championed the cause of reconciliation between religion, especially theistic religion, and modern science. His 2007 book *The Language of God: A Scientist Presents Evidence for Belief* announced and explained his belief that theistic religion and natural science need not be at war with each other but can, in fact, integrate and cooperate.

And yet, modern Western society continues to wrestle with an imagined intrinsic conflict between theistic religion and science. Signs of it appear everywhere. Fundamentalists of all religions resist science at every turn while (mostly) making use of its products. Some Christian homeschooling textbooks show Adam feeding the dinosaurs—because a literal reading of Genesis points to their coexistence only a few thousand years ago. Leading scientists continue to snipe at religion itself. Noted molecular biologist Francis Crick (1916–2004) famously declared that "Christianity may be OK between consenting adults in private but should not be taught to young children."[2]

The war between science and religion has many causes, all of them based on misunderstandings and limit-transgressions. As every college student knows, it really began with the Galileo affair in the early seventeenth century when Catholic astronomer Galileo Galilei (1564–1642) refused to be quiet about his proof of

science back to *Christianity: The Savior of Science* (Grand Rapids, Mich.: Eerdmans, 2000).

2   Crick quote in Robin McKie, "Genius Was in His DNA," *The Guardian,* September 16, 2006.

the sun-centered solar system. The Catholic Church and secular rulers knew he was right, but they wanted to tell the people that the earth is not the center of the solar system in their own way and at their own time. Galileo refused and was put under house arrest. Popular beliefs that he was tortured and even killed by the Inquisition are myths. What Galileo did that really launched the modern war between science and theology was declare science's independence from theology. According to him, science, based on observation and mathematics, has the final authority in matters of nature. Theology has final authority in matters of salvation. And thus began the struggle. Religious leaders and theologians did not want to acknowledge science's independent authority, and scientists refused to bow to religious authority. The irony is that by the twentieth century Galileo's claim that theology has any authority at all, over any areas of life, came to be denied by many scientists and philosophers! The religious authorities started the fight by resisting the truth of Galileo's findings, but the secular rulers of the science establishment (universities) claim to have ended it by proving religion to be mere superstition.

The Modern Decline of Metaphysics

Underlying much of the conflict throughout the eighteenth and nineteenth centuries, however, was *metaphysics* versus *science*. That is, gradually, not only organized religion but metaphysics itself came under attack by scientists and philosophers enamored with science. Throughout most of the eighteenth century, enlightened religious thinkers turned away from pseudoscience—treating the Bible as a handbook of cosmology, for example—to metaphysics and natural theology to support and defend theistic belief. Science was used as a tool for supporting theistic metaphysics. Deism emerged as a leading option for reconciling modern religion and theistic metaphysics. Then came the devastating discoveries of David Hume, the skeptical Scottish philosopher who argued that metaphysics itself is dead because it is ultimately unreliable. Immanuel Kant drove the nail in natural religion's coffin by arguing that the human mind is incapable of having knowledge of anything except *appearances*. The whole quest for knowledge about ultimate reality, apart from revelation and faith, was pronounced a dead end. Twentieth-century science's objections to religion seem to lie in two claims. First, that modern philosophy has killed metaphysics and religion is by nature metaphysical. All real knowledge is empirical and *only* of appearances; there is no reliable method of studying what cannot be observed empirically. (Thus, an alliance between positivism and modern scientism.) Second, that religion has a kind of built-in resistance to change and progress, that it is a drag on discovery, whereas science has produced much good.

Fundamentalist antiscience religionists, on the other hand, rage against science that it has a kind of built-in bias against revelation, faith, and the supernatural, and, if science has its way, it will always push religion aside and possibly even persecute religious believers. This wing of the debate views science as limiting reality to the empirically observable and demeaning both spirituality and morality with a kind of attitude that whatever can be done must be done (by science). They can point with some justification to the atom bomb, the ecological crisis, and the sexual revolution, fueled by modern methods of birth control, as evidence of the ungodliness of science.

Fundamentalism versus Science

One event in the modern war between science and religion stands out as especially emblematic of why both sides are so hostile to each other: the infamous Scopes Monkey Trial of 1925—especially as fictionalized in the play and movie based on it entitled *Inherit the Wind* (1955). The trial really happened in Dayton, Tennessee, and became so famous because it was the first live event broadcast nationwide by radio, then a relatively new household entertainment appliance. It was also famous because two giants of the war between science and religion faced off—representing their respective ends of the spectrum. William Jennings Bryan (1860–1925), a popular American politician who served as Woodrow Wilson's Secretary of State and ran for president twice, prosecuted the young high school teacher who allegedly violated the state law against teaching evolution. (Bryan volunteered to pay the teacher's fine should he be convicted; the issue was not the teacher or even the law but, from Bryan's perspective, the specter of Social Darwinism should "godless evolution" be widely accepted.) The newly organized American Civil Liberties Union (ALCU) brought in as defense attorney nationally famous lawyer Clarence Darrow (1857–1938). Darrow was noted as a defender of the weak and advocate of science, including evolution. He was probably an agnostic with regard to religion.

The trial was a devastating defeat for anti-evolutionism and fundamentalism. Bryan, who took the stand to testify against evolution, made a fool of himself. Darrow used scalding rhetoric to make Bryan and evolution's opponents look ridiculous. Baltimore reporter and columnist H. L. Mencken (1880–1956) called the anti-evolution fundamentalists who swamped the courthouse to support Bryan and the anti-evolution law "Booboisie"—a pun that caught on for religious redneck denizens of the Bible Belt. The teacher, Scopes, was convicted and fined one hundred dollars. Bryan paid his fine. But it was a Pyrrhic victory for fundamentalism. Popular opinion responded that the fundamentalists were antiscience obscurantists. Fundamentalists began to establish their own schools to protect their children and youth against not just naturalism but science itself. Most such Bible colleges never taught courses in science until years later when they evolved into liberal arts colleges and universities.[3] A residual suspicion, if not hostility, toward science itself remains strong in many conservative

---

3   For the true story of the Scopes Trial, as opposed to the fictionalized version of *Inherit the Wind*, see Edward J. Larson, *Summer for the Gods: The Scopes Trial and America's Continuing Debate Over Science and Religion* (New York: Basic Books, 2006).

Christian circles. Public schools often teach the Scopes Trial by having students read the play *Inherit the Wind* as if it were factual and not fictionalized. It represents Bryan and conservative religion in the worst way possible. Christian colleges and universities still exist *partly*, anyway, to protect Christian youth from the scientism and hostility toward religion that exists in many secular (and even some church-related) institutions of higher education.

As Plantinga masterfully demonstrates in *Where the Conflict Really Lies*, however, the real conflict is *not* between science and religion and not even between evolution and religion; it lies instead between the metaphysical belief system *naturalism*, often confused with science, and *science itself.*

Distinguishing Science from Naturalism

The whole key to resolving the conflict between science and theistic religion lies in maintaining boundaries between them while at the same time celebrating points of real contact and possibilities of integration between them. Swiss theologian Emil Brunner laid out the elements of a truce between Christianity and science in his *The Philosophy of Religion from the Standpoint of Protestant Theology*. Brunner began by admitting and decrying religion's role in the totally unnecessary war and admitting modern science's value. Modern science, he declared, has by its amazing discoveries required religious traditions to discard many relics of "primitive science."[4] He rightly declared that theology has no business intervening in the framing of scientific hypotheses.[5] Speaking of evolution as a case study he averred that "it should never have entered the head of any Christian theologians to intervene in the controversy over Darwinism, so long as the framing of evolutionary theories was confined in a strictly scientific manner to the domain of what is open to observation."[6]

---

4   Brunner, *The Philosophy of Religion*, 171–72.
5   Ibid., 172.
6   Ibid., 172.

This means, however, Brunner argued, that *science*, too, must keep to its limits. He laid much of the blame for the unnecessary war between science and religion at the doorstep of scientific monism, by which he meant what we have called *naturalism* and *scientism*.[7] These he declared "superstition"! The Swiss theologian wrote that science itself does not undermine true Christian faith; that only results from a false understanding of science or a false understanding of Christian faith.[8] In other words, the common confusion of science with naturalism and the tendency of some scientists, to say nothing of dilettantes of science, to think science is the one and only source of knowledge.

On the other hand, Brunner had strong words for people of faith who oppose science itself, as opposed to naturalism parading as science. Their problem, he proposed, was failure to free the real message of the Bible (what Barth called its *Sache*) from its cultural clothing.[9] In other words, their problem is *literalism* of biblical cosmology, genealogy, etc. According to Brunner, and surely he was right about this, "Impossible it is that any essential position of Christian faith should be affected . . . by changes in the scientific view of the world."[10] Of course, much depends on what one considers "essential positions of Christian faith." Brunner was talking about *basic Christian metaphysics and doctrine*, not the age of the earth, for example.

Theologian-philosopher Tresmontant, while strongly resisting *syncretism* between metaphysical structures, especially between the biblical-Christian worldview and its alternatives, daringly affirmed that *theology, cosmology*, and *the positive sciences* must be coordinated and integrated. He even went so far as to declare that the Hebrew-Christian cosmology—view of the physical universe and how it works—is accountable to the sciences.[11] What

---

7   Ibid., 174–75.
8   Ibid., 183.
9   Ibid., 173.
10   Ibid.
11   Tresmontant, *Christian Metaphysics*, 67.

he meant, clearly revealed in the context, is what evangelical theologian Bernard Ramm (1916–92) meant in his controversial 1954 book about science and religion entitled *The Christian View of Science and Scripture*. Throughout that attempt to correct fundamentalism about science, Ramm argued that *theology must take into account the material facts of science* and not dodge them or deny them. When something is truly a fact of science, such as the sun-centered solar system, theology must adjust to it.

However, going back to Brunner, no material fact of science can conflict with basic Christianity understood properly—not as cosmology but as spiritual metaphysics. Science does not have within its purview any ability to falsify biblical-Christian metaphysics or to establish as necessarily true *naturalism* or *materialism*, however much some scientists and philosophers attempt to *misuse* science to do that.

CHAPTER 7

Biblical-Christian Humanism

One of the perennial questions of philosophy is "What is man?" Today, in the twenty-first century, we ask, "What is the human?" or "What is humankind?" in order explicitly to include both sexes. From ancient times until now all philosophers and theologians have wrestled with answers. Modern Western philosophy has been especially obsessed with humankind's nature and existence. The great Enlightenment essayist Alexander Pope (1688–1744) declared humanity the center of philosophy: "Know then thyself; seek not God to scan. The proper study of mankind is man." Christianity has always included beliefs about humankind such as the *imago dei*, the image of God, and original or inherited sinfulness, and great debates have evolved around them in Christian theology. The Bible contains many teachings about humankind without placing humans at the center of everything; God remains the center of the biblical story. However, the biblical story is about "God *for* us," not God "in and for himself," and so humanity is nearly always in view—as God's covenant partner and sometimes as God's cocreator. There is a dark side to the Bible's story about humanity, however, and that includes a necessary *reservation* about humanity's ability to be faithful to the covenant with God. Evil is nearly always attributed to humanity's rebellion against God even when a powerful anti-God force called Satan is named as instigator of the rebellion.

Contemporary Non-Biblical, Non-Christian Views of Humanity

Over the centuries of Christianity many Christians have adopted views of human nature and existence *contrary* to biblical metaphysics. This book is a call to Christians to embrace the biblical narrative as primary in developing beliefs about reality; humanity is an important part of reality and the Bible has much to say about us. Some of the Bible's view of humanity is subtle, implied, assumed, but it is nevertheless discernable—at least in its basic outlines. And it stands in stark contrast to many alternative philosophical and religious views of humanity. A major concern of this book is to help twenty-first-century Christians clean their lenses, so to speak, of foreign, alien elements that have replaced or become combined with the biblical picture of reality. Many Christians' lenses are tainted with non-Christian stains that cause their perspectives on humanity to be unclear, confused, and distorted.

Tresmontant rightly asserted that not every view of humanity, "anthropology," is consistent with biblical religion.[1] In this case, "anthropology" refers not to the popular image of archeology digging to discover ancient human artifacts but to the philosophical study of human nature and existence. Tresmontant rightly concluded that, according to the Bible, humanity has a supernatural destiny as the crown of creation and that this "involves certain metaphysical implications and presuppositions,"[2] such as the existence of human *freedom* and *responsibility* as well as humans' distinctive *capacity for God*.[3] Also, humanity's distinctive nature rules out certain contrary metaphysical beliefs such as Gnosticism—the second-century (and beyond) idea that the body is the seat of sin and evil and that the soul is a spark of the divine, an emanation of the divine substance. Tresmontant warned,[4] that throughout the ages and still today even Christians often succumb to the Gnostic myth and confuse it with biblical thought. In fact, he wisely asserted, the two stand in absolute and stark contradiction.

During the late twentieth century, especially in the 1980s and 1990s, a spiritual movement swept across Europe and North

---

1   Tresmontant, *The Origins of Christian Philosophy*, 95.
2   Ibid., 109.
3   Ibid., 110.
4   Ibid., 113.

America dubbed by many the "New Age movement." There was really nothing new about it except its public promotion of Gnostic ideas about humanity and its eclectic blending of Eastern mysticism with Western esoteric, occult beliefs and practices. It was, for all practical purposes, however, a new manifestation of Gnosticism—especially as it bled into Christian circles and became known to many as "esoteric Christianity" or just "New Age Christianity." This is a classic case of syncretism—the perennial temptation to blend unbiblical beliefs with biblical ones and the succumbing to that temptation by many thoughtful and sincere Christians.

One effect of the New Age movement among Christians was a growing belief in *reincarnation,* including karma—the law of cause and effect especially associated with Eastern religions such as Hinduism and Buddhism. New Agers *added* reincarnation and karma to Western Gnosticism with the result that many Christians embraced beliefs totally alien to the Bible and Christian tradition. At the core of the New Age movement, however, was the ancient and idolatrous belief in the divinity of the human person, whose higher self was said to be always already one with God. Many New Agers adopted monism as their basic metaphysical outlook. New Thought ideas easily blended with New Age Gnosticism, giving the New Age movement a Christian and modern feel.[5]

At the opposite end of the metaphysical-anthropological spectrum from New Age thought is *secular humanism*. Like the New Age movement, it was around in some form long before the public became aware of it and conservative Christians identified it as a major threat to society. Like New Age Gnosticism, secular humanism

---

5   Many people, including many Christians, tended to associate the New Age movement only with superstitious beliefs in the magical power of crystals and with astrology, etc. Many dismissed it as unworthy of being taken seriously because they thought it had no philosophy within or behind it. However, there were and are serious thinkers within the New Age movement who eschewed the more sensational aspects that made headlines and episodes of television talk shows. Among them were British philosopher George Trevelyan (1906–96), author of several books on New Age thought including *A Vision of the Aquarian Age* and *Operation Redemption*, and American spiritual thinker and writer David Spangler (b. 1945), author of many books and articles on New Age spirituality and philosophy. Both were metaphysical thinkers who incorporated aspects of Gnosticism, New Thought, and Eastern mysticism into their philosophical-religious anthropologies.

includes a metaphysical vision of human nature and existence that is strictly contrary to biblical anthropology and yet has such a strong influence on modern Western culture that many Christians unwittingly adopt aspects of it. Originally, *humanism* was a term for a new discovery of and belief in human cultural creativity during the Renaissance of the fifteenth and sixteenth centuries. Especially in southern Europe it was a revival of ancient Greek and Roman philosophy and art and a renewal of appreciation for humanity's goodness. In northern and central Europe it was more distinctly Christian with an emphasis on the *imago dei* in humanity—that humanity was created in God's image and likeness—and that it was not destroyed but endures in humankind as the source of human creativity and dignity. Erasmus was a major leader of the northern Renaissance, especially in philosophy and theology. He emphasized human freedom and responsibility as well as God's grace and taught that humanity had the God-given ability to do much good.

Original humanism, then, was Christian humanism. During the twentieth century, however, especially in America, humanism came to be associated with *secularism*—belief that humanity is alone in the universe and that religion and spirituality are not necessary for the full flowering of human potential. Two humanist manifestos were published declaring humanity's autonomy from God and religion and essential goodness and dignity apart from religion. The first, published in 1933, was known simply as the Humanist Manifesto and was signed by a group of mostly agnostic or atheist scholars. The Humanist Manifesto II, an updating of the first manifesto, was published by another group of scholars in 1973. Both declared the special dignity and worth of humanity within an essentially *naturalist* metaphysical perspective.

The publication of Humanist Manifesto II created a furor in America, with fundamentalist Christians claiming that it expressed the belief system being taught in American public schools and calling for Christians to home school their children in order to protect them from the secularizing effects of the public schools.[6] Numerous books poured forth attacking and defending secular humanism. On the secular humanist side a leading advocate and defender was philosopher Paul Kurtz (1925–2012), who published *In Defense of Secular Humanism* in 1983—partly in response to the conservative Christian attacks on it.

Many, perhaps most, participants in the controversy over the New Age movement tended to ignore its metaphysics, which was and is a form of *Gnosticism*, believing that the human soul is divine or one with God—not by grace but by nature. Many, perhaps most, participants in the controversy over secular humanism tended to ignore that its metaphysics is a form of *naturalism*, which believes the human person is merely a highly evolved animal with no need or capacity for God and no supernatural aspect. But secular humanism specifically added to naturalism the belief in humanity's special dignity and worth above all other species, even though naturalism itself cannot rationally justify such a claim.

These two modern anthropologies are mentioned here only to illustrate unbiblical answers to the question "What is humanity?" swimming about in culture and offering themselves as viable perspectives on human nature and existence. Very seldom do their offerings come obviously labeled "unbiblical" or even "New Age" or "secular humanist." They have blended into the fabric of mainstream European and North American culture, however, and it takes a concerted effort to resist their influence. Because the Bible itself uses the same words for *spirit* for both the supernatural dimension of humanity and for God, many Christians are seduced into adopting New Age or Gnostic beliefs about the divinity of the human soul or spirit. Because of the tremendous achievements of

---

6   Among other conservative Christians Tim LaHaye (1929–2016) especially led the charge against secular humanism in books like *The Battle for the Mind* (1980). LaHaye's leadership in the antisecular humanism movement among conservative Christians was a source of controversy even among some Christians who thought he did not understand secular humanism well or that he was extreme in his tendency to associate secular humanism with Satan.

science and the fact that it is often taught wrapped in a naturalistic and optimistic-progressive view of reality, many Christians are seduced into adopting a secular humanist perspective of humanity as essentially good without taking into account humanity's dependence on God and humanity's brokenness due to sin.

Throughout Christian history various philosophical ideas about humanity have impinged on Christians. *Platonism* and *Neoplatonism* influenced some of the early church fathers such as Origen to think of the body as the "lower nature" of humanity, while the soul, mind, or spirit was the Godward aspect striving for release from earthly entanglements. Aristotle's philosophy influenced some medieval Christian thinkers such as Aquinas to consider reason as the source of humanity's special dignity and worth. Monistic idealism influenced some Christians to confuse humanity with God—a special temptation throughout the nineteenth century, the optimistic century of liberal Protestantism in Europe and America, during which belief in the infinite perfectibility of man was pervasive. Hegel's dialectical monism of Absolute Spirit was enthusiastically embraced by many Christians as the key to overcoming Protestant orthodoxy's generally very negative view of humanity as having lost the image of God due to sin, as well as promoting belief in the perfectibility of humanity. At the same time, especially in Britain and America, some philosophers began to promote pragmatism and utilitarianism as alternatives to biblical-Christian anthropology; human beings were defined as problem solvers with the natural capacity to transcend themselves and their environments. The *good* was defined as what *works* to enhance human happiness, and many Christians, especially in America, rushed to adopt that perspective, combining it uncomfortably with biblical-Christian ideas of humanity.

The Biblical-Christian View of Humanity

The biblical view of humanity can easily be summarized in a nutshell by reference to two Psalms—8 and 14. Psalm 8 builds on the idea of humanity as created in God's image and likeness, specifically mentioned in Genesis 2, and asks and answers the perennial question "What is humankind?"

> What is mankind that you are mindful of them, human beings that you care for them? You have made them a little lower than the angels and crowned them with glory and honor. You made them rulers over the works of your hands; you put everything under their feet: all flocks and herds, and the animals of the wild, the birds in the sky, and the fish in the sea, all that swim the paths of the seas. LORD, our Lord, how majestic is your name in all the earth! (vv. 4–9)

Throughout the biblical narrative runs a theme of humanity as created good and remaining *in essence* good, possessing special dignity and value over the rest of creation *because* humanity was created in God's image and likeness and assigned by God to be his *created cocreators* in relation to the rest of creation. Like the rest of creation, humanity is portrayed in Scripture as *dependent but good*. Unlike the rest of creation, humanity is there portrayed as possessing a special goodness in relation to God, reflecting God's own nature *as gift* without being in any way equal with God.

Psalm 14 presents the counterpoint that is equally true and important for a holistic biblical-Christian understanding of humanity:

> The fool says in his heart, "There is no God." They are corrupt, their deeds are vile; there is no one who does good. The LORD looks down from heaven on all mankind to see if there are any who understand, any who seek God. All have turned away, all have become corrupt; there is no one who does good, not even one. (vv. 1–3)

The apostle Paul quotes this psalm in Romans 3. Pervasive throughout Scripture is the theme of humanity's corruption, brokenness, and depravity, and it is always pinned to humanity's willful rebellion against God and his covenant plan for them. Some Christian theologians refuse to encapsulate these two biblical themes in a metaphysical framework, preferring instead to leave them juxtaposed in paradoxical tension—humanity's essential goodness and humanity's evilness. Others have borrowed heavily from various philosophies to explain the apparent paradox metaphysically. We will look at some of these alien-to-the-Bible philosophical explanations soon.

Tresmontant dared to claim that the Bible itself contains an implicit metaphysical anthropology *not dependent* on any extrabiblical philosophy for explanation. That is not to say he claimed it is a perfectly rational anthropology in the modern sense of "rational"; he did not. Neither Tresmontant nor Cherbonnier claimed that about Christianity; they did not deny mystery in biblical metaphysics. On the other hand, they claimed that the biblical perspective on reality *fits the facts of experience* better than all alternatives and nowhere better than here—in its account of human nature and existence: "the human condition."

Tresmontant correctly and proudly asserted the Christian and biblical view of humanity as *good*. Both the Bible and Christian tradition have exalted and magnified human nature rather than denigrated it.[7] On the other hand he also rightly steadfastly rejected any idea of humanity as divine by nature (Gnosticism) while acknowledging what the Eastern Christian tradition calls "divinization" (*theosis*) or what he preferred to call "the supernatural destiny of man."[8] By this he meant "union with God" without equality with God.[9] In other words, union with God that is personal, not substantial (blending of essences), and yet metaphysical. It is non-monist and yet a real union that transcends nature. And it is gift, not achievement. The biblical basis for this divinization of humanity is 2 Peter 1:4, which specifically states that God makes

---

7   Tresmontant, *Christian Metaphysics*, 85.
8   Ibid., 105.
9   Ibid., 106.

his people to participate in the divine nature. This has to be interpreted in light of the whole of Scripture, which emphasizes the fixed metaphysical interval, ontological difference, between Creator and creature. It does not mean, as many New Agers would have it, that the soul is always already "one with God" or capable of achieving "oneness with God." It means that humanity can be united with God in a personal way, receiving God's abundant life as a gift by grace. This is distinctly *supernatural* in the sense of being a divine gift, not fulfillment of a natural capacity in humanity.

This *supernatural destiny of humanity* is undeniable evidence of the Bible's positive affirmation of humanity as essentially good even if existentially estranged, fallen, and broken due to sin. Tresmonant correctly argued that orthodox Christianity defends human nature against all who would denigrate it.[10] Even *corporeality*, having a physical body, is good, part of God's creative plan for humanity.[11] Nothing is clearer in biblical thought and Christian tradition than the goodness of the material, physical world including the body.[12] This is based on the creation narrative of Genesis as well as on the bodily resurrection of Jesus and humanity's own future resurrection taught by Paul in 1 Corinthians 15 as corporeal, bodily.

Tresmontant would be the first to admit that this optimistic biblical view of humanity must be counterbalanced with a realistic assessment of human corruption and evil. Key to *biblical metaphysics in anthropology*, however, is that evil, brought about by sinful rebellion against God, has distorted humanity's relationship with God but not human nature itself.[13] The essence of man is the image of God and humanity's supernatural destiny, which is already at work in those who belong to God by grace and faith. These have *prior actuality* in terms of humanity's existence; sin, brokenness, corruption, and fallenness are posterior to the image of God and

---

10   Ibid., 86.
11   Ibid.
12   Ibid., 87.
13   Ibid., 97.

goodness in terms of metaphysics. Twentieth-century Protestant theologian Tillich expressed this as humanity's being "essentially good but existentially estranged." That is, humanness is the original creation of humanity and God's intention for humanity, and that remains real. The evidence is the *incarnation*: Jesus Christ was the "true human" *because* he was sinless. Salvation, then, becoming Christlike by grace, receiving divinization, union with God by grace, does not take one *out* of true humanity but *restores* true humanity.

The Reality of Humanity's Brokenness

Yet, the inferior reality of humanity's brokenness remains essential to a holistic biblical view of humankind. What must be avoided is any hint that this brokenness, however exactly understood doctrinally (Catholics and Protestants tend to differ about "original sin"), results from a "twist of human nature."[14] Manicheism must be strictly avoided, as it dualistically blames sin and evil on matter, on bodies. Manicheism is "one of the hidden heresies that distorts Christianity."[15] It is evidenced in any belief that sin and evil are *necessary* in human existence because of some flaw in human nature itself. Instead, the biblical narrative always places the blame on the misuse of the good gift of freedom, not on God or human nature itself. This is why the Bible refers to the "mystery of iniquity" (2 Thessalonians 2:7 KJV). Sin is mysterious because it results from the misuse of something good— freedom—and is absolutely irrational. No reason can be given for it.

A key biblical category virtually unknown to philosophy is the *heart*. Throughout Scripture sin and evil are traced back to the heart of the human person. This is to say that it is not rooted in the person's nature or body or even ignorance but in the will. The concept of heart is key to biblical metaphysics in the areas of anthropology; it is essential to understanding the Bible's account of evil which, as Cherbonnier said, can be summed up with the phrase "hardness of

---

14   Ibid., 98–99.
15   Ibid., 89.

heart."[16] Tresmontant agreed stating that, biblically speaking, both sin and stupidity result from hardening of the heart.[17] What does the Bible mean by *heart*? Certainly not the organ that pumps blood. Rather, the heart is the "root of all our reasoning."[18] It is not under the control of reason as philosophically defined. In other words, it is not pure reflection based on objective observation and logic. The Bible makes the *mind* posterior to the *heart* in terms of *behavior*. The heart is the "centre in which are taken the fundamental decisions."[19] "The heart is that original freedom from which understanding and knowledge proceed."[20] This is completely different from the traditional Greek-inspired thinking about knowledge and understanding which begins with mind and reason. "To know the good is to do the good" is *not* the biblical perspective; it is the Greek and generic philosophical perspective that underlies the modern idea that education is the solution to everything. According to the biblical story of humanity, behavior is controlled by the heart more than by the mind or reason. Tresmontant poetically expressed the biblical idea of sin: "In the depths of his heart begins a dance. Man becomes a stranger to himself, *alienated*."[21]

Humans Are "Damaged Goods" by Their Own Fault/Fall

In the biblical story, then, humans are *damaged goods*. Their *nature* is good because it was created by God in his own image and likeness with a supernatural destiny, but they are *damaged* by their own infidelity to God's calling and purpose for them. They are *responsible* for their damaged condition, not because they violate reason with rebellion, but because they devise rebellion in their hearts and their minds, and actions follow the disposition

---

16   Edmond La Beaume Cherbonnier, *Hardness of Heart: A Contemporary Interpretation of the Doctrine of Sin* (Garden City, N.Y.: Doubleday, 1955).

17   Tresmontant, *A Study of Hebrew Thought*, 123.

18   Ibid., 117.

19   Ibid., 119.

20   Ibid., 123.

21   Ibid., 121.

their hearts have created. Tresmontant, Cherbonnier, Brunner, and others intent on going back to the source—the biblical story—for Christian metaphysics and anthropology agree that responsibility requires *freedom*.[22] Cherbonnier spoke for all of them (and numerous other Christian thinkers) when he wrote that

> The Bible consistently acknowledges human freedom. It is presupposed by all its key words, such as sin, repentance, forgiveness, love, and covenant. Consequently, though not intentionally philosophical, it contains by inference what is probably the most thorough understanding ever written of what it means to be a free agent.[23]

According to Brunner, *freedom and responsibility* together comprise the "formal image of God" *not* destroyed by or lost in the fall of humanity into sin.[24] He distinguished this from the "material image," which he defined as *"right relationship with God."* Sin, beginning freely in the heart, alienates the human person (and all of humanity in general) from God *against reason.* Therefore, the material image is forfeited responsibly. But the formal image can never be destroyed; it is why the human person is able to hear and believe the Word of God and it is what makes him or her full of dignity and value above the rest of creation.

Cherbonnier expressed the whole point of this book when he wrote about theology's compromise with pagan and secular philosophies—especially in the sphere of understanding humanity. According to him, Christians attempting to make their faith intellectually respectable wedded it to great metaphysical systems of thought alien to biblical truth. Most of them undermine, if not destroy, human freedom.[25]

---

22   Tresmontant, *Christian Metaphysics*, 90–98; Cherbonnier, *Hardness of Heart*, 29–38; Brunner, *The Philosophy of Religion*, 68.

23   Cherbonnier, *Hardness of Heart*, 38.

24   Emil Brunner, *Dogmatics II: The Christian Doctrine of Creation and Redemption*, trans. Olive Wyon (London: Lutterworth Press, 1952), 55–61.

25   Cherbonnier, *Hardness of Heart*, 36.

Non-Biblical, Non-Christian Anthropologies to Avoid

In sum, not only theologians, but ordinary lay Christians and priests, pastors, and others have uncritically assumed that the Bible is only about *ethics* and not at all about *metaphysics,* or they have uncritically assumed that its morsels of metaphysical insights need a ready-made extra-biblical metaphysical framework in order to be complete and acceptable to the mind. Thus, they have turned repeatedly to pagan and secular philosophies such as those mentioned in previous chapters and/or in this one (viz., New Age and secular humanism). Often that adoption is piecemeal and even unconscious, but it still can corrupt biblical-Christian thinking and nowhere is that more evident than in *anthropology*—thinking about human nature and existence.

Now is the time to turn, however briefly, to some of these extrabiblical, non-Christian philosophical and religious anthropologies and examine them in the light of the biblical story of God and humanity. Many books have been published laying out in detail various ancient and modern views of man or human nature. Leslie Stevenson's *Seven Theories of Human Nature* (1987) and Perry LeFevre's *Understandings of Man* (1966) are two among many such surveys. Particular proposals for understanding humanity abound and proliferate. But all or most reduce to a few basic metaphysical outlooks that determine what can and cannot be believed about human nature and existence, including about human persons.

Gnostic belief about humanity underlies *New Age humanism* and began in the first or second century as an intensification of certain strains of Greek thought about humankind. For some Greeks and Romans influenced by Greek thought and for Gnostics, "life in the flesh is irremediably corrupt."[26] For Greek philosophy in general, evil was grounded in matter: "Matter is at fault."[27] Often

---

26   Carl A. Raschke, *The Interruption of Eternity: Modern Gnosticism and the Origins of the New Religious Consciousness* (Chicago: Nelson-Hall, 1980), 39.

27   Tresmontant, *A Study of Hebrew Thought*, 11.

accompanying this pessimistic view of the sensible was Greek philosophy's generally negative view of time and history as cyclical. Most Greek philosophers did not go as far as the Gnostics (or later Manicheans) to view matter *itself* as evil. The point for them was that matter, including the body, is *limiting*, a drag on the soul or spirit, which yearns to be free of worldly limitations. Gnostics (and later Manicheans) specified matter itself as evil and as the seat of all evil. This "Greekish" way of thinking about humanity, to whatever degree, contrasts with Hebrew thought in that the former is *dualistic* while the latter is not. For Greek thought, and all its derivatives, evil and tragedy result from good souls being trapped in matter and time.

Greek-Gnostic cosmogony and anthropology conflict with biblical-Christian thought at two crucial points. For Christians, especially, the most important point of conflict is the *incarnation*. The incarnation alone, Tresmontant averred, rules out any dualism that pits body and soul or body and spirit against each other. For Greek thought, incarnation can only be a *downfall*.[28] Tresmontant also rightly pitted such Greek dualism of anthropology against Hebrew anthropology, which allowed no dichotomy between the material and immaterial aspects of the human being.[29] According to Hebrew thought, embedded and assumed in the biblical narrative, the human person does not "have a soul" but "*is* a living soul."[30] The Bible distinguishes strongly between the creator and his creation but not as strongly between body and soul.[31] This makes a significant difference in terms of *salvation*. The biblical-Christian idea of salvation, rooted in Hebrew thought, is *redemption of creation*, including the sensible world of time and matter and including bodies. According to Paul in Romans 8, redemption will be a kind of *resurrection of creation*—a liberation of the world itself from

---

28   Ibid., 80.
29   Ibid., 90–91.
30   Ibid., 94.
31   Ibid., 95.

"bondage to decay," which is not blamed on a fall *into* matter or time. Paul affirms the redemption of *bodies* in 1 Corinthians 15 and compares believers' bodily resurrection in the future with Jesus's bodily resurrection.

Greek thought, including Gnosticism, which Tresmontant rightly saw as influential throughout Western history, regarded the immaterial aspect of the human person, the soul or spirit, as naturally divine—a stray spark of God's substance trapped in matter and time yet longing for return to its spiritual home above. That return was and is often thought of as blending back into God. According to Tresmonant, drawing on biblical anthropology, the *pneuma* (spirit) in the human being is *supernatural* but *not divine*. It is supernatural in the sense of *leaning toward God*. The human spirit is that aspect of man that makes encounter with God possible.[32] But even though supernatural in terms of *telos*—calling, purpose, goal—the human *pneuma* is *created*. According to the biblical story, then, "man is a spiritual animal."[33] That's impossible for the Hellenistic mind to accept—except when it has been Christianized. Ancient Greek thought and historical and modern Gnosticism invariably regarded the spiritual and the animal (natural) as incapable of harmony. Tresmonant succinctly summed up the biblical-Christian view by asserting that the reality of created human spirit makes possible the indwelling of God's Spirit.[34]

Greek-inspired anthropology, then, in varying ways and to varying degrees tends dualistically to affirm on the one hand humanity's *true divinity* and on the other hand humanity's *imprisonment in matter, space, and time*. Biblical-Christian thought about humanity, in contrast, denies humanity's divinity yet affirms the *true dignity* of humanity because it is made in the image of God and its spirit has the capability of hosting the Holy Spirit. It also

32   Ibid., 107.
33   Ibid., 108.
34   Ibid., 109.

affirms the *goodness* of the body and its participation in redemption, and its divine destiny along with the spirit in heavenly, supernatural existence. Much Christian thought has drunk deeply at the wells of Greek-Gnostic thought about humanity, dualistically denigrating this-worldly existence in matter, space, and time and over-spiritualizing salvation as escape from that. One example of that is the common contemporary Christian belief in the immortality of souls as opposed to the resurrection of body-souls (whole persons). "Immortality of souls" refers to the Greek belief that souls, being sparks of the divine, are naturally immortal, incapable of real death (extinction of the true, inner self, which is spiritual). The biblical narrative knows nothing of that; in its place it presents souls (persons) as always dependent on God for existence, for life, and as destined at best for resurrection, not eternal immaterial-spiritual existence in some purely spiritual dimension away from the world.

At the opposite end of the spectrum of anthropologies lies *secular humanism* rooted in *naturalism*—the metaphysical vision that says nature is all that is real and that denies any supernatural spiritual dimension to reality, including humanity. This contrasts with biblical-Christian humanism, which elevates humanity *above the rest of creation* as having a supernatural-spiritual dimension in spirit open to Spirit (God's) and as being *created in God's own image and likeness*. These together make the human being a living soul—unique among the rest of God's animal creatures. As a God-related living soul, the human person has unique dignity and worth *different in kind*, not just *different in degree* from other species. Brunner expressed biblical-Christian humanism succinctly: "In spite of sin, man is the most glorious of the creatures of God."[35] Explaining further, he wrote, "Therefore it is not permissible to deprecate or abuse man. Even in his sin man is yet honourable, since he still bears the image of God within him, even though it be obscured and

---

35 Brunner, *"Nature and Grace,"* 41.

'painted over.'"[36] Jewish philosopher-theologian Heschel argued that "if man is not more than human [animal], then he is less than human [unique among the animals]."[37]

Secular humanism stands in stark contrast with biblical-Christian humanism, just as naturalism stands in stark contrast with biblical-Christian belief in creation. Both are *reductionistic*—reducing reality to what observation can (in principle) discover and know. Both are rationalistic while, as Plantinga showed about naturalism, being self-referentially absurd. (Here *absurd* is not meant as an insult or denigration; it is only meant in its philosophical sense of "illogical.") There exists no better expression of secular humanism than Kurtz's book *In Defense of Secular Humanism*. Kurtz, a professor of philosophy at the State University of New York, surprisingly (and shockingly to some secular humanists!) admitted that for some people secular humanism, or naturalistic humanism, functions as a kind of religion.[38] However, it is certainly a religion without belief in God or anything supernatural; for the secular humanist nature is all there is and humanity is solely part of nature. Kurtz made no secret of his belief that secular humanism is a form of naturalism:

> Most humanists take man as a part of nature, even though man has his own unique dimensions, such as freedom. There is no break between the human mind or consciousness on the one hand and the body on the other, no special status to personality or "soul," and especially no privileged or special place for human existence in the universe at large. Thus, all claims to human immortality or eschatological theories of history are held to be an expression of wish-fulfillment, a vain reading into nature of human hope and fancy.[39]

---

36 Ibid., 42.
37 Heschel, *Man Is Not Alone*, 211.
38 Paul Kurtz, *In Defense of Secular Humanism* (Buffalo, N.Y.: Prometheus Press, 1983), 116.
39 Ibid., 65.

Kurtz, speaking for most, if not all, secular humanists, was not afraid to draw some of the inevitable conclusions from this naturalistic view of humanity. For him, secular humanists "accept the fact that human existence is probably a random occurrence existing between two oblivions, that death is inevitable, that there is a tragic aspect to our lives, and that all moral values are our own creations."[40] For him, as for most secular humanists, religion tends to contribute to the alienation of humanity from himself and nature. "The more he [the human] exalts God as the Father image, the more he demeans himself."[41] And yet, in contrast to some naturalists, Kurtz and other secular humanists affirm a specialness to humanity. He alluded to this in the above quote as humanity's "unique dimensions." Among them he noted (throughout *Defense*) freedom, reason, creativity, and conscience. Much of the book revolves around explicating a naturalistic ethic for secular humanism—one absolutely independent of anything transcending nature. Again, Kurtz bit the bullet and admitted that, on the basis of nature alone, there can be no moral or ethical absolutes *beyond those chosen by humans* themselves.[42] Yet, like other secular humanists such as philosopher Kai Nielsen (b. 1926), author of *Ethics without God* (Prometheus, 1990), Kurtz strove to establish a *relative* morality and ethics for humanity, one consistent with naturalism. For him, as for many, perhaps most, secular humanists, that involves some form of *utilitarianism* in which humans are obligated to care for humanity as a whole; the greatest good for the greatest number is the golden rule in this secular humanist ethic.[43]

One might legitimately ask Kurtz and other secular humanists "Why?" Why should a person *not* opt instead for hedonism—an ethic based solely on self-interest? His only answer was to insist that such persons are obviously not prepared for moral autonomy (whatever that

---

40   Ibid.
41   Ibid., 66.
42   Ibid., 66.
43   Ibid., 68–69.

means exactly).[44] Kurtz went so far as to insist that a holistic humanist ethic depends on "deontological considerations"—belief that "the good" cannot be defined solely by consequences but must also include *duty*. But he never provides a clear or convincing answer to the question of metaphysical *grounds* for humanitarianism. He simply *asserts* that a non-humanitarian is possibly a "moral monster."[45] The big question lurking in the background is a metaphysical question about *meaning* grounded in some *ultimate reality*. Lacking any transcendence, other than human self-transcendence, Kurtz, together with other secular humanists, had to admit that human life has no absolute purpose or meaning. Feebly, however, he claimed that human life has real meaning and value because humans create them by striving for happiness and discovering enjoyment in life now (as opposed to hope for a future fulfillment after death). Meaning, purpose and value are discovered in striving for the good life in this life.[46]

But *what is the good life?* That is the question that any humanist, religious or secular, must answer. And the answer, whatever it may be, depends on some vision of ultimate reality, some belief about human nature and existence in relation to ultimate reality. Kurtz and other secular humanists affirm a good life that looks not totally different from that affirmed by most religious people, including most Christians. Concern for the common good was important to him. But the question is "Why should I be concerned for the common good *if* I can avoid being disadvantaged by being concerned only with myself, only with my own good?" All he and other naturalists can say is "Moral monster!" They cannot explain *why* living according to self-interest alone makes one a moral monster.

There is another vision of secular humanism, also based on naturalism, that poses an entirely different answer to the issue of ethics and morality. That is *Social Darwinism* such as that espoused

---

44   Ibid, 51–52.
45   Ibid., 54.
46   Ibid., 42.

(without calling it that) by philosopher-novelist Ayn Rand. Rand, author of many novels including the ever popular *Atlas Shrugged* (1957), argued that naturalism does not yield a humanitarian ethic but one centered on self-interest. Survival of the fittest is the law of nature, and if nature is all there is, then any policy of action that inhibits the strong and empowers the weak is against nature. She condemned pure altruism as evil because it goes against nature which, for her, was highest reality and supports self-interest above all else.[47] She only allowed charity, altruism, when it was in one's own self-interest. What would Kurtz say? Possibly that Rand was a "moral monster," but more likely (because he was extremely intelligent) that she was partly right and that altruism *is always in one's own self-interest* because the flourishing of humanity, the betterment of the common good, is good for every self. However, *if* a person is convinced that he or she can flourish, be happy, and be fulfilled on the basis of self-interest alone, the only argument a secular humanist can give is to call him or her a "moral monster" not ready for "moral autonomy."

Eristics around Anthropology—Human Existence

The above is an exercise in what Brunner called eristics. It is not intended as *disproof* of secular humanism or naturalism. The point is that on the basis of naturalism *alone* one cannot establish objective morality or ethical absolutes. And on the basis of naturalism alone, an ethic of self-interest is most, well, natural. In other words, contrary to what most secular humanists believe, including Kurtz, Rand was right in the sense of being *most consistent*. But, ultimately, there can be no rational argument against Rand's version of naturalism. If one presupposes, with naturalists, that nature is all there is, then there is no reason to suppose that humanity is higher, better, of greater dignity, value, and worth than other species. Such a high appraisal of humanity is nothing more than

---

47   See Ayn Rand, *The Virtue of Selfishness* (New York: Signet, 1964), 45 and throughout.

self-assignment. It has no metaphysical grounding and therefore is simply a belief without basis or foundation. Even Rand's ethic of self-interest is inconsistent insofar as one cannot derive an "ought" from "is" (the naturalistic fallacy). That one "ought" to act always out of self-interest may be a choice, but without something transcendent providing the metaphysical basis for the "oughtness," it lacks moral force. Ultimately, it all comes back to Plantinga's argument in *Where the Conflict Really Lies* that naturalism itself undermines truth itself. If naturalism is believed, there is no basis for believing it is true.

Most conservative Christians recoil in horror when they hear of secular humanism. Unfortunately, they also recoil in horror at the very idea of humanism, even though *true humanism* is *biblical-Christian humanism*. Christians need to recover and reclaim the concept of humanism for themselves. It was a mistake to ever allow naturalists to own it. Naturalism alone can never establish or preserve the ultimate dignity and worth of human life or ethical absolutes; naturalism alone can only consistently yield an ethic of self-interest.

Also unfortunately, many Christians have integrated aspects of naturalistic humanism into their perspective on reality. This is rarely, if ever, conscious, but naturalism is such an influential idea in modern Western cultures that it's difficult to resist entirely. Many Christians recoil almost in horror at the very word *supernatural*. That's partly because the word itself has been so abused (e.g., equated with occultism or miracles on demand) but also, for some Christians, because it offends belief in and commitment to reason and science. It doesn't need to, as explained earlier, but modernity has convinced many that it inevitably does so. Many Christians, wanting to be both modern and Christian, adopt a kind of deistic middle way—relegating miracles to the past (Bible times) and denying the possibility of miracles in modern, Western societies. More to the point of humanism, however, many Christians influenced by modernity adopt a relativistic, utilitarian ethic devoid of absolutes. Cultural relativism is not unknown in certain Christian circles—especially academic ones. Especially in certain politically conservative Christian circles, Rand's objectivist ethic of self-interest, a form of social Darwinism, is popular and manifests in strenuous opposition to charity, especially welfare programs to help the weak and disadvantaged. The irony is that, once understood rightly, naturalistic, secular humanism can be observed at work in many places where it is condemned.

Interlude 7

Two questions especially hover around and lurk within all discussions of biblical-Christian ideas of humanity. They are the questions of *freedom* and *sin*. Throughout the centuries of Christian reflection on the biblical story, different concepts of both have arisen and often divided Christians against each other. Almost all Christians affirm both ideas—freedom and sin—but numerous interpretations of both have become well established and create tremendous confusion. Just because a Christian talks about "human freedom" or even "free will" does not mean much; these ideas can mean different things. Also, just because a Christian talks about "sin" or even "original sin" does not mean much; these ideas can also mean different things.

The concern of this book is not *doctrine* per se. The concern is to explore and explain *basic Christian metaphysics, the biblical perspective on reality*. It would be delightful to be able to leave the matter with "biblical-Christian metaphysics requires belief in *both* freedom and sin," but these concepts are so fraught with controversy, even among Christians, that some discussion of them is necessary to clear the air, so to speak. What do they mean and not mean for what has here been called "Christian humanism"?

Historical Christian Beliefs about Freedom and Sin

Much Christian thought has been devoted to the issues of freedom and sin. Differences about them have contributed heavily to denominational divisions. Unfortunately the biblical story does not include a specific, detailed explanation of them and leaves the door open to different interpretations, especially about the details.

An old saying is that "the devil is in the details," and that's certainly true here. Almost all Christians throughout two thousand years have agreed that humans are free and also bound to sin, that sin is pervasive in human existence and yet people sin freely and are responsible for their choices. But when anyone bores down into what these Christians mean by these terms and concepts, trouble begins. For example, Augustine, the father of Western Christian thought, argued that everyone has free will but only those in a state of grace have true freedom. Many Christians agreed with that and still do. But for Augustine "free will" only meant choosing without external coercion or compulsion. It did not mean being able to do otherwise. This view of free will is called "compatibilism" because it is compatible with determinism. Augustine was a determinist; he believed all of life is ultimately determined by God's sovereignty according to a divine plan *and* that inherited sinfulness bound the will to sin until it is freed from that bondage by God's grace. Before the fall into sin people were free not to sin; afterward everyone (except Jesus Christ) is born *not* free *not* to sin. True freedom is grace restoring the image of God and liberating a person from bondage to sin.

At the same time as Augustine a group of Christians argued against his divine determinism and also against his view that inherited sin destroys humans' ability not to sin. They argued that this idea ruins responsibility. Some of them, known as Pelagians (after Augustine's nemesis Pelagius [354–420]), went so far as to deny inherited sinfulness entirely and argued that everyone is born pristine, as Adam was created, with free will to sin or not to sin. Many Christians sought middle ground between Augustine and the Pelagians. At least since the early fifth century, then, a debate has raged within Christianity itself over free will, true freedom, and sin—that is, about the human condition *in light of the fall.*

Is it possible to dig back through or bypass the layers of theological debate about these matters and find some bedrock ideas about them in the biblical narrative itself? What ought Christians to believe about them insofar as they want to be guided faithfully by biblically informed metaphysics? Is this perhaps another case where, even at the highest levels of Christian theology, *philosophy* has intruded to misdirect attention away from the biblical story to what the Bible must mean based on some other perspective?

For example, many critics of Augustine's theology believe he was overly influenced by Neoplatonism and never wrested his mind completely free of Manicheism. Did these extrabiblical thought forms guide Augustine, who established a kind of norm for especially Western theology (Catholic *and* Protestant), away from biblical thought about these matters and toward an approach corrupted by non-Christian perspectives? To suggest that is almost to utter heresy in many conservative Catholic and Protestant circles where Augustine's theology is still believed to be normative.

Our guides, however, ask us to consider that possibility and to go back to what the Bible actually says about these matters and what it clearly assumes about them—without feeling duty bound to adhere to a particular theological tradition such as that started by Augustine. Tresmontant, Cherbonnier, Brunner, Heschel, and other retrievers of biblical metaphysics all together ask us to consider the possibility that the biblical story of God and humanity yields an outlook on human nature and existence that is different from Augustine's and the received theological tradition that derives from him. That is not to say they reject Augustine's thought *in toto*; it is only to suggest that he may have been wrong in some areas— especially with regard to sin and freedom.

Important Definitions of Terms

Before delving into what our guides and especially the Bible have to say about these matters, however, it will be helpful to some readers for us to define certain terms and concepts relevant to them. *Fatalism* is the common belief, found in many ancient Greek sources, that all of life, all of reality, is determined by impersonal forces and that people have no control over them. Expressed in a popular idiom fatalism says, "What will be, will be." Fatalism is a form of *determinism*—belief that all of life, all of reality, is controlled by either personal or impersonal forces such as nature, God, or karma. *Divine determinism* is belief that a personal God foreordains and renders certain all that will happen. Most Christian divine determinists, such as Augustine and John Calvin and their theological heirs, believe that God uses secondary causes such as persons' wills, decisions, and actions to bring about what he has designed, ordained, and is rendering certain. What happens is not necessary, but it is certain because of God's sovereign control. Many determinists believe in a kind of *free will* called "compatibilism"— that persons are free when they are not being forced to do something against their wills even if they could not do otherwise than they do. *Nondeterminists*, sometimes called "free-will theists" (especially as Christians), believe God does not design, ordain, and render certain everything that happens but gives creatures the dangerous gift of genuine "power of contrary choice"—ability to resist God's will such that God foreknows but does not foreordain everything that happens. *Open theists* are those who believe God creates an "open future" such that even he does not know all that will come to pass. They are free-will theists who go farther than most with regard to God's foreknowledge as limited.

Those categories cover most of the Christian theological territory with regard to *freedom* in the sense of *free will* and *determination*. Now it will be helpful to many readers for us to define terms and categories with regard to *sin*—especially among Bible-believing Christians.

Some Christians believe *sin* is a hereditary disease of the soul; everyone since Adam and Eve (except Jesus) is born with an inherent guilt and/or tendency that make actual sinning inevitable. This is one form of *original sin* espoused by Augustine and embraced by many Catholics and Protestants. Other Christians, especially Eastern Orthodoxy and Wesleyans (followers of Methodist founder John Wesley who appear in numerous Protestant groups) deny inherited guilt but embrace inherited corruption such that actual sinning is inevitable as part of the maturation process (at the "age of accountability"). Eastern Orthodox Christians especially emphasize that what is inherited from Adam and Eve is *mortality-death* rather than guilt or corruption. Orthodox and Catholic Christians deny *total depravity*—the belief common among conservative Protestants that sin has shattered the image of God in human persons and that every part of them is so damaged by sin that they cannot even accept God's grace without a special, supernatural infusion of grace transforming the soul. Many Protestants accept some form of total depravity. However, liberal, progressive Protestants generally deny original sin as an inherited disease of the soul and emphasize inherent human goodness.

What the Bible *Really* Says about Freedom and Sin

With that survey out of the way, we can proceed to an examination of the biblical narrative and how our chosen guides understand the nature of freedom and sin. All of them *reject determinism* and *inherited sinfulness* while embracing *human solidarity in sin and God as sovereign over all outcomes.*

We began this tour of Christian metaphysics, the biblical perspective on ultimate and penultimate reality, with the prophet Isaiah, who strongly emphasized *both* God's all-determining sovereignty *and* human responsibility for sin, which is treated as primarily idolatry. Especially chapters 40–48 emphasize that the entirety of world history, the rise and fall of nations, is in the Lord's hands; he alone decides the outcome of all events. Nothing falls outside his knowledge, wisdom, and control. Proverbs 16:33 sums up this prophetic theme about God's sovereignty: "The lot [dice] is cast into the lap, but its every decision is from the LORD." This theme of God's control over history and nature is an overriding one that cannot be missed or minimized. God is in charge like nobody and nothing else.

But does this mean *determinism*? Does the biblical narrative support the idea, common in the history of philosophical theology and much Christian theology—going back to Augustine in the fifth century—that God *designs, ordains,* and *renders certain* everything that happens down to the decisions of people—even their sinful dispositions and actions? That would be very difficult to reconcile with the equally important emphasis throughout the biblical narrative on humans' responsibility for sin and defection from God's will. Those theologians and philosophers who have embraced divine determinism do so while having to admit that it is logically irreconcilable with human responsibility. They simply leave the matter in the realm of mystery and disagree with Luther, Calvin, and Edwards's attempts to inspect God's mysteries too closely and rationally.

The biblical narrative, on the other hand, throughout *implies* that God's sovereignty—although over all such that nothing escapes it—permits room for human free will as the power of alternative choice—the ability to do otherwise than God wishes. Everywhere God blames people for their sins, not himself. Their hardness of heart is their own doing, not God's. Reason not only strains to accept the paradox offered up by divine determinists; it breaks apart when attempting to embrace *both* absolute, all-controlling divine sovereignty *and* human responsibility for sin. Also, extreme versions of God's sovereignty such as divine determinism cannot avoid verging close to *pantheism* or what some philosophers call *theopanism*—the idea that God is all there really is; all is merely an extension of God. Without some degree of creaturely autonomy and freedom the ontological interval between God and creation so crucial to Christian metaphysics threatens to close.

Are God's and Creature's Agencies Noncompetitive?

Often, when this issue of God's sovereignty and human freedom arises in discussions of Christian theology and philosophy, some people will appeal to a so-called "noncompetitive" view of God's agency and human agency. That is, God's agency, active-bringing-it-about that things happen and are the way they are, surrounds, indwells, and undergirds creaturely agency. Creatures' agency, such as human decisions and actions, whether creative or destructive, cannot compete with God's because all creaturely ability is dependent on God's power "on loan," as it were. This is, of course, a highly speculative and extrabiblical rationalization of divine determinism that does nothing to solve the problems mentioned above—human responsibility for sin and the all-important interval between God and creation that must not be abridged. If anything, it simply intensifies these problems.

The Bible everywhere and throughout *assumes* a competitive agency arrangement between God's will and work and human wills and works. Not "competitive" as necessarily morally opposed but "competitive" as in "not the same"—somewhat "over against" ontologically—in terms of being juxtaposed rather than perfectly unified. Human responsibility for sin requires such; otherwise it is not sin unless God is a sinner (which is inconceivable). For sin to be *sin* it must be responsible disposition, decision, and action. It has to arise within the human heart even if it is inspired by outer temptation (as in the narrative of humanity's fall in Genesis 3).

Of course, another "escape" is, as mentioned before, simply to eschew reason and appeal to mystery when considering God's sovereignty-as-determinism and human responsibility for sin. Tresmontant, however, rightly declared that Christian thought, at its best, including the church fathers, seeks to rid itself of myth and foster reasonable belief.[1] That does not mean Christian thought has to adapt to modern, rationalistic canons of reason (e.g., positivism or even foundationalism) but only that it must not revel in contradictions. Mystery is one thing; contradiction is something else. A sheer logical contradiction is always and everywhere a sign of error,

---

1   Tresmontant, *The Origins of Christian Philosophy*, 15.

whereas mystery can be a sign of transcendence. Cherbonnier agreed completely with Tresmontant that basic reason cannot be abandoned even in theology. Reason, including especially the law of non-contradiction, is part of the created goodness of the world and of human nature. "When what a man says in the morning cannot be reconciled with what he says in the afternoon, he must have been arguing from a false premise."[2] The law of non-contradiction is a God-given safety alarm to warn against falsehood.

The lingering question is whether belief in both divine determinism and human responsibility for sin is mystery or contradiction.

Taking the Biblical Narrative Seriously: God's Risk Is Part of God's Sovereignty

Fully aware of the biblical emphasis on God's sovereignty over all things, Tresmontant rightly clarified that alongside that emphasis is God's freely chosen creation of free cocreators.[3] This is a paradox but not a contradiction.[4] It implies *risk* on God's part.[5] Clearly, for Tresmontant, this is all based on God's voluntary self-limitation or self-restriction of power as explained earlier. For him, the Bible and the best of Christian thought view history as an "unpredictable invention of two separate liberties bound together in a common enterprise."[6] The common enterprise is covenant-fellowship between God and creatures and eventual union between them that does not dissolve distinction. But because of the awful gift of free will, "the oak is not in the acorn."[7] In other words, history contains novelty, the unexpected, surprises, detours, but God is omniresourceful in bringing it all around to his predestined goal in spite of creaturely resistance. However, some will be lost along the way.

---

2   Cherbonnier, *Hardness of Heart*, 101.
3   Tremontant, *A Study of Hebrew Thought*, 149.
4   Ibid., 151.
5   Ibid., 152.
6   Ibid., 36.
7   Ibid., 37.

Admittedly, this is the way the biblical narrative plays itself out—in spite of several verses in Isaiah that *seem* to imply God's absolute control over everything down to the minutest details. Throughout God's lamentful relationship with his people, from Adam and Eve to the redeemed saints of Revelation, there is joy, disappointment, regret, relief, and burning jealousy on God's part. Can all that be dismissed as mere anthropomorphism? According to Tresmontant and many others, that's not possible. An anthropomorphism is a figure of speech pointing beyond itself to something in God. If all that emotion arising out of genuine interaction with free creatures is merely figures of speech, what does it point to in God? Rather than teaching something true about God it would be putting a mask on God who, in reality, is more like Aquinas's *Actus Purus* (pure actuality without potentiality) and Aristotle's "Thought Thinking Itself" than the God of Abraham, Isaac, and Jacob.

Because of sin, then, human freedom must be understood as *power of contrary choice* granted by God in an act of awful love and risk—for the sake of fellowship. Cherbonnier strongly affirmed human freedom against pagans (Greek philosophy), secularists (naturalistic determinists), and Christian determinists (Augustinians and Calvinists). According to him, the Bible's emphasis on *covenant* inevitably implies creaturely freedom of choice; the Bible is not philosophy, but it presents a profound picture of free agency.[8]

Free Will and Fallenness Both Affirmed

Cherbonnier distinguished rightly between *free will,* which is never absolute and is a part of God's good gift of creation in human persons, and *fulfilled freedom*, which is found only in *agape*—which is the love for others to which persons are called by God. "Human freedom is only *fulfilled in agape,* . . . conversely, it [is] progressively *destroyed* by sin."[9] Sin is the opposite of *agape*: hardness of heart toward God

---

8   Cherbonnier, *Hardness of Heart*, 38.
9   Ibid., 132.

and others and a turning in on oneself by one's own choice. It gradually binds the will by itself to itself and away from its own calling and destiny in love of God and others. "Men have contrived to entangle themselves in a web of enmity extending from camouflaged rivalry to overt conflict."[10] This is not only an individual choice as the early Christian heretic Pelagius taught, but neither is it a divinely imposed fate sovereignly designed and rendered certain by God "behind the scenes," so to speak. Cherbonnier adamantly denied the Augustinian notion of original sin as any inherited evil and put in its place the more biblical idea of a solidarity of humanity in sin.

Cherbonnier suggested, even argued, that *both* Augustine (divine determinism, inherited sin) *and* Pelagius (individual responsibility and absolute free will) were *wrong* while *both* were also *right*. The solution to the age-old theological debate lies, he insisted, in the biblical metaphysic of *solidarity*. What is most real is interpersonal relationships that are both emotional and free.[11] The Bible knows nothing of isolated individuals.[12] For it, "human relations comprise a network carrying positive and negative charges."[13] Sin, then, is not merely individual; it is something deeply engrained in social systems and institutions.[14] According to Cherbonnier, then, all people are sinners because they are born into a human network of sin—a "web of enmity." And yet, individuals freely embrace this sin as their own and harden their hearts against *agape*, against God. Therefore they are responsible. *Why* all do this is unanswerable; all that can be said with assurance is that all do it.

Responsibility for sin cannot be transferred away from the individual who acts freely, but it can be and must be *shared* by all because sin is transmitted as well as chosen.[15] For the Bible

---

10 Ibid., 133.
11 Ibid., 137.
12 Ibid., 126.
13 Ibid., 127.
14 Ibid.
15 Ibid., 138.

responsibility "is always *mutual*,"[16] because no person is an island. The Bible views humanity as *communal in solidarity*. Cherbonnier applied this biblical metaphysic of human solidarity and interconnectedness with individual freedom of choice to ethics. He used as his case study *capital punishment*. Based on the biblical insight about individual responsibility balanced with mutual solidarity he argued that society should bear some responsibility for the conditions that contribute to a criminal's misconduct. "His execution would merely enable them to ignore their own culpability in the sin, to transfer to a scapegoat the guilt which all share."[17] Therefore he advocated life imprisonment for murder combined with rehabilitation during the incarceration.

For Cherbonnier, this alternative view of freedom and sin, shared and individual responsibility, forms the basis for Christianity's social dynamic.[18] While salvation is, of course, in one sense individual, it is also in another sense social. A problem in one part of society is all of society's concern.[19]

To sum up, then, in the biblical account of humanity, *true freedom* is being in God's love, living a truly human life of *agape* love toward God and others; *free will* is the limited but real power of contrary choice that makes the individual fully but not exclusively responsible for hardness of heart which is the essence of *sin*. *Sin*, hardness of heart, is both universal, such that every person is born into it, and individual, such that each person who is morally aware embraces it, hardening his or her own heart together with others. *Responsibility*, guilt, is both individual and communal. God's *sovereignty* is God's overall control of history, directing it and guiding it to its destiny chosen by him—in spite of human resistance. This picture alone reconciles all that the Bible says about God and humanity into one harmonious story of good creation, communal defection,

---

16   Ibid., 137.
17   Ibid., 139.
18   Ibid., 141.
19   Ibid.

divine call to covenant resulting in both conflict and congruence, and ultimate consummation of God's plan to bestow divine mercy and restore the image of God on those willing to be redeemed. It also reconciles the best impulses of two strands of Christian thought, each of which picks up on one theme of the biblical narrative— either God's sovereignty and humanity's sinfulness or God's love and mercy and humanity's responsibility for sin. As Cherbonnier wrote, Augustine and Pelagius were "brothers under the skin,"[20] each partly right and partly wrong.

---

20   Cherbonnier, *Hardness of Heart*, 101.

Appendix: A Model for the Integration of Faith and Learning

A colleague in a Christian university told me: "I don't try to integrate my Christian faith with my research or teaching; I leave my Christian faith outside the laboratory and classroom and pick it up again when I go home and to church." Another colleague said that as a Christian he believes one thing to be true, but he believes its opposite to be true when conducting his research and teaching his discipline. These rejections of the *integration of faith and learning* are all too common on Christian campuses and yet they represent betrayals of the reasons for those campuses' existence. Most Christian colleges and universities were founded for the purpose of integrating the basic biblical-Christian metaphysic with all the subjects being taught. This project became especially important for pastors, parents, Christian administrators, and donors when *secularism* became prominent in Western cultures and philosophies like *naturalism* began to creep into the human and natural sciences.

The Rise of the Faith-Learning Integration Movement

During the 1960s and 1970s, a new wave of interest in the integration of faith and learning arose especially in American Christian institutions of higher education. Christian philosophers such as Arthur Holmes (1924–2011) published several major volumes expounding the need for and explaining the mechanics of faith-learning integration. A scholarly journal dedicated to faith-learning integration was launched: *Christian Scholar's Review*. I was its chief editor during the 1990s. Many Christian colleges and universities began requiring faculty members to attend workshops and seminars on faith-learning integration and, as part of their tenure process, write papers explaining how they integrate the Christian faith with their research and teaching. Whole organizations such as the American Scientific Affiliation contributed to exploring integration of Christian belief with scholarly research.

My life in American Christian higher education tended to track with the rise and decline of this project. I attended a Christian college and seminary and then, after earning my doctorate in Religious Studies at a secular university, taught more than thirty years at three well-known American Christian universities where talk of faith-learning integration was very hot with administrators promoting it and some faculty pushing back against it. I concluded that the slow decline of emphasis on faith-learning integration on Christian campuses has two causes. First, faith-learning integration itself has often been poorly explained. I have sat through attempted explanations of it with growing frustration as its promoters presented the project in ways almost guaranteed to cause resistance. Second, some Christian scholars, even ones teaching in Christian colleges and universities, have been reluctant even to attempt the integration of faith and learning for a variety of reasons. Some have feared that participation will cause them to lose respect, even credibility, among their secular counterparts in the academy of scholars. Others have feared that their research projects and teaching will be limited by a conservative religious ideology that hinders academic freedom.

My intention here is to provide a model of faith-learning integration that at least partially relieves these tensions and problems and paves the way toward a new emphasis on and acceptance of the project.

Challenges to Faith-Learning Integration

One problem hindering faith-learning integration has been a certain ambiguity about the faith part of the integration project. What is meant by "faith" in "faith-learning integration"? Is it the personal, individual relationship with God called "conversional piety" by some theologians? Is it Christian spirituality? How would that be integrated with, say, biology or astronomy? Actually, the major promoters of faith-learning integration, especially among evangelical Christians, have meant by faith, in this context, *the biblical-Christian perspective on reality* such as has been explicated throughout this book. It is often called "the Christian worldview." A problem with that, however, is that different disciplines use *worldview* in different senses. *Worldview* can mean *life philosophy or cultural habits or political ideology.* So when scholars even in Christian colleges and universities hear that they are to integrate "the Christian worldview" with their research and disciplines, much confusion is aroused. What the gurus of faith-learning integration have normally meant by *faith* and *worldview* in this instance, however, is the *biblical-Christian metaphysical perspective on reality*: the basic philosophy presupposed by and encoded in the Bible. That could be made clearer by many who instruct Christian faculty at new faculty orientations and workshops on faith-learning integration.

However, this encounters a very serious problem. Many evangelical Christian colleges and universities hire faculty members who confess Jesus Christ as Lord and Savior but who have very little, if any, real knowledge of Christian philosophy or theology. Many of them graduated from secular high schools, colleges, and universities. When they hear "faith-learning integration" during new faculty orientations, they automatically assume the "faith" referred to is their personal faith, their spiritual relationship with God through Jesus Christ. Then, when administrators and others who instruct them about faith-learning integration disabuse them of that simplistic notion of faith, they feel entirely inadequate to practice the integration expected. Then, at least occasionally, they are offered instruction in the Christian worldview that includes a great deal of baggage—denominational or confessional theology—and is itself confused and confusing.

At one Christian university, for example, faculty members across the spectrum of disciplines—from medicine to social work to mathematics to foreign languages to Christian ministry—were told by the president and his surrogates that the faith part of faith-learning integration included "Seed Faith." Seed Faith was the founder's version of the so-called prosperity gospel of health and wealth through "word-faith" (positive thinking and speaking). This may be an extreme example, but this writer has heard faith-learning integration explained to faculty members in many confusing ways that were guaranteed to cause consternation if not outright resistance.

A great deal of resistance to faith-learning integration might be avoided simply by explaining it clearly and correctly—as it was intended by its main modern proponents, most of whom were evangelical philosophers and theologians. However, I have found *even some of their explanations confusing,* which is one reason for this book and especially this appendix. Of course, admittedly, my explanation of faith-learning integration may not fit every context, but it is hopefully flexible enough to be adaptable to different institutional and confessional situations. This explanation of faith-learning integration will be made in a series of numbered points.

A Basic Assumption Underlying Faith-Learning Integration

First, a basic assumption of faith-learning integration is "all truth is God's truth whatever its source." This principle is rooted in the biblical idea of God as Creator and sustainer of all reality (evil being nonreality, absence of the good) and in the example of the apostle Paul's quoting Greek poets and philosophers in Athens (Acts 17). It is also rooted in the second- and third-century Christian Apologists such as Justin Martyr, Athenagoras, Theophilus, Clement of Alexandria, and Origen—all of whom taught against Christianity's critics that its basic truths are consistent with the truths discovered by the Hellenistic philosophers. None of them adopted Hellenistic philosophy uncritically; all of them attempted to show that what truth exists there belongs to Christians *because* the God of the Hebrews and of Jesus Christ is the author of all truth—wherever it may be found.

This first principle of faith-learning integration *does not mean*, however, that all *theories* are true or from God. It means simply that *when something is believed to be true by a Christian it must be believed to belong to God as its ultimate source*. All true truth (as opposed to false theories that claim to be true) belongs to God because God is one and the ultimate source of all that is good, true, and beautiful. The alternative would be unthinkable—from a biblical-Christian perspective.

This first principle of faith-learning integration *also does not mean* that all truth has already been revealed or discovered; it does not rule out *secondary sources of truth*. Human research *discovers truth*, *creating* human *knowledge*. Whenever truth is discovered, however, a Christian owes it to God to give him the credit *for it being true*.

Perceptive readers, thinking critically, might now observe and raise a problem with this account of truth. Is it not the case that *even God learns* some things in the flow of time? Some Christians will deny that and insist that God's omniscience is timeless and eternal, that all truth, past, present, and future, is already known to God. Even then, however, some things will come into existence in the future flow of time, in history. What could it even mean to claim that a future terrorist act, for example, is already God's truth?

Surely the prophets, apostles, and Christian philosophers thought of this and by "all truth is God's truth" did *not mean* that evil acts of the future are "God's truth" *except that God will allow them and even rule over them*. However, the principle "all truth is God's truth" surely refers to *timeless truths—axioms and principles of creation revealed and/or discovered by human research*. The point of the principle is *not* that a Christian scholar must *mention God* in connection with every fact; it is that *God is the ultimate arbiter of truth such that if something is discovered to be true it cannot be independent of God.*

It helps in these matters to give examples. What would be an alternative to "all truth is God's truth"? During the thirteenth century in Catholic Europe new ideas about the universe were flooding in from Muslim Spain. Much of it was based on Aristotle's philosophy and cosmology and seemed to conflict with biblical-Christian thought. A Christian philosopher named Siger of Brabant (1240–84) suggested what has come to be known as the "two-truths theory." According to him, at least according to his critics, one can and sometimes should believe one thing as a Christian and its opposite as a philosopher. An example was the doctrine of creation. Philosopher Aristotle and his Spanish translator (into Latin) and interpreter Averroes taught that the universe is itself eternal. Christian tradition taught that creation is temporal, not eternal. Siger, so his critics claimed, encouraged educated, intellectual Christians to believe both—as philosophers to believe that creation is eternal and as Christians to believe that creation is temporal (has a beginning). This two-truths approach was condemned by the Catholic Church. Thomas Aquinas opposed it and sought *critically* to integrate Aristotle's philosophy with Christianity.

This dualistic two-truths approach to seeming tensions and conflicts between Christian thought and secular thought is exactly what administrators of Christian colleges and universities wish to avoid and a major reason why faith-learning *integration* is the ideal. Some version of, or something like, two-truths thinking is the main alternative to faith-learning integration in Christian institutions.

Biblical-Christian Metaphysics Central to Christian Thinking

Second, faith-learning integration assumes that the biblical-Christian world and life perspective, metaphysic, is rooted in divine revelation and therefore forms the center and foundation of all Christian thinking. There is a sense in which this perspective on reality is itself revealed or tied to revelation which often takes narrative form. This means that, *insofar as the biblical-Christian perspective is faithful to revelation, it is the controlling paradigm for all Christian thinking.* Alternative paradigms are (as explained in this book): monism, emanationism, dualism, naturalism, and panentheism. Faith-learning integration asks every faculty member of a Christian college or university, every researcher in a Christian organization, to *see the world, reality, through Christian eyes, to allow the Bible to absorb the world.* But this *assumes* there is, indeed, a biblical metaphysic. This book is a contribution to the explication and understanding of that biblical metaphysic *for the sake of faith-learning integration* (as well as simply for Christian enrichment, for discipleship of the mind).

An important caveat is in order right here. *Some* Christian college and university administrators *occasionally* add *other* beliefs to the basic Christian metaphysical perspective on reality. An example was cited earlier—the evangelist-founder-president of a Christian university who insisted that faculty members consider "Seed Faith" part of the biblical-Christian perspective on reality. I left that university as soon as this expectation dawned on me. It was not always stated explicitly, but any faculty member who remained long enough came to realize it. *Some* Christian colleges and universities may very well *add* confessional doctrines to expectations of faculty for faith-learning integration. This writer believes this to be a mistake, however, and it only adds a further dimension to dissent. It's all well and good, for example, for a Christian college or university president to ask prospective faculty members to confess belief in the Trinity, but it's something else to ask them, once hired, to integrate belief in the Trinity with their discipline. The Trinity, while true, is not part of what is meant by "faith" in faith-learning integration even if it is part of what is meant by the confessional stance of the university and its faculty.

That God is creator of all, ruler over all, supernatural and personal, living and active, is relevant to every discipline taught in a Christian college or university. That God acts in history and that the supernatural realm is real are relevant to most disciplines—even if only as background beliefs. That God is triune is true for all evangelical Christian colleges and universities but *not* relevant for every discipline taught. I realize some critics may object to this, but I would challenge them to show how belief in the Trinity is relevant to, say, astronomy or the study of modern revolutions or economics.

Faith-Learning Integration the Purpose of Christian Higher Education

What gave rise to the existence of modern Christian colleges and universities was the rise of *secularism* as a result of the Enlightenment. Very quickly, even institutions founded by Christians were swept up in the secular wave of culture with religion relegated to a corner if not total obscurity. One result of that process was the creation of Bible colleges that confronted secular higher education by rejecting many of the modern arts and sciences. In addition, Bible colleges concentrated almost exclusively on indoctrination, with the Bible being treated as a textbook on virtually every subject. Gradually, however, *some* of these fundamentalist-founded institutions came out of their anti-intellectual and counter-cultural shells of sheer obscurantism and began to teach courses in modern sciences and use textbooks by leading secular scholars. The integration of faith and learning was developed as an alternative to *three threats*—anti-intellectual obscurantism (common in the Bible colleges movement), secularism, and two-truths thinking. The basic idea was and is: Let's focus the "faith" part of higher education, especially outside biblical and theological studies, on what C. S. Lewis called *Mere Christianity* and what before that Scottish philosopher-theologian James Orr called *The Christian View of God and the World*. And let's insist that our post-fundamentalist, newer evangelical Christian higher education in arts and sciences be based on that *together with* the material facts of scholarly research and let's integrate them with each other. Obviously that was and remains an ambitious and tension-filled project, but it is what *defines* post-fundamentalist, evangelical higher Christian education.

No Final Conflicts between the Sciences and Christianity

Third, a basic working assumption of this faith-learning integration was stated by theologian Emil Brunner in *The Philosophy of Religion from the Standpoint of Protestant Theology* (1937): "Impossible it is that any essential position of Christian faith should be affected . . . by changes in the scientific view of the world."[1] By "scientific" Brunner meant *wissenschaftlich*—the German word for all the sciences. And by "scientific view" he did not mean every theory proposed by scientists. By "essential position of the Christian faith" he meant basic elements of orthodoxy, not every interpretation of the Bible ever held by someone. All that is clear from the context.

All thinking Christians should humbly agree with Brunner that by their amazing progress and discoveries the modern sciences have required certain traditional Christian beliefs to change.[2] Surely he was thinking of the Galileo fiasco. But he also meant what fundamentalists mean by "young earth creationism" or "scientific creationism," which posits that the whole universe is only a few thousand years old and rejects evolution entirely. He laid down the rule that theology has no business intervening in the framing of scientific theories and hypotheses.[3] At the same time, according to Brunner, *science* must keep to its limits.[4] Conflicts between them arise when science oversteps its legitimate boundaries. Science, for example, sometimes wrongly includes *naturalism*—the philosophy that nature is all there is. That is not within science's purview to say;

---

1   Emil Brunner, *The Philosophy of Religion from the Standpoint of Protestant Theology*, trans. A. J. D. Farrer and Bertram Lee Wolf (London: James Clarke, 1937), 173.

2   Ibid., 171–72.

3   Ibid., 172.

4   Ibid.

when it is said by a scientist he or she is speaking as a philosopher, not as a scientist. The same is true, however, when theologians or Bible interpreters attempt to make statements about cosmology or nature based on literalistic readings of ancient biblical texts without acknowledgment of their cultural conditioning or nonliteral genre.

Speaking to conservative Christians who bring Christianity into conflict with modern science Brunner stated, "It should never have entered the head of Christian theologians to intervene in the controversy over Darwinism, so long as the framing of evolutionary theories was confined in a strictly scientific manner to the domain of what is open to observation."[5] On the one hand, Brunner argued, conflict between the sciences and theology arise from failure by Christians to free the essential message of the Bible from its cultural forms.[6] In other words, the whole, tragic Galileo fiasco could have been avoided if Christians had recognized and acknowledged that the Bible is not a book of physical cosmology—"how the heavens go." For centuries Catholic and Protestant Christians had *interpreted* the Bible using Aristotle's metaphysics and a literal interpretation of some passages that should have been recognized as figurative (e.g., "four corners of the earth").

Where the Conflicts Really Lie

On the other hand, Brunner asserted, much of the perceived conflict between the sciences and Christianity arises from scientific monism, which he labeled "superstition"![7] By "scientific monism" the Swiss theologian meant what later thinkers called *scientism*— belief that science is the path to all knowledge and that it will provide all the solutions to life's problems. Scientific monism was implied by the world's smartest woman quoted earlier in this book who wrote in her column that biology reduces to chemistry and

---

5   Ibid.
6   Ibid., 173.
7   Ibid., 174–75.

chemistry reduces to physics so physics is the most important science. This expresses reductionism based on a hidden metaphysical materialism.

Brunner's point was that in the ongoing war between science and theology there is plenty of blame to go around. But his concluding point (of this discussion) was conflicts between science, philosophy and culture, on the one hand, and real Christian beliefs, on the other hand, arise from misunderstandings.[8] He could have mentioned, and probably intended his readers to think, "theology," too, as a source of much misunderstanding giving rise to unnecessary and even false conflicts.

Brunner's main thesis is one every Christian should take very seriously: "The conflict between faith and science has never been serious nor one that affected central questions."[9] It has never been serious because it has been based on false premises and assumptions about faith and science. It has never affected central questions because the central questions of both Christian faith and modern science lie in different realms. Science ought not to ask about ultimate reality; that's philosophy's and theology's realm. And, ultimately, philosophy can speculate about ultimate reality but only theology is based on revelation *from* ultimate reality. Theology ought not to ask about or attempt to answer issues of science— insofar as science sticks closely to its realm of studying observable nature and nature's laws.[10]

Brunner averred that philosophy, more than science, gives rise to real conflicts between Christian faith and perceived secular truths.[11] He did not mean all philosophy or philosophy in general but *particular philosophies*. Philosophy and theology raise some of the same questions, and their answers sometimes actually do fall into conflict. Theology claims to base its answers on *revelation*;

---

8   Ibid., 183.
9   Ibid., 173.
10   Of course this includes legitimate, necessary deductions from observation.
11   Ibid., 173.

philosophy never does that but claims to base its answers on *reason alone*. There is no necessary conflict between faith in revelation and proper use of reason; conflicts between faith and philosophy arise when philosophy claims to answer life's ultimate questions relying on reason alone. Brunner's whole point was that there is nothing essentially, necessarily wrong with secular reasoning in science and philosophy in and of themselves; where they go wrong and create conflicts with Christian truth is in their hubris, their tendency to place sole faith in reason alone and forget that, for example, reason alone, including both science and philosophy, cannot answer life's ultimate questions (including about evil).[12]

What it all comes down to, then, is that the integration of faith and learning does *not* preclude genuine scientific (*wissenschaftlich*) research or real philosophical analysis and even speculation—so long as these do not claim absoluteness, overstep their boundaries, or make metaphysical claims that cannot be proven and conflict with essential elements of the Christian view of life and reality rooted in revelation.

That means, however, that *there are* points of conflict between *Christian faith*, understood as a worldview, a metaphysical vision of reality, and *certain theories* proposed and even claimed as knowledge by scientists and philosophers. None of those, however, are necessary, provable, or certain. And Christian scholars, working within Christian organizations dedicated to Christian faith as a worldview, ought to avoid teaching them as truth insofar as they actually do conflict with and undermine it. What it does *not* mean is that every *interpretation of the Bible* or *traditional belief* held by Christians is sacrosanct and impervious to criticism and need for revision in light of the *material facts of science* and *logic*. Faith-learning integration depends on Christians holding lightly to traditional beliefs and interpretations that are not crucial to the metaphysical vision of reality required by the biblical story.

---

12   Ibid., 187.

Strata of Reality and Gradations of Faith-Learning Integration

Fourth, faith-learning integration *must* take seriously another basic insight of Brunner's: the "strata of reality" and "corresponding gradations of the sciences."[13] In other words, as he never tired of pointing out in many of his books, there are layers of reality, and some of them are more open to faith-learning integration, which also leaves them more open to real and necessary conflict between Christian faith and scientific theorizing. For example, there is no such thing as Christian mathematics; mathematics, and probably also physics, are disciplines where conflict between Christian faith and research's conclusions are rare if even possible. That is because they do not deal with the central concerns of biblical revelation which have to do with *God and humanity*—personhood. The closer one comes to the study of persons, however, the more potential there is for real conflict between revelation, Christian faith, and theories posited by scientific researchers. That is to say that, for example, *sociology* and *psychology* often include theories about human nature and existence that cannot be reconciled with revelation. That could hardly happen in mathematics.

At the same time, conversely, mathematics has less to contribute to Christian faith than, say, sociology and psychology. The possibilities for both conflict and integration abound in the latter two sciences. That is because, Brunner argued, *idolatry* is a serious problem in the human sciences and hardly exists in mathematics and physics insofar as they stick to their proper methods and realms of research. And that is because *sin* is a basic datum of revelation that secular sociology and psychology rarely take into account. The same could be said of the *imago dei*—the image of God in the human person.

This means it is ludicrous for administrators of Christian colleges to demand that *mathematicians* account for their success or

---

13   Ibid., 174–75.

lack of it in integrating Christian faith with their discipline. But it is not ludicrous, it is even important, for administrators of Christian colleges to require scholars in the *human sciences* to account for their success or failure in integrating Christian faith, understood properly, with their disciplines.

It is conceivable, of course, that a mathematician or physicist might violate Christian beliefs by *making an idol* out of numbers or natural laws or mathematics in general. A Christian professor of physics who teaches that nature's laws cannot be suspended even by God would, of course, be falling into conflict with basic Christian metaphysics. But there are no such things as "Christian mathematics" or "Christian physics." There might be, however, "Christian sociology" or "Christian psychology"—in the sense of sociology and psychology worked out in light of revelation *and* the best of modern secular research brought together in mutual information. And it is much more likely in these disciplines than in the former for widely held theories to conflict with revelation. However, *insofar as they are more than theories*, insofar as they are material facts, indisputably true, Christian faith must take them into account and *reinterpret revelation in their light*.

Illustrations and Example of Conflicts between Christianity and Theories

Specific examples will help shed light on these fairly abstract principles. A Christian professor of psychology who teaches that *all behavioral dysfunction is explainable by "nature and nurture"* will necessarily fall into conflict with revelation and the basic Christian perspective based on it. Why? Because *sin* cannot be reduced to behavior caused by "nature and nurture." A Christian psychologist will have to make room for the categories of *sin* and *evil* in his or her teaching. One example of a psychologist who did that is M. Scott Peck (1936–2005) who, in *People of the Lie* (1983), argued for the inclusion of "evil" as a category of human behavioral dysfunction.

He was not merely "baptizing" some other, already recognized, mental or emotional disorder as "evil." Rather, through his own experience as a therapist and research as a psychologist Peck came to believe in the existence of genuine evil transcending anything secular psychology had previously acknowledged.

Another example is a Christian professor of communication theory and practice who teaches that "*if they have not learned, you have not taught.*" In this common axiom "they" stands for students or listeners in general, and "you" stands for a teacher or communicator of ideas. A Christian cannot say that and be consistent with revelation, the Christian worldview, because it conflicts with the nature of human persons as communicated by revelation and believed by Christians throughout the ages on the basis of revelation. In the gospels Jesus taught but some of his hearers did not learn because of their *hardness of heart.* The axiom does not take into account the reality of the *darkened mind* and *ears deaf to truth* because of sin.

An example from the other direction, from science to the reinterpretation of revelation, is the *social solidarity of evil.* Much modern social science demonstrates the dependence of human persons on social structures, a finding which can enrich and deepen Christian understanding of *original sin* as not only inherited corruption but also as the *social pressures of injustice* that contribute to sin and evil. Walter Wink (1935–2012) was a theologian and social scientist who interpreted sin in light of the demonstrable effects of deep social structures on individuals and communities. Racism, in other words, he argued, is not just a choice but a social reality, a social disease that should be considered one of the "principalities and powers" the apostle Paul refers to in Ephesians 6:12 (KJV). A contemporary theology of human sin and evil that does not take these insights into account is probably inadequate.

The problem with examples and illustrations is that people tend to latch onto them and remember them while forgetting the principles they are meant, however inadequately, to illustrate! The point of offering them here is not to use them as litmus tests for faith-learning integration but simply to illustrate how it might be done adequately or inadequately—often without intentionality. Readers are encouraged to come up with their own examples and illustrations—primarily from their own experiences of learning or teaching (or both) in Christian learning contexts.

The point here is simply that the faith part of faith-learning integration is *not* an ideology or complete system of ideas like a systematic theology. Unfortunately, in some Christian learning environments, some systematic theology such as Charles Hodge's three-volume *Systematic Theology* (1873) or one of its many later (mostly one volume) paraphrases is used as the faith side of faith-learning integration. Sometimes it is applied rigidly and even physicists and mathematicians are expected to read it, know it, and use it as the faith part of faith-learning integration. That is expecting far too much of laypeople and it is wrongly identifying a system containing much speculation with revelation itself.

Rather, the faith part of faith-learning integration is or should be the basic perspectives of the Christian blik, the metaphysical vision of reality necessarily implied by the biblical story of God, creation, and humanity. That means that *every* Christian teacher in *every* Christian school should be sufficiently familiar with the Christian metaphysic to integrate it with his or her discipline and research and teaching, avoiding teaching theories or ideas that contradict it but instead enriching it with material facts and ideas that make it even more relevant and applicable to everyday life.

Questions to All
Your Answers

Many Christians' faith exists as a loose collection
of unexamined clichés and slogans borrowed from
songs, devotional books, sermon illustrations, and
even the internet. Too often this belief system (if
it can be called a "system") lacks coherence and
intelligibility; it can hardly be expressed, let alone
defended, to others. The problem with folk religion is that it too easily withers under the on-

slaughts of secularism or seemingly reasonable answers provided by cults
and new religions. Christianity has a long tradition of intellectual examination of other faiths and its own beliefs. Socrates said that the unexamined
life is not worth living; great Christian minds of all the ages have believed
the unexamined faith is not worth believing. Reflective Christianity is
Christian faith that has subjected itself to the rigorous questioning of
Scripture, tradition, reason, and experience. It is mature Christian faith
that goes on believing even as it questions what it believes. The goal of
this book is not to destroy anyone's faith but to build it up by placing it on
a firmer foundation of critical examination. Ten popular Christian clichés
are subjected to critical inquiry and interrogated to discover whether they
contain truth or are in error. In most cases the conclusion is—both. The aim
is not to tear down straw men but to demonstrate a path toward stronger,
more mature Christian belief.

Against Calvinism

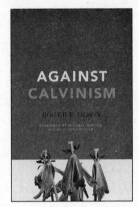

Calvinist theology has been debated and promoted for centuries. But is it a theology that
should last? Roger Olson suggests that Calvinism,
also commonly known as Reformed theology,
holds an unwarranted place in our list of accepted
theologies.

In *Against Calvinism*, readers will find scholarly arguments explaining why Calvinist theology
is incorrect and how it affects God's reputation.
Olson draws on a variety of sources, including
Scripture, reason, tradition, and experience, to support his critique of
Calvinism and the more historically rich, biblically faithful alternative theologies he proposes.

Addressing what many evangelical Christians are concerned about
today-so-called "new Calvinism," a movement embraced by a generation
labeled as "young, restless, Reformed"—*Against Calvinism* is the only book
of its kind to offer objections from a non-Calvinist perspective to the current wave of Calvinism among Christian youth.

As a companion to Michael Horton's *For Calvinism*, readers will be able
to compare contrasting perspectives and form their own opinions on the
merits and weaknesses of Calvinism.

Available in stores and online!

How to Be Evangelical without Being Conservative

(Available in ebook only)

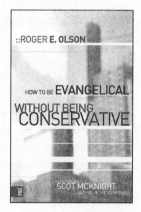

Many people equate evangelical Christianity with conservatism in religion, politics, theology, and social attitudes. Some are scandalized by any separation between them. As one evangelical pastor's wife declared to a church group, "We are a conservative people!" In fact, however, evangelicals have not always been conservative; radical stances on doctrines, worship, social norms, politics, and church leadership have often marked evangelicalism in the past. The 2007 movie *Amazing Grace* about William Wilberforce's protracted battle against the slave trade featured a small group of British evangelicals committed to abolition. The same radicalism characterized much of American evangelicalism in the years before the Civil War. In recent years the American media have portrayed the evangelical movement as a conservative force in society sometimes equating it with fundamentalism and puritanism. The missing piece of the story is, however, that both fundamentalism and puritanism contained radical elements that opposed the status quo. This book sets forth evidence that the link between evangelicalism and conservatism has not always been as strong as it is today in the popular mind, and it will provide suggestions for contemporary evangelicals who want to remain evangelical (and not become "post-evangelical") without identifying with conservatism in every way.

Available in stores and online!

Four Views on the Spectrum of Evangelicalism

Four Views on the Spectrum of Evangelicalism compares and contrasts four distinct positions on the current fundamentalist-evangelical spectrum in light of the history of American fundamentalism and evangelicalism.

The contributors each state their case for one of four views on the spectrum of evangelicalism:

Kevin T. Bauder: Fundamentalism
R. Albert Mohler Jr.: Conservative/confessional evangelicalism
John G. Stackhouse Jr.: Generic evangelicalism
Roger E. Olson: Postconservative evangelicalism

Each author explains his position, which is critiqued by the other three authors. The interactive and fair-minded nature of the Counterpoints format allows the reader to consider the strengths and weaknesses of each view and draw informed, personal conclusions.

The Counterpoints series provides a forum for comparison and critique of different views on issues important to Christians. Counterpoints books address two categories: Church Life and Bible & Theology. Complete your library with other books in the Counterpoints series.

Available in stores and online!